ENDORSEMENTS

"In any organization, a successful approach to leadership includes engagement that spans more than a list of perks and employee benefits. It's an ongoing pledge to create an environment and community where people want to work and where they can do their best work. From a career of leadership experiences and the voices of visionary leaders across industries, Bethel Thomas outlines how creating a culture of inspiration, sense of purpose, and pride can motivate teams to reach new heights."

— **Dr. James Downing**, President and CEO, St. Jude Children's Research Hospital

"Bo Thomas has demonstrated the best effort yet of intellectually challenging today's "Malignant Normality." This book provides a refreshing lens of a new leadership perspective. His 7 Inspiring Leadership Practices are exceptional. If you are genuinely interested in leadership, read this book now!"

— **Don Hutson**, Co-author of the NY Times and WSJ Bestseller, *The One Minute Entrepreneur*

"*Reinventing Leadership* gives us a profound understanding of how leadership must be reinvented if we are to inspire and enjoy a "better normal." Bo Thomas calls on all of us to be leaders, and to lead "from an ethical heart, with a moral compass and courage." I have known

Bethel (Bo) his entire career. He not only writes about a new kind of leadership, but he also lives what he is encouraging each of us to do."

"Through a combination of storytelling and real-life experiences, Bo Thomas offers a new leadership framework for this era. His seven "non-negotiable and inspiring leadership practices" create a roadmap for leaders who want to serve and build community. Traits such as compassion, collaboration, and empathy are essential for success and the meaningful change of systemic inequities. Bo invites the reader to embrace and unleash their full potential wherever they lead."

"Bo Thomas describes what "better normal" leaders do: Work to make broken systems better to improve lives. We chose to solve hunger at Tusk, especially for children. It's not sexy, but it's a calling for leaders who want to make a difference in the lives of others. It's the inspiring leadership that knits our fragile society together, and we need so much more of what Bo encourages us to do!"

"I am thrilled with this book. My search for something more inspiring than a "return to normal" is over. Bo Thomas's call for a "Better Normal" is the answer I was seeking, and he details it in a strong, convincing, and hopeful manner. *Reinventing Leadership* is powerful, a must-read regardless of your life role. All of us must lead with urgency if we are to create healthier organizations, communities, a stronger democracy, and a healthier planet. Thank you, Bo, for this gift of yourself."

— **Carol H. Rasco**, Former Director of the Domestic Policy Council under President Clinton, leader for a more helpful government, and former CEO of the largest literacy non-profit in the country, Reading is Fundamental (RIF).

"I embraced endorsing this book because of who Bo is. When I worked with him, I thrived because he lives and leads the leadership he writes about. He's penned a book with a new calling. Ask yourself, 'How can I use this new leadership model to influence, inspire, and impact those around me?' You'll forever be grateful for what you did."

— **Jill Robinson**, Assistant Dean of External Relations and Strategic Partnerships for the Jack C. Massey College of Business, Belmont University

Dr. Bethel "Bo" Thomas: "I am honored to salute you and to endorse your new book on transformative leadership. The U. S. Department of Transportation continues to benefit from the work started with your consulting group more than 20 years ago. The visionary assessment of the future focused on safety, the environment, the economy, and equitable access continues to lead and influence transportation and infrastructure philosophy, collaboration, innovation, and policy in the 21st century. Thank you."

— **Rodney E. Slater**, former U.S. Secretary of Transportation

"Bo Thomas challenges us to reinvent leadership. His wide-ranging look at leadership for the future draws upon four decades of personal leadership experiences and new insights into the power of inspiration.

With a new humanizing leadership language, post COVID leaders will be well equipped to create a "Better Normal"."

— **Jerry Williams**, Executive Director Emerita, 25-year CEO of Leadership Nashville, a national model for bridging community leaders with community issues.

REINVENTING
LEADERSHIP

Leading to Inspire a
"Better Normal"

Bethel E. Thomas, Jr., PhD

IngramSpark Publishing | Nashville

Reinventing Leadership: Leading to Inspire A Better Normal
© 2023 Bethel Thomas

Published by IngramSpark Publishing l Nashville, Tennessee

ISBN
Hardcover 979-8-9871913-0-9
Paperback 979-8-9871913-1-6
eBook 979-8-987-1913-2-3

Printed in the United States of America

For further information on bulk purchases or arranging a speaking event, please contact

Bethel Thomas at BoThomas5566@gmail.com
BoThomasBooks.com.
linkedIn.com/in/Bo-Thomas

TABLE OF CONTENTS

ACKNOWLEDGEMENTS

Some of the people I want to acknowledge are people who have influenced my leadership career with their writing, but most of the people I acknowledge are people who influenced me by who they are, how they led, or how they lived.

Mentors, Authors, and Researchers: The opportunity to "reinvent" leadership after what we learned in 2020-2021 was just waiting for someone to create a new leadership perspective and model. We already had great leadership information from previous authors and researchers who had left us their own unique gifts. I am grateful to them all, but I particularly thank Tom Peters who I was fortunate enough to get to know and learn from in the summer prior to the release of his ground-breaking book, *In Search of Excellence*. Tom added early fuel to my leadership fire.

A special word of gratitude to Todd Trash and Andrew Elliot who left their gifts of research into the power of inspiration. To Abraham Maslow and Carl Rodgers, psychologists, I thank for their lasting impact on solidifying the fact that we all need unconditional love and a sense of belonging to be fully human and reach our potential. A big thank you to Robert Jay Lifton and a diverse group of 26 of his colleagues, all highly respected in the science of human behavior: psychiatrists, psychologists, and mental health experts. I thank them for their courage to act on their moral compass and civic "duty to warn" about "malignant normality" in their book, *The Dangerous Case of Donald Trump.*

I especially want to thank Brené Brown whose work with vulnerability opens a new leadership door for any leader who cares to enter and become a better human being and leader. Hopefully, Brown's work will lead to a much-needed new wave of women leaders and women authors where the premium leadership skills are the ones women know best. The old "soft skills", the relationship skills, are now the new "hard skills" that leaders for a Better Normal must embrace.

All the above folks left leadership gifts that are interconnected. As a result, they reveal an even larger gift of leadership synergy that I hope will inspire a new generation of leaders and a new commitment from organizations to build cultures of inspiration. I am so grateful to you all.

Literary Management Group: I am particularly thankful that I found Bruce Barbour, Founder of the Literary Management Group, whose family has a rich tradition with books and publishing. Notable to me was the fact that Bruce's father helped Dr. Norman Vincent Peale publish the masterpiece, *The Power of Positive Thinking.* Dr. Peale gave one of his last interviews before his death to Bob Fisher and me in Pauling, New York, as we were writing *Real Dream Teams.* Bruce and I immediately connected. He sensed my urgency about the unique message of this book and helped me move it along quickly with his team.

IngramSpark: The Ingram family and Ingram Industries are a rare gift to Nashville. My friend, Orrin Ingram, was particularly sensitive when I shared my concern about the slow process of traditional publishing in 2022. Orrin quickly put me with Alexandra Burlason, Craig Pollock, Jenna Hall, and Kayla Thompson at IngramSpark. This book is in front of future leaders now as opposed to later because of Orrin and his broader family.

The Belmont University family. I put my consulting practice on hold to join my long-time consulting partner, Bob Fisher, who had become President of Belmont University in Nashville three years earlier. Bob and I wrote the book *Real Dream Teams* and then lived our best real dream team experience at Belmont. I am particularly grateful to my friend, co-author, co-consultant and colleague for the invitation to join him on the Belmont leadership journey. Bob, our lives and families have been connected since our children were small. I am blessed by your friendship gift of a lifetime.

I also thank a coalition of colleagues and leaders at Belmont who helped inspire a major transformational change in higher education: Susan West, Paula Gill, Jason Rodgers, Steve Lasley, Thomas Burns, Todd Lake, Pat Raines, Cathy Taylor, Phil Johnson, Cynthia Curtis, Jeff Cornwall, Bernard Turner, John Gonas, Rick Byrd, Betty Wiseman, Jill Robinson, Kate Mosley, Debbie Coppinger, Sarah Cates, Cindy Painter, Jose Gonzalez, Boyd Smith, Joyce Searcy, Willie Young, Fred Kendall, Vicky Tarleton, and Jon Roebuck.

I especially thank visionary Belmont Trustee leaders who fanned the flames of transformation and were change leaders: Larry Thrailkill, Marty Dickens, Milton Johnson, Janet Ayers, and Gordon Inman. A special thanks to Development Advisory Committee Board members Steve Hewlett, Steve Horrell, Helen Kennedy, Randy Smith, Cynthia Leu, and the late Clayton McWhorter for their unconditional support of me and the Advancement team.

Nashville Colleagues. My leadership friends included many in the Nashville community with our vision of becoming Nashville's university. We partnered with governors, mayors, the city council, the Nashville Healthcare Council, the Chamber of Commerce, and Convention Visitors Bureau in historic public-private partnerships.

There are multiple leaders, many in the groups noted above, that I appreciated who were eager to be real partners on big initiatives in the transformations of Belmont and Nashville. These included Phil Bredesen, Bill Purcell, Karl Dean, Bill Haslam, Ralph Schulz, Janet Miller, Butch Spyridon, Tommy Frist, Jr., Agenia Clark, Jim Cooper, Lisa Quigley, Keel Hunt, Haley Hovious, Jerry Williams,

Cordia Harrington, Cal Turner, the late Richard Treadway and the late Darrell Freeman.

Music City was like a magnet for creative talent, many who influenced me. Part of the allure of music-rich Belmont were Nashville friends in the music business like Mike Curb, Wayland Holyfield, Bard Herbison, and Mark Wright. I am deeply grateful for their leadership in working with me, James Elliott, and other Belmont leaders to create the first-ever accredited song-writing major in the country. Eugenia Winwood, Paul Kwami, Laynge Martine, and Beverly Keel are other special friends who helped me more fully appreciate the inclusive, humanizing, and universal language of music.

The USA Department of Transportation Leaders. Kudos to this team of leaders. Collaboration was necessary and essential for the new multi-modal transportation model envisioned by Rodney Slater to become a reality. The Presidential appointee, Secretary of Transportation leader Slater was a model for "Better Normal" leadership, "visionary and vigilant" in pursuit of excellent transportation solutions, always inviting and inspiring other leaders to own and implement the vision. Bob Fisher and I were honored to work for over three years with Secretary Slater and a powerful "guiding coalition" team that included transportation leaders who became colleagues and friends: Jerry Malone, Mort Downey, Jane Garvey, Commandant James Loy, Jack Basso, Melissa Allen, David Sanders, Kelly Coyner, Ashish Sen, Ken Wykle, Jolene Molitoris, and Carmen Jones.

St. Jude Children's Research Hospital Leaders. This is a "Great to Greater" organization, and a universal model for making our world a better place. This book would not have been, well, this book, without St. Jude. I cannot thank Dr. James Downing enough for his willingness to share his personal journey from researcher to CEO-leader with me. Summer Freeman earned kudos for sharing relevant documentation of the St. Jude journey from Danny Thomas to the St. Jude strategic thinking and acting process, to the Global Initiative, to the Inspiration4 space flight, to St. Jude's relationship with war-torn

Ukraine. Thanks to Dennis Reber and Thonda Barnes for graciously providing insightful information related to the distinctive nature of the Leadership Academy. To Rob Clark, for opening doors and helping me connect, thank you. Finally, I am grateful to Marlo Thomas who invited me to want to know more about St. Jude back in 2015 with her inspiring video acceptance of her father's induction into the inaugural class of the Tennessee Healthcare Hall of Fame at Belmont University.

Leadership Relationships. From over 300 groups with whom I have consulted and/or joined on leadership journeys, I want to say thanks to a few leaders in particular because of the humanity that permeated their leadership. Their accomplishments are many, but who they are is more important than what they did: Charles Nabholz, Elaine Eubank, J. D. Gingrich, Allen Weatherly, Pat Averwater, John Steuri, Bill Hubbard, Jerry Adams, Milt Honea, Sherman Tate, Jo Luck, Steve Seitz, the late Paul Williams, and Carol Rasco.

My friend and spiritual mentor, Michael E. Williams, had a strong impact on my thinking about ethical leadership and leaders with character. He was a retired Methodist minister and Storyteller in Residence at Martin Methodist College (now University of Tennessee Southern) when he died tragically in 2018. I am grateful to University leaders Mark LaBranche, Judy Cheatham, John Collett, Bill McAlilly, Richard Warren, and Byron Trauger for their leadership in helping secure the legacy of Michael Williams and assuring that rural storytelling will become a part of the fabric of this new university in rural south-central Tennessee. These leaders have consistently reinforced the concept of the "ethical heart" and modeling core values in how they lead.

David Plazas has encouraged my writing for several years as the Opinion and Engagement Director of the USA Today Network newsrooms in Tennessee and The Tennessean. I am grateful for the important role of journalism in American life, and the journalism commitment to ethics and truth-telling. I particularly appreciate David for his transparency, his leadership as Chair of the Tennessean's

Diversity and Inclusion Task Force, and his help in making me a better writer.

Charles Neal deserves a very special word of thanks. My good friend since college days at UT Knoxville, he has encouraged me throughout the writing process to write for every-day leaders of all stripes as well as any business, spiritual, or political person anywhere who leads fellow human beings. Thank you, Charles, for being the first to say, "You are really advocating for resetting and reinventing leadership." Thus, the title.

My Home Family. I have learned most about the human side of leadership from those closest to me. My grandson dropped numerous gems of leadership wisdom through Friday night sleepovers and movies he selected, and we discussed. Son-in-law Chris has been an invaluable contributor with his high-tech skills, easy pathways to information, and a sense of humor that kept all in perspective. My sister, Carolyn, has been a strong advocate for my work from day one.

The book is dedicated to the three women I grew up with, literally. I had so much to learn about being a husband, a father, and a friend. I am thankful and grateful for Rubye Lynn, my wife and life-partner, and our daughters Elizabeth and Steph for their patience, unconditional love, wisdom, and gift of family. Our daughters are so darn smart and kind. It's a shame the gene pool doesn't run upstream! These three women have been passionate, caring and encouraging in their support of this work and fundamental in shaping my awareness of the inequities women and others experience every day. Thank you for inspiring me to write honestly about the painful reality of "normal" and the danger of "malignant normality", to "not settle" for a traditional leadership book, and helping me sustain the beliefs that "we all have a leadership voice" and "we can do better". You are my heart. I am eternally grateful and blessed.

DEDICATION

To my wife, Rubye Lynn, daughters Elizabeth and Steph: Thank you for insisting that I write about painful truths and hopeful opportunities, and to trust being me in the process. I am forever blessed by your caring, endless support, and for teaching me to be a better human being. You are the loves of my life.

INTRODUCTION

The phrase, "one wild and precious life" is from Mary Oliver, the Pulitzer Prize-winning poet. In her poem, the "Summer Day," she asks a series of questions about who made the world. Could it have been the swan, the black bear, even the grasshopper? Then she reflects on how she spent her day paying attention to nature and strolling through the fields. The poem shifts dramatically to personalize the last four lines, asking me and other readers to consider a shockingly beautiful and urgent question:

"Tell me, what else should I have done?
Doesn't everything die at last, and too soon?
Tell me, what is it you plan to do
With your one wild and precious life?"

The first time I saw and experienced this question, it was as if Mary Oliver herself was speaking to me. It struck me as timeless and a question for any age group and every person. It was electric and emotional. It was an out-of-the-blue challenge to think differently about life, my life and the lives of others. Mary Oliver's question stirs us to think about life from a totally new perspective.

In the book, *The Mission of a Lifetime: Lessons from the Men Who Went to the Moon*, astronauts recalled how seeing the earth rise from their position on or near the moon exposed the fragility of earth; all humanity as one human race moving on a tiny globe through space.

From that new perspective, hatred of other neighbors on planet earth, cruelty, divisiveness, and war seemed unimaginable. Our one humanity, our vulnerability, and interdependence were overwhelmingly clear.

The Mary Oliver question and the astronauts view of fragile earth frame the perspective for a new leadership model and a significantly new role for leaders after the shattering events that unfolded in 2020.

REINVENTING LEADERSHIP: WHY NOW

2020 will forever be remembered as the year that changed our perspective on life, leadership, and the broader world. Our fragility, vulnerability, and human preciousness were painfully exposed by four powerful realities converging in one historic moment:

1. The virus-related pandemic,
2. Long-standing, man-made structural inequities with severe negative consequences for women, people of color, LGBTQ, poor, and other marginalized people,
3. Uninspiring bureaucratic leaders and,
4. The emergence of toxic leaders and the creation of a dangerous "malignant normality" emboldened by millions of good people and the thousands of political, business, media, and religious leaders who were actively supportive of, complicit with, or silent about toxic leaders.

The convergence and crystallization of these four powerful forces, all at one time, have created the biggest leadership crisis of our lifetime. "Normal" as we have known it prior to 2020 has been exposed as ugly, mean-spirited, insensitive, and destructive. Human beings have been the losers. Some people seem to be looking for new ways to make

> The convergence and crystallization of these four powerful forces, all at one time, have created the biggest leadership crisis of our lifetime.

life more difficult for others. Basic human rights and the core values of democracy are being dismissed and violated. The honest realities of "normal" are painful, disappointing, and sad. We can't go back to normal. The magnitude of the crisis creates a new sense of urgency about leading and leadership. The crisis demands that we lead for something more, something better than the normal that has been exposed. It is up to hundreds of thousands of new leaders with a new perspective on life, leading to embrace the fragile, vulnerable, and precious lives they lead to create a "Better Normal": at home and work, in the community, country, world, and for the planet.

"In the end, perhaps the greatest blessing conveyed by the lessons of spiritual genius that Tippett harvests in *Becoming Wise* is the strength to meet the world where it really is, and then to make it better." Our journey throughout this book is to meet the world and leadership where they really are, and then lead to make them better.

The "one wild and precious life" and "one human race on fragile earth" perspectives change everything for leadership and leaders. The new perspectives place a premium on human life and reveal how much more we want and value from our personal and professional lives. There is a profound new awareness of how important relationships are, at home and work.

"Life is short" resonates in new ways. As we will discover in more detail later, during the pandemic millions of people discovered their current jobs to be unfulfilling and uninspiring. As a result, they quit and began their search for more meaning and purpose. In addition, working from home during the pandemic created a new life balance few had experienced. A slew of studies emerging in 2022 indicate that hybrid workplaces, a combination of office and work from home, are not only preferred by employees but employees are more productive! The benefits of hybrid outweigh the costs of being in the office full-time for employees and organizations.

The radical converging of the four powerful driving forces in one year has been the ultimate wake-up call for leaders. Millions of people are frustrated, angry, hurting, and feel betrayed by their leaders and their companies.

Multiple systems and policies created by leaders in the past are inequitable. We now know that over 70% of us have been marginalized to some degree for years with less opportunity than the other 30%. Many political leaders have and are exploiting the discontent and anger with misinformation, providing human targets to blame and vent anger. The culture wars are dysfunctional and divisive. They thrive on creating fear of our fellow human beings. These wars, like all wars, are destructive and unsustainable. No longer can business, political, or religious leaders be silent or complicit with policies and actions that dehumanize the very people they lead. It is not us versus them. It is us. It is we the people.

After 2020, democracy, politics, religion, business, education, medicine, human rights, and the environment are now linked and connected by the culture wars. The new world has sadly become a battleground in all arenas, and it impacts us all directly. The culture wars have a negative impact on humans everywhere. They lead to policies and laws that marginalize people further, the people you live with and work with. Leaders everywhere are called to create a "better normal" and a "we the people" common good.

REINVENTING LEADERSHIP: WHY ME?

The events of 2020 were the tipping point for me to write about leading. The values and ethical principles that I learned and most of us have honored for years were openly violated in 2020 and 2021 for all to see. Powerful people were living out different values. Power, control, blame, and dehumanizing behaviors have become common and normal. Sandbox and kindergarten values of play fair, tell the truth, and respect others are being trashed. Millions of good people seem to be saying it is ok to ignore the common values they grew up with in churches, synagogues, and mosques. The "OK" has become a resounding silence or open compliance with toxic political leaders. The result has morphed into a malignant normality that is dangerous and a threat to all of us. There is nothing "OK" about the leadership of toxic people. There is nothing normal about dehumanizing actions, behaviors, and policies.

I felt strongly that it was time to address this as the leadership crisis of our lifetime. I felt it would only get worse if we didn't call malignant normality by its name and become advocates for what is right. Toxic leaders have boldly asserted themselves into every aspect of our lives. The consequences of doing nothing was unacceptable. A bold new leadership response to the trending malignant normality was urgent.

Why me? Well, simply put, I am uniquely positioned to write about leadership at this moment. My career spans over 4 decades of leadership and relationship-building. I have examined the leadership elephant from trunk to tail. I have consulted with over 300 organizations related to leadership, team building, and strategic planning. I co-authored *Real Dream Teams,* based on the research and best practices of highly effective teams. I have been a practicing psychologist, a leadership coach, a university professor, a parent, and a husband. I am one of the few authors who actually stepped into the leadership arena before writing about it, helping lead the transformation of a major university from a "good to great" one. I am passionate about leadership that inspires the best in others and treats people as the number one asset. I have seen and heard the pain and anger of marginalized people and the hunger of people for leaders to stop blaming others and seek solutions that make things better for all.

In truth, I was not sure anyone else would be willing to write about the dangerous trend of Malignant Normality. I was not sure anyone else would write about the failure of current management models to address the magnitude of the human inequities that past leaders created, and we inherited. I was not sure anyone else would call out the brokenness of the leadership that got us to 2020.

WE CAN DO BETTER

The common theme I hear from others and share throughout this book: "We can do better." Leaders are now called to lead with character, courage, and compassion to affirm with actions and new policies that the people they lead are indeed the most important asset and most valuable stakeholder in any enterprise. Leaders must now inspire people to channel their frustration and anger into building equitable and better work environments, healthier communities, and a more peaceful world. Democracy and the organizations of the future will thrive on their talented people, all their people. "We the people" is in our DNA.

The leadership myths are many, but the most common myths are these: 1) only a few can lead, 2) leaders are born not made, 3) most people need to be managed, supervised, and controlled, and 4) only a few leaders at the top are capable of making the really important decisions. We now know that these are myths. These old beliefs are simply not true. They are now as dated as "flat earth" thinking. We now know that all can learn to lead, either in reaching personal goals or leading others.

YOU CAN LEAD

I want you to know in the first few pages of this book that this book is written for you. If you picked up this book and are reading this sentence, I want you to trust the new truths about leadership. All point to you and others with whom you work. The number one truth is that you can lead. All of us can lead at given times. We all can step up and make things better. I share this with you now knowing that most people simply have never thought of themselves as a leader because of the old myths. Supervisors, coordinators, managers, and other people who do the work every day think they are simply their titles. That's it. No one ever suggested they lead. No one told them they could lead. Therefore, most leadership books are read by those few who already think they are leaders and by academicians. Frankly, I am not writing for the people in my leadership circles. I hope they will read this book, become more inspiring, and improve their leadership. But I am writing this for all those people, maybe like you, who never thought of themselves as leaders or never been asked to lead.

TURNING CRISIS INTO OPPORTUNITY

So, you have a leader within, just waiting to emerge at home, at work, or in the community. It doesn't matter whether or not you are extroverted, introverted, young, older, a college graduate or not. Leadership can be learned. I recommend that every company, large and small, teach all their people how to lead and why it is so important for all people to lead. This book will help you learn how to lead for a better tomorrow by inspiring others and helping make others more successful.

This is a different book on leadership. Here's more about my tipping point for this unique work. Someone needed to identify and connect the four unprecedented forces that converged that changed everything and transformed the role of leaders. Someone needed to write about inspiration as the "only" key that consistently unlocks and sustains our best individual and collective thinking and acting. Someone needed to call out "character," "moral compass," "compassion," and "ethical leadership" as being essential for any leader: business, religious, or political. Someone needed to sound the alarm about the growing malignant normality.

This book on leadership is different in that it is written from a human growth framework rather than a traditional management framework. Management models, by definition, are about managing people rather than leading human beings. Therefore, "how" we treat others becomes a priority. Humanizing work and community is a priority. Compassion and kindness are priorities. You will hear new voices of leadership who use or have used their platform to inspire, influence, and lead for a better world that include Maya Angelou, Taylor Swift, Malala Yousafzai, Michelle Obama, BTS, Serena Williams, Michael Phelps, and Simone Biles.

This new perspective of leadership shows the relationship and synergy between seven existing leadership practices that inspire and tap into the underutilized discretionary potential in each of us. The new leadership perspective and new leadership model create a moral imperative for all people to embrace and inspire character, courage, and the common good. I hope you feel as compelled to read and learn as I felt compelled to be the "someone" to write about the moral and leadership opportunity of a lifetime.

> The new leadership perspective and new leadership model create a moral imperative for all people to embrace and inspire character, courage, and the common good. I hope you feel as compelled to read and learn as I felt compelled to be the "someone" to write about the moral and leadership opportunity of a lifetime.

This new model at this moment can make a difference for all who now lead and for the millions more who can discover the leadership potential within themselves. Since all can lead, "millions" is the right term. In the world of the future, the most innovative and progressive companies will invest wisely in greater economic security for all their people. They will invest in leadership development, relationship-building, creativity, and emotional intelligence training for all people in the organization. People will be the most important asset and they will create more value for all the stakeholders, joining the healthy trend toward stakeholder capitalism. Since all people have the potential to lead more in their personal or professional life, we need many more leaders throughout every organization. Leaders who have earned followers will be there to primarily inspire, empower, coach, and make others successful. As you will learn, the new leadership model is built on the best practices of what we know about leadership and what inspires others. One of the best practices is rethinking old assumptions, like assumptions about leadership that turn out to be myths. This book is about reinventing leadership and creating a Better Normal.

THE CASE FOR "BETTER NORMAL" LEADERS

I realize I am sounding the alarm for an army of new leaders with a new perspective for creating better normal organizations and better communities. I strongly believe that "Better Normal" is possible and that the old normal is not good enough. And, since I am a new voice for several readers, I want you to understand a little more about me. I will share more at various stages in the book about my learning pathways to this leadership endeavor and why I feel so compelled to write with urgency about leadership.

I grew up in rural America in the small town of Smithville, Tennessee, small as in 2450 people. My mother was a church organist and piano teacher, which meant I took piano lessons and played in music recitals. I was her worst student, but I learned to love music. Meals were often delayed because mother was playing and singing at the piano. My dad was the county agricultural agent for Dekalb County, which meant 4-H Club for me, milking cows, and working in the family garden. Who would have thought our little 8 acres three blocks from the County Court House and the center of town would bring so many daily chores to my door! It did mean a kinship with my friends who lived on real farms with more chores than me. Social life centered around school, sports, and church and I raised my hand for any event anywhere any time.

Depression era parents and post WWII meant saving money, a one-car family, quilts with family history, limited spending, little travel, and big work ethic. Smithville was a church-centered small community where parents heard of misbehavior before one got home from school or church. "Being good" and "being polite" were heavily rewarded.

In short, what I learned in kindergarten and throughout my early years in small town America became the ethical seeds for my leadership development:

- From church: Do the right thing. Be kind to humans, animals, and the planet. Be humble. Help others.
- From church and school: Play nice with others, be fair, tell the truth, be trustworthy. Learn from others.
- From sports: In team sports, when the team wins, we all win. I win when I help others be successful. It's not about me. Be collaborative. Assists are as important as scoring. By the way, democracy and organizations are team sports.

Basically, these became non-negotiable core values or guiding principles for me. There were gatekeepers everywhere in my little community. If you cheated, treated people badly, or were untrustworthy, everyone knew. Trust was everything. Most people reached agreements on a handshake or by "I give you my word." My little world grew exponentially after leaving home for college. I struggled going from a little pond to a bigger pond. As I mentioned earlier, I was shocked that not everybody played by the same rules I did. But I kept raising my hand, being curious, being persistent, and graduate school inspired me as I discovered how I could make a difference in a bigger arena. It was a path of constant discovery and becoming, but I found a way to live up to my potential.

In short, the core values that we learned in kindergarten, churches, synagogues, temples, and mosques about truth, love, relationships, and a power greater than ourselves, shaped our lives. They shaped mine. I believe that these same core values should absolutely shape how we lead and how we treat others.

Part one of the book makes the case for leading change through the lens of a new leadership perspective and a new model for leading. The revelations of 2020 do create a new urgency about leadership and the role of leaders. I will make the case for a revolutionary change in traditional leadership and show the necessity for the 7 non-negotiable leadership practices that inspire the best in others.

Part one of the book explores the three big discoveries from 2020, each discovery earning its own chapter and creates urgency for the reinvention of leadership:

Chapter 1. Getting back to Normal is the Enemy of a Better Normal,

Chapter 2. This moment is The Greatest Leadership Opportunity of our Lifetime, and

Chapter 3. A Culture of Inspiration is the only culture that invites:

- Character, courage, compassion, and the common good,
- Leveraging underutilized and untapped potential,
- Individual and collective passion,
- Sustainable peak performance, and
- Invites **everyone to lead**, help others be successful and exceed even their own expectations.

I am hopeful that this book will be the tipping point for you to lead. This book was written for you. I am actively recruiting you to lead, to visualize your leadership potential and then act to make a difference with your "one wild and precious life." For those of you already leading, I am recruiting you to lead even more effectively and invite your colleagues to embrace becoming leaders.

Honoring our One
Humanity And Making
a Difference With Our
Leadership Is Inspiring

PART I

THE NEW LEADERSHIP PERSPECTIVE

CHAPTER ONE

NORMAL IS THE ENEMY
OF A BETTER NORMAL

"As our case is new, so we must
think anew, and act anew."

— ABRAHAM LINCOLN

We do live on a tiny planet with fragile humanity all around. In families, workplaces, and play spaces, we have so much more in common than we have differences. We all love, bleed, feel the pain of loss, experience joy, and thrive on hope for the future. We all have been exposed in new ways. We are vulnerable. We are incurably human. Our new awareness and better understanding of others, our new perception of humanity, allows us to honor and appreciate people in a new way. The new world creates a huge gap between what we used to call "normal" and where we are now. We must rethink everything. Returning to the old normal is not an option. As one local leader said the other day about gun violence. "Why would we want to get back to normal? Normal is killing us." We need a Better Normal and American leaders of all stripes need to lead in ways that inspire and enhance human life. All of us are invited to think, act, and become intentional about what we plan to do with our one wild and precious life and the lives of others in this new world. Most of all, this new world boldly invites us to think differently about leadership. Those who lead, educate others, and parent have a chance to reset how they lead, educate, and parent from a powerful new perspective.

THE HUMAN COST OF THE FOUR POWERFUL FORCES: THE STARTLING RESHAPING OF LEADERSHIP

"If you keep doing what you have always done you will keep getting what you always got." This old saying has fresh and urgent meaning after 2020. The stark new reality after 2020 means we can't keep doing what we have always done as leaders. The magnitude of the combined forces, all in one year, has disrupted normal life and normal leadership responses.

Let's look more closely at what happened in 2020 and early 2021 and why this moment in history is so unprecedented. It is so unprecedented and the consequences so significant, that the "normal" of the past is a step back in time. The magnitude of the opportunity calls for better leaders, better and healthier organizations, communities, and a stronger democracy. The new world of 2020 and beyond is a game changer for leaders and leadership. "Getting back to normal" is not an option for any leader or any organization.

BRUTAL REALITY: THE NEW LEADERSHIP CHALLENGE

When I taught my first college class, an introductory Psychology class, I was terrified. I was only 6 years older than the youngest student in the class. I was overprepared and had a sledgehammer of notes for a small-hammer 50-minute class. I had cut my face while shaving in the morning of this class, cut enough to require a band aid. I explained in the opening minute of class that "I was thinking about the presentation to the class and cut my face while shaving this morning." Then I proceeded to over-lecture, ending the class 5 minutes beyond the allotted time. After all the students left the classroom, I found a note on the desk at the front of the room. "How kind of someone. A compliment on my first day," I thought. But I opened it to read these words. "Next time, think more about your face and cut your lecture."

As I write about the reality of what happened in 2020 and beyond, I know I am sounding an alarm. I don't know how to "cut" the facts without glossing over the seriousness of the painful consequences of normal.

So, hang with me as we look at the consequences and the human cost of the four converging forces of 2020. It is not very pleasant nor very comfortable nor inspiring. It is the bad news before we get to the good news. The bad news is very bad. The good news is very, very good.

I know many of you would say, "Skip the bad news and go directly to the good news and the inspiring practices." In essence, I am saying that we can't appreciate the amazing leadership opportunity we have if we don't quickly acknowledge the shocking threat to leadership posed by the brutal reality of 2020. A sneak peek at the good news tells us that there are multiple examples already of organizations that have never accepted the norm as good enough. There are just too few. I will focus on the best of the best of leadership from the past and will share those gifts of leadership as we create a new model that inspires the best in others. St. Jude Research Hospital in Memphis, for example, has gone from "great to greater" in the past few years, inspiring the best of everyone from Memphis to Ukraine with its global network. They have become a model for breaking the mold of normal and doing breath-taking work in finding cures for pediatric cancer and saving lives. We will feature St. Jude, W. L Gore & Associates, Belmont University, and other more open

> A sneak peek at the good news tells us that there are multiple examples already of organizations that have never accepted the norm as good enough. There are just too few.

organizations as models and offer them as hope for "humanizing" any organization for a Better Normal. After all we have learned about the leadership crisis and opportunity, any organization can create a vision and mission that lead to making a difference with their people, the people they serve, their community, and the world. Our best leadership days are ahead of us. Absolutely. Leaders now have a moral imperative to inspire character, courage, and the common good. With the exposure of millions of marginalized people, there is a strategic "just cause" available to any organization. And we know how to be intentional about building leadership for any enterprise. There is so much good news and an explosion of new leaders for a better normal is just waiting to happen.

But first the bad news, simple because the human impact of the "normal" we have been living is so unfair to so many people who you and I work with every day. We know, without question, that new leaders, like you, everywhere are the ones who must enter the arena to help make things fair, equitable, right, and better for the people they work with every day.

So, for the next few pages, I am inviting you to walk in the shoes of the countless number of people whose life will never be the same because of Covid; enter the world of the millions of people who have had less opportunity because they were born black, brown, LBGTQ, or poor; feel the frustration and hurt of those who don't feel valued or appreciated by bureaucratic managers or toxic leaders; and experience the unfairness and sadness of systems and structures that have to some degree marginalized up to 70% of us. All these people are us.

The most powerful impact of the four forces that emerged in 2020 are best seen through the lens of the human impact, those most affected. Obviously, the devastating impact of each of the forces is a book in itself, so I will just note a few outcomes to show the enormity of the stressful and disturbing consequences. All of us felt the impact, some more than others.

COVID-19 PANDEMIC: THE FIRST DRIVING FORCE THAT SHOCKED AND STARTLED US

The threat of a virus we had not seen or experienced before exposed in vivid detail the fragile and vulnerable world our astronauts saw from their moon perspective. Covid-19 became the common enemy, the alien from outer space that invaded the inner space of all humanity. Only this alien is invisible. Being the most powerful country in the world with an abundance of resources did not protect us. In the first year, more of us were infected and more of us died in these United States than in any other country.

We were not world leaders in our response to this common threat and more lives were lost as a result. The Covid-19 crisis was unprecedented and unique for government and private sector leaders as well as educators and parents.

The continuing threat of virus-related pandemics alone demands a new perspective on leadership and a new model for leaders for the future. Virus-related pandemics, then, are the first of four major forces that create a crisis and opportunity for new leadership and more leaders.

THE HUMAN COST OF THE VIRUS PANDEMICS: A FRACTION OF THE COST

- Millions of people around the world died. According to estimates from the Center for Disease Control between February 2020 through March 2022 there were over 955,223 deaths in America. Many said their last goodbye to a loved one over the phone.
- About one-third of those infected experience long-term symptoms, meaning that over 30 million working Americans may have or have had long-Covid, negatively impacting their ability to function at work or home.

- According to the U. S. Bureau of Labor Statistics, in March of 2022, there were more than 10 million job openings due to the virus, limited day care, school interruptions and people looking for more value and economic security from work.
- The negative impact of the virus was more pronounced for those more vulnerable including people of color, the poor, and those unable to obtain health care coverage. The human impact was brutal. We all lost.

The spotty national, regional, and local leadership response to the virus pandemic and to the welfare of millions of American people and their families has become normal. We can do better in dealing with virus-related pandemics and public health issues that impact everyone.

THE MAN-MADE SYSTEMIC CRISIS: THE SECOND DRIVING FORCE FOR NEW LEADERSHIP

The crisis gets worse. The new world order is just as dramatically impacted by what we have learned about our man-made issues created by years of structural and systemic inequities. We see clearly the most vulnerable of the vulnerable in all of humanity. Our broken systems and the inequities within them have been exposed. The brokenness has been there for years, just below the surface. My friend, Lisa Quigley, a long-time political observer and now project leader of a Tusk Philanthropy initiative to bring food security to thousands of children, said recently, "The table has been set for years related to widening economic disparity and food insecurity in every state. The 2016 to 2020 era just made it worse. We have the knowledge and resources to fix our broken systems."

THE HUMAN COST OF MAN-MADE SYSTEMIC INEQUITIES

The current eco-systems and infrastructures, the old normal and status quo, assure for millions of American workers one or more of the below:

- Continued poverty,
- Poor health and limited affordable healthcare,
- Inadequate funding for children and teachers in public education,
- Environmental erosion,
- Gender inequities in pay, leadership opportunities, and lack of day care for young children.
- Systemic racism reflected in less opportunity for jobs, promotions, education, bank loans, leadership, choice of neighborhoods; criminal justice, policing inequities; greater exposure to gun violence; greater infant mortality.

The above outcomes of systemic inequities have become standard operating procedures and normal. We can do better.

If you are a leader or want to develop your inner leader, the marginalized are people like you, people who you work with, your friends, and your colleagues. Your fellow human beings. As a leader, you often must be their voice and have their back. They should know you are willing to fight for them in the workplace and community. Many of you have been on the receiving end of less opportunity. It is up to you to help create environments where equity and inclusion are the norm.

The man-made dysfunctional systems with pandemic-type impact are just as shocking and stunning as the virus-related pandemics, and they add a new layer to the painful new perspective on humanity and our shared vulnerability.

"This isn't a snow day where you're waiting for the sun to shine and the world to return, because the world we have lived in for so long in many ways is never coming back," says Jamie Metzl, technology futurist and co-founder of OneShared.World. "This is an all-hands-on-deck moment for the country, the world, our species. Everyone has a role to play to build back something better than what is being destroyed." Most people in most organizations and American neighborhoods spend inordinate amounts of time worried about economic security. Personally, I know I have had every opportunity to succeed. Those opportunities are reflected in my education, jobs with retirement benefits, health/dental/vision insurance, and thus, economic security. I have had ease of access to multiple other opportunities. I now know that I have benefited from an unfair system. All people deserve the same opportunities in the systems of the future.

UNINSPIRING BUREAUCRATIC LEADERS: THE THIRD DRIVING FORCE FOR NEW LEADERSHIP

In addition to the covid virus pandemic and the structural, man-made inequities of pandemic impact, a third factor adds to the urgency for new leadership: the full awareness of the continuing negative human impact of traditional bureaucratic leaders. This third driving force is an overall leadership issue where too few people are expected to lead and make strategic decisions.

Traditional Bureaucratic Leadership

Unfortunately, the documentation related to bureaucratic leadership had not been encouraging before 2020. The bottom-line results of the studies related to workplace morale and job satisfaction are staggering and stunning. Research from various sources tells us that millions of people come to work every day uninspired and poorly motivated because of the relationship with their boss, manager, or supervisor. The day-to-day operations most often are delegated to managers and supervisors who do just that: manage and supervise. Broad-based leadership is minimal and old terms like bosses and subordinates prevail, but do not inspire. In addition, bureaucracies cannot keep pace with the rapidly changing marketplace and bureaucracies underutilize their people talent. Bureaucratic leaders have either learned "by doing," gone to traditional business schools to learn how to manage people or been promoted without leadership training. They most often have not spent intentional time learning and capitalizing on their people skills. Fortunately, some have sought leadership coaches to help them become better leaders.

THE NEGATIVE HUMAN CONSEQUENCES OF BUREAUCRATIC LEADERSHIP

- A high percentage of people in the workplace say their relationship with their manager or leader is unsatisfactory, negatively impacting all they do at work. Ninety-one percent of 1,000 employees surveyed in a recent Interact/Harris Poll said their leader lacks the ability to communicate well.
- Almost half of American workers report never being appreciated or recognized once by their manager in the last year. In 365 days. Not once.
- A high number of people say they comply at work and save their best for the weekend.
- People are often fearful of sharing their ideas or best thoughts, negating opportunities for innovation and entrepreneurship.
- Being vulnerable, transparent, and compassionate are viewed as weaknesses by many people in bureaucratic leadership positions.
- Strategic plans do not adequately address the systemic and structural inequities described above.
- The trailblazing Gallup Research clearly indicates that people don't leave organizations as much as they leave bosses and managers. The attrition rate has been much higher for over-controlling bosses during the working remote era than for those leaders who learned to adapt. Uninspiring bureaucratic leaders create a talent and economic drain on the organization.

The above consequences of Traditional Bureaucratic Normal Leadership are the norm in many organizations. We can do better.

TOXIC LEADERS AND THE MALIGNANT NORMALITY TREND: THE FOURTH DRIVING FORCE

Stay with me as we talk about malignant normal leadership and the normalizing of unacceptable and dangerous patterns of behavior. This emerging leadership model runs counter to every good model of leadership. It plays on fear, manipulation, and deception.

THE NEGATIVE HUMAN COST OF TOXIC LEADERSHIP

- The polarized political environment and culture wars are dysfunctional, abusive, and hurtful.
- Leaders in powerful positions have modeled divisive, destructive, and harmful behaviors, normalizing behaviors that we once considered "not normal," unacceptable and dangerous. Thus, the new term "Malignant Normality" has emerged and spreads like an undiagnosed cancer when unchallenged. The term, "malignant normality," was first used by Robert Jay Lifton, M.D., and is adapted here to describe leaders who try to normalize dangerous and unethical behaviors. Dr. Lifton writes that "we need to avoid uncritical acceptance of this new version of malignant normality and, instead bring our knowledge and experience to exposing it for what it is."
- The modeling of the behaviors described above appeal to the dark side of human behavior and gives active permission for others to act in harmful ways.
- Hate crimes, white supremacy and hate groups, and gun violence have increased exponentially over the last five years.
- Women, Black, Brown, Indigenous, LGBTQ and all poor people make up 70% of the adult population in the country. They

already are marginalized with a double standard that translates into less opportunity and malignant normal leaders increase the level of pain.

- Millions of people lack economic security in the wealthiest country in history and the wealth gap has widened. Millions of school age children are food insecure.

Malignant Normality is now a part of "normal." This trend is dangerous. This is not who we are. We can and must do better.

THE NEW LEADERSHIP PERSPECTIVE: A NEW VOICE

Toxic leaders have no power when other leaders and other people find their voice, refuse to be silent and refuse to be complicit. The counter to toxic leaders is leaders who lead to inspire others and lead for the good of all. The most common name today for Better Normal organizations are "Open Organizations."

"Open organizations" are open to learning from everyone and invite creativity and innovation. Open organizations are emerging now that tap into the reservoir of underutilized human potential by acting on the fact that all people can discover their passion and lead. Leaders in open organizations are already providing models for a better way to lead. All organizations need more people to lead and leaders for the Better Normal are already leveraging their people talent to move their enterprise toward long-term sustainability, creating value for all stakeholders. Traditional bureaucratic organizations, still dominant in 21st century America, have too many supervisors and managers and too few leaders.

John Kotter has been a thought leader on change and leading change for over 25 years. He, Vanessa Akhtar, and Gaurav Gupta wrote in the January 2022 issue of The Kotter Chronicle about their new book, appropriately named *Change.* Among several insights on the changes needed in response to Covid, supply chain issues, and inflation is this.

> "What we've learned is that organizations that can effectively adapt and pivot quickly in this context are those that create an environment that fosters more leadership, from more people. We need many more people constantly looking for opportunities and taking action to capitalize on them."

Imagine the possibilities when leaders see their roles as helping make the amazing people around them successful. Think of the implications for learning in any organization and what this means for investing in new leadership learning opportunities for everyone. Our new leadership model recognizes people as the most important asset for any enterprise and taps into the "wild and precious" lives to lead for a Better Normal and a better world. Leadership needs to expand exponentially. You can make this your opportunity.

Albus Dumbledore, one of the most beloved of the Harry Potter characters and the most powerful wizard of his time, knew that Harry would eventually defeat the Dark Lord only if he would be prepared enough when the time came. Dumbledore knew he must be the one to help prepare Harry for that right moment. I feel as if Dumbledore is speaking directly to us as leaders after 2020 when he spoke to Harry about troublesome times. "Dark times lie ahead of us and there will be a time when we must choose between what is easy and what is right." And then, Dumbledore adds, "It is our choices that show what we truly are, far more than our abilities."

There is no going back to normal and traditional bureaucratic leadership as the dominant norm. Toxic, malignant normal leadership will never be a recommended model for any successful leader. Our choices do "show who we truly are." We are called at this time to live and lead for a Better Normal, one that prepares us for dark times and times of great opportunity.

LITMUS TEST FOR LEADERS IN THE NEW WORLD

The litmus test for leaders has always been simple:

One, would you want this person to lead your enterprise?

Two, would you want your child or grandchild to model their character and behavior after this leader?

Three, can this person be trusted to tell the truth?

Four, does this person unite and inspire others?

A healthy democracy, healthy families, and healthy organizations are built on people telling the truth and being trustworthy. Good leaders tell the truth. Only when we have the truth and good information can we make good decisions and accomplish great work. Only when we want the best for all around us can we be truly successful.

> The litmus test for leaders has always been simple.

GOOD GUYS AND BAD GUYS

I was 7 years old when I become a regular at the movie theater on Saturday afternoon in my little hometown of Smithville. Old Western movies, good guys and bad guys, and 10-cent popcorn were the draws for me. Hopalong Cassidy was one of my cowboy heroes. What a cool name, huh? I ran across a picture of young me in a Hopalong T-shirt recently. Not too shabby. I had gotten a toy holster and six shooter the previous Christmas. I guess pistols back then were called six shooters since a real cowboy had only six shots before having to reload from the extra bullets on his belt. At any rate, the play-like holster and gun were just what I needed to live into my cowboy fantasy at the time.

A real cowboy, I reasoned at the time, needed a "handle" of some kind, a name that really distinguished him from others. If I was going to walk the five blocks down main street to the Saturday afternoon matinee and protect myself and Smithville from bad guys on the prowl, I needed a name that fitted a tough good guy with a six shooter. I was too young to chew and spit tobacco like a real tough guy, but my love of lemon drops would be good enough. So, for a short moment in my young life, I became the Lemon Drop Kid. How dare anyone confront the Lemon Drop Kid, spitting lemon drop juice and carrying a gun on his way to and from the movie on a Saturday afternoon. And it worked. I was never confronted by a bad guy. Not once. Smithville was an even better place to live because of the Lemon Drop Kid! (By the way, it was open carry for toy guns when I was growing up. Even then, I outgrew the need for open carry of toy and real guns by age 9, leaving the wild west behind).

We still have good guys and bad guys, good leaders and leaders in title only. We have discovered that the "bad guys" pack a lot of power but are not riding white horses. They stand out anyway. They are the toxic leaders and, unlike the imaginary bad guys in my hometown who I never had to confront as a kid, these real-time "bad guys and gals" confront us every day. Toxic political leaders have now entered the arenas of science, healthcare, women's health, medicine, public education, library science, gun proliferation, the media, and the environment. They seek to make decisions for medical doctors, scientists, journalists, educators, psychologists, teachers, sociologists, librarians, and other professionals. For example, in some states, up to 70 % of K-12 teachers have considered leaving because politicians at state and local levels have made their jobs even harder. This kind of normal is not okay. Toxic political leaders and media sources that thrive on misinformation are the reason business leaders, religious leaders, educational leaders, and other political leaders are called to lead differently and advocate for the people they lead. As noted earlier, many superstars are using their platform to provide hope for a better world.

There are already thousands of leaders in the Better Normal camp. We just need many, many more.

My career-long study and practice of leadership time and again leads to the magic of relationships, inspiring leadership practices, and the beautiful untapped human potential available in all of us. I remind new leadership learners often of this fact: we have so much more evidence available to us today that reinforces our focus on inspiring leadership practices and the essential relationship between the leader and the people with whom the leader works.

REINVENTING: CREATING A NEW LEADERSHIP NARRATIVE

We absolutely have the power to change narratives. Examples are everywhere but one of my best examples came from an unlikely source one Friday night.

Friday night is movie night and sleep-over with our grandson. Bo is now 11 and this has been a delightful ritual for the last 7 years. If you are a parent or a grandparent, you are saying, "Enjoy this moment while you can." We are. One of the movies we have watched many times by popular demand is called "Ferdinand," a bull with a big heart who changes the narrative of how we think of bulls. We first see young Ferdinand at a Spanish bull-training camp, watering a small flower and savoring its fragrance. His fellow bulls are emulating their fathers, fighting each other nearby. The fathers and the sons all aspire to be chosen for the arena as the worthy bovine opponent for El Primero, the famous matador. Ferdinand is the exception. He knows at an early age he doesn't want to fight, and he doesn't want his proud, muscular father to fight either. When Ferdinand's father is selected for the big fight, he promises Ferdinand that he will make him proud and come back victorious over the matador. Of course the father never comes back, and a sad Ferdinand runs away only to be rescued by little Nina and her father. Ferdinand happily finds himself on a flower farm, unconditionally loved by Nina and his new farm family. The plot thickens as Ferdinand grows up to be as big and strong as his dad.

He is mistaken near the flower market for a fighting monster bull, captured and returned to the bull-fighting academy.

Ferdinand quickly learns that two things happen to bulls at the academy. They either are selected to fight in the arena, or they go up the hill to the chop factory to be slaughtered. He has already seen two of his fellow bulls hauled off for the chop factory fate. Even though no bulls have ever escaped the academy, Ferdinand is determined to escape and determined to take his fellow tough guy bulls with him. He assures his reluctant fellow bulls there's a better life out there and encourages all to go with him. They do agree and even rescue the two bulls trapped in the chop house. "It's not just about me. There is a better world out there, trust me." They all make it out, and Ferdinand assures they all are safe before he is finally captured, for the second time. But this time, as you might imagine, he ends up being forced into the arena where El Primero is waiting along with thousands of bull-fighting fans, eager to see another traditional fight and fatal outcome for the bull.

Here's where the narrative changes dramatically. After multiple attempts to spear Ferdinand, Ferdinand gets nicked by the sword, shows his power and strength, picks El Primero up with his horns. Starring the frightened matador in the face, he gently lowers him. Then Ferdinand sits down in front of El Primero, refusing to fight and courageously leaving himself vulnerable and open to the worst fate. A new show of power for a normal bull. But Ferdinand is different. The fans erupt with "Let him live" and the flowers intended for the matador reign down for Ferdinand. Nina runs into the ring, hugs Ferdinand, and all the bulls end up with Nina and her father on the flower farm and a future of fragrance and sunsets. A better normal if you will.

This movie resonated with so many children of all ages with its powerful message of being who you are, being proud of who you are, using power to be sensitive to others and helping others, and that it is very possible to change a narrative. We want our grandson to be tough and gentle, to find as many alternatives to fighting as possible. There are multiple implications for young men and for leaders who want a better normal. Bullies don't play, work, or lead well.

This leadership book creates a new narrative for leaders and leadership. We have looked at the destructive and unfortunate negative consequences of the four driving forces that emerged in 2020. The curtain has been pulled back. There's no turning back. The good news is that we have lifesaving, healing, inspiring, and transformative options to the old normal. The new leadership narrative creates a leadership language that can permeate and inspire any enterprise or family.

In summary, we are on a leadership journey that capitalizes on learning from "what we know" and we know a lot about these four driving forces that have converged at this moment. We will learn from the pains of traditional "Bureaucratic Normal" and toxic "Malignant Normal" leadership. We will learn a new inspiring "Better Normal" leadership model that thrives on the best of what we know about leadership and relationships, human potential and discretionary energy, the power of passion and inspiration, and how you and everyone can help make those around them successful. We can also accept and learn from the other discoveries from 2020 that we are fragile, vulnerable as well as beautifully imperfect and powerful. We have a common and shared humanity. We all can lead.

This is really good news! The sky's the limit.

HELPFUL DEFINITIONS FOR THE NEW LEADERSHIP NARRATIVE

As you read the definitions below, I hope you see yourself as part of this new leadership narrative. Most of you have experienced the pain and unfairness of the old normal. Most of us know we can do better and there is hope in acknowledging the broken systems of leadership. Now, we can all be a part of the reinventing leadership process.

As we continue, I will use the term "leader" frequently. Every time you see that word, I am talking about you and to you. In the next few pages, you will learn why inspiration is critical to your leadership and you will learn to apply each of the 7 inspiring practices.

Normal. The way things were prior to the shocking events and revelations of 2020: Virus-related pandemics; man-made structural inequities that perpetuate unequal opportunities and marginalized people; severe environmental crisis; dangerous politicians in powerful positions; misinformation and conspiracy theories; fear of shared humanity/diversity/inclusion; uninspiring bureaucratic management; and status quo mentality. This is the new normal, not the Better Normal.

Leadership. The art and practice of inspiring others to exceed expectations, want to work collaboratively for a higher calling, and help make others more successful.

Leaders. People with character, courage, and compassion who inspire the people around them to be more successful and lead for the good of all.

Inspiration. Inspiration-based leadership creates an internal desire in others to exceed expectations, raises levels of self-esteem, creativity, and collaborative behavior, and increases motivation to innovate and accomplish things beyond one's comfort zone. Inspiration is internal and vastly superior to traditional external incentives and the key to helping others be successful. Leaders can create a culture of inspiration by learning the 7 inspiring leadership practices.

One Humanity. The belief that all people are equally human and equally deserving of respect, dignity, equity, justice, and truth.

Humanizing. A term at the core of a culture of inspiration where work is designed for humans to grow and thrive. "Humanizing" encapsules the "one wild and precious life" concept, the astronaut view of fragile planet earth with one human race, Maslow's Hierarchy of Needs growth model, and "high-touch," relationship practices.

"People are our most important asset." The leader assumption at the heart of "Better Normal" leadership, the inspiring leadership practices, and the "moral imperative" to seek the best for all people with whom the leader works and lives.

"Better Normal" Leaders. Leaders who engage and inspire others with character, compassion, and courage for the common good. They rise above normal and new normal, creating a "better normal" where all are invited to lead either in their personal or organizational life. They lead with win-win thinking and acting. They use their courageous voices to do the right thing and align their actions with their core values. They help make their work process and those around them more successful, speak for the people they lead, and protect the environment.

"Bureaucratic Normal" Leaders. Leaders who still lead primarily with a traditional management model of leadership after 2020, have a bias for top-down control, and expect only a few people to lead and many more to manage and supervise. They lead with a combination of win-win and win-lose thinking and acting. They often are silent or compliant with systemic inequities and malignant normality.

Toxic, "Malignant Normal" Leaders. People in leadership positions after 2020 that still attempt to "normalize" behaviors that we once considered cruel, de-humanizing, dangerous, and outside what we would call normal. These are toxic, fear-based leaders, use anger to control others, and they expect others to be loyal and unchallenging, including the media. They lead with a combination of win-lose and lose-lose thinking and acting that benefit them. Their power comes from other people who are silent or complicit with "malignant normality." Good leaders unable to confront "malignant normality" unwittingly become part of the leadership crisis.

Win-Win Thinking and Acting. When leaders value all the stakeholders and act to create outcomes that are beneficial to all.

Win-Lose Thinking and Acting. When leaders value some stakeholders more than others and act in ways that benefit some at the expense of others. Zero-sum outcomes.

Lose-Lose Thinking and Acting. When leaders become so angry and/or driven by power, control, greed, or revenge, most people lose, creating a dangerous cycle of unproductive and dysfunctional outcomes. Ultimate outcome is war.

Marginalized People. People who traditionally have had less opportunity because they were born Black, Brown, Indigenous, LGBTQ, or female. Others who often experience marginalization are physically disabled, mentally compromised people as with depression, and those limited by socio-economic status. Marginalized populations are groups and communities that experience discrimination and exclusion (social, political and economic) because of unequal power relationships across economic, political, social and cultural dimensions. Inequity of opportunity includes but is not limited to jobs, careers, salaries, job benefits, education, bank loans, location of neighborhood, voting, healthcare and health insurance, transportation, policing, leadership positions, physical safety, economic security, and psychological safety.

Up to 70% of the American population and workforce are made up of people who are marginalized and have experienced unequal opportunity to some degree in their lives.

The Moral Imperative for Leaders. Strategically and intentionally lead with a moral compass to provide more understanding, opportunity, equity, and advocacy for marginalized people and the environment, making a difference for their organization, communities where they serve, and the world. New leaders will advocate for their people and intentionally counter "malignant normality" and toxic leaders.

Intentional Leadership. Specific leader actions and practices that inspire all people to want to be successful and act with character, courage, and compassion.

Leaders intentionally align actions, behaviors, and practices with core values and guiding principles.

Reinvention. We use "reinvention" here to discuss the total redo of leadership: inviting every person to lead, completely changing the leadership narrative and language, dropping "management models" and adding "inspiring, humanizing leadership models", breathing fresh air into "people are our most important asset", expecting that leaders lead in the community and with the environment, and challenge a new army of leaders to lead with an ethical heart, confront toxic leaders, and create a better normal. Reimagine!

The Challenge
is So Great
The Opportunity for
Good So Compelling
The Positive Impact
So Enormous
We Cannot
Afford to Fail

CHAPTER TWO

THE LEADERSHIP OPPORTUNITY OF A LIFETIME

"If you're always trying to be normal, you will never know how amazing you can be."

— MAYA ANGELOU

There has never been in my lifetime or yours a greater need for inspiring leadership or a greater need for more people to lead. Many historians are calling this current era "the test of our lifetime," for leaders, leadership, even democracy. What an opportunity! Leaders, managers, supervisors, educators, religious leaders, politicians, parents, and the millions of people who can discover the leader within and can seize this unique moment in history to make a difference. We have an opportunity to think anew and act anew. We will take the first steps on a new leadership journey. You ask 100 people what leadership means, you will get 100 different answers. There is no common leadership language. The journey is an invitation to a new conversation about leadership, starting with why leadership today is so inadequate for the complex challenges we face. You will discover that the leadership challenge is so great, the opportunity for good so compelling, the positive impact so enormous, we cannot afford to fail.

As a current or emerging leader, today is the "test of your lifetime." To pass the leadership test, a big portion of the test is built around the leader's ability to create psychological safety for colleagues. I doubt many leaders have heard the term, psychological safety, or talked about the term recently. I will talk more about it later, but psychological safety is a recent discovery in leadership circles and is fundamental to Better Normal leadership. In essence, psychological safety is essential for human growth, individually and collectively. Think of a work environment where people know their leader cares about them, knows they can risk being vulnerable, express themselves honestly, feel understood, and know their leader is committed to acting to make them successful. To do this, leaders must take the time to know the diverse group of people they lead. This is new territory. It is what Brene Brown, PhD, calls willingness to interact in the "arena" and what Elizabeth Thomas, PhD, calls "fostering brave spaces." Leaders are inviting colleagues to engage in diversity and equity conversations with courage and humility. As Thomas points out, "talking about social justice issues and past inequities can be difficult and uncomfortable." She describes the discomfort as a "healthy tension" where the goal is understanding and learning from the rich diversity in work environments. This is the same "healthy tension" often created by the gap between an undesirable current reality and a desirable future vision.

Think about the first time you tried to ride a bicycle, or skate, or water ski, snow ski, swim, or speak in front of a group. Any new experience. Nervous stomach. Butterflies. There is always tension and discomfort. Healthy tension is inherent in change and learning. Learning is a process of being open to new information, letting go of old information or misinformation, and adopting new ways of thinking and

> As a current or emerging leader, today is the "test of your lifetime."

acting. I will share some helpful tools later for making these conversations a part of any leader's journey with the new "people skills" that help leaders learn more quickly and become more successful. But the intentional investment in creating psychological safety and fostering brave spaces means people are heard, are seen, are respected. Everyone learns together. Everybody benefits. People are willing to volunteer their best when they feel "listened to." As a leader, you are inviting your colleagues to join you in this greatest-ever leadership opportunity to make a difference.

We know from the Gallup research alone that people are more productive when they know you care about them as a person and care about what they are thinking and feeling. Some leaders have been guided by the following principle of caring: "People don't care how much you know till they know how much you care." However, caring is not top of mind behavior for many of us. "Intentional" means deliberately making it top of mind. "Intentional" means purposely deciding to, and then actually doing it. "Intentional" means showing empathy for others, showing concern for the families of people with whom you work, expressing interest in knowing people more on a personal as well as professional level. We will talk about setting appropriate boundaries as we seek to be more transparent, vulnerable, and courageous as leaders. That said, leadership for a Better Normal does call us to reset everything we know about leadership and develop new habits. New habits take time and practice. I will invite you to be very intentional about your application of each of the seven practices as we go through this leadership journey. My hope is that you act differently, experiment with new behaviors after each inspiring leadership practice.

My grandson attends Snowden public elementary school in Memphis, a school that reflects the wonderful diversity of the city. A first grader at the time, Bo and I were sitting on the front porch steps one

> As a leader, you are inviting your colleagues to join you in this greatest-ever leadership opportunity to make a difference.

Saturday morning after the Friday night sleep-over at our house. We were talking mostly about his collection of Hot Wheel cars, and I used the word "habit" in talking about our Saturday morning habit of playing with his cars. I then asked him if he knew what the word "habit" meant, thinking this was a little teaching moment for Pop. Without hesitation he said, "Be proactive, begin with the end in mind, put first things first, think win-win, seek first to understand, synergize, and there's one more." My shocked response was, "Good grief, where did you learn that?" His reply, "It's a program at school." The program is called, "The Leader in Me."

Well, if you're familiar with Stephen Covey's work, *The Seven Habits of Highly Effective People*, this leadership program for elementary students is based on those leadership principles that top leaders around the country have been learning for years. All students at Snowden Elementary are assigned leadership roles and many decisions are made by students, not teachers. All the teachers and school staff are trained in the program and how to recognize and reinforce the habits when they see them in class, in the cafeteria, and on the playground. Countless students have their spirits lifted each day by being trusted, complimented, or shown their worth and potential by an adult. The adults in the school believe that they lead by communicating a child's worth and potential so clearly that children are inspired to see it in themselves. According to Covey, this is what good leadership is about and this is the heart of the program: every child, every person, has a leader inside. My grandson does, I do, you do.

By the way, do you see the implication for where you work and live? Doesn't this just blow you over?

If communicating worth and potential so clearly that children are "inspired to see it in themselves," why not communicate worth and potential as clearly at work with the adults we lead and at home with family members?

The emerging new world will require a critical mass of leaders to lead change and create healthier and stronger organizations, government, churches, synagogues, temples, schools, and families. Imagine what would happen if we all thought about "the leader in me," either leading one's own life from a different perspective or leading others from a new perspective. What if we all thought about inspiring people to see their worth and potential? Can you imagine the positive impact that would have on work, home, community, and the world?

We have all been given a chance to rethink and redo our thoughts and actions related to leadership for this new world. We know more about leadership than we have ever known. We know that it is not about power, control, or titles. We know it's about inspiring people to see their worth and potential for good. We know it is about inspiring others to want to struggle together and use their collective gifts to reach a shared dream.

Only recently, however, have we had enough information to tell us that all leadership roads lead to inspiration as the catalyst for best efforts and great outcomes. Only inspired people give their best. Only inspired people, working together get extraordinary results.

We have all the information we need to create a new leadership perspective for the complex world of the future. We now have the keys to inspiring leadership that match the magnitude of the opportunity created by Covid-19, pandemic-type systemic issues, uninspired bureaucratic leadership, and toxic leadership. We can see we need all people to lead within their sphere of influence.

WHY ONLY INSPIRATION AND INSPIRING LEADERS CAN CREATE A BETTER NORMAL

Only when inspired do we choose to commit our discretionary energy for our best thinking and acting and sustain our desire to strive for extraordinary results both individually and collectively. Inspired performances in sporting events often garner a comment like "she, he, they left everything on the field, court, slope, or track. No one could ask for more." Inspired people are capable of heroic efforts. We see it in sports, in schools, at work, when people are in the arena and giving their all. The process of becoming inspired and exceeding expectations looks something like the flow of steps below:

Inspiration ⟶ Courage ⟶ Use of Discretionary Energy ⟶
Passion ⟶ Sustained Effort ⟶ Exceeded Expectations

The "first step" in this journey to the greatest-ever leadership opportunity begins now. Join me as we explore the pathway to inspiring the best in ourselves and others:

- Learn how inspiration consistently leads to peak performance.
- Explore the urgency for informed and inspiring leadership in the new world of pandemics and unremarkable leadership.
- Discover the "leader in you" and form a new perspective on leadership.
- Think deeply and identify your own core human values and ethical compass as well as that of your organization, school, and family.
- Create your personal leadership invitation for others to join you in the search for a culture of inspiration that values each person and all the lives of those you lead, parent, teach, and who share your world.
- Discover the seven non-negotiable practices of leaders that inspire the best thinking, collaborative actions, and extraordinary results.

- Become super intentional. Learn to implement the practices of inspirational leaders and begin making a difference in your leadership at work, home, and community.
- Begin to think about the importance of understanding the experience of all the systemically marginalized people you lead. Think about what economic security means to you and what it would take to create that kind of security for the people you lead. More later.

I have always had a strong belief that my life matters and that I can make a difference. Mattering and making a difference is deep down important to us all. It is at our core as a primary life motivating force. We want our lives to matter. As human beings and leaders, we often get discouraged in this quest to make a difference. "Difference is only a difference when it makes a difference." I want to encourage you to believe you can make a difference as a leader. I know that inspiration is the catalyst to exceeding expectations. It really took me a while to discover what inspired me. I tend to be optimistic and determined, so I have to dig deep for more determination when disappointed with not making as much difference as I would like. So, when I do exceed my own expectations, or when a team I lead exceeds expectations, it is highly rewarding. I cherish those times and they sustain the strong belief that my life matters, and I can make a difference. I mention this now because we know the path to "making a difference" with leadership. I will do my best to describe that path as we move through this new model for leadership that maximizes the opportunity for you to make a difference as well as inspire others to make their unique difference.

Something else. I know I am challenging you to believe that you can lead or if you are already leading in some capacity, to learn some new leadership practices and to perceive leadership from a new

> Mattering and making a difference is deep down important to us all.

perspective. I know this is new terrain for many leaders. Even good leaders who already inspire others will want to push leadership to new levels in their organization. New terrain just means new learning opportunities. In the touching novel, *Wish You Were Here,* by Jodi Picoult, Diane, the leading character, finds herself trapped on one of the Galapagos islands, shut down at the beginning of Covid and the only tourist on this beautiful island. Her frustration of being trapped there with no transportation out for several weeks is countered by her gradual discoveries of a new pace of living, the natural beauty around her, different people, and a new language. While there, she reflects on her ultra-busy life in New York, her work as an art dealer at Sotheby's, and the detailed plan she and others have for her life. "Busy is just a euphemism for being so focused on what you don't have that you never notice what you do. It's a defense mechanism. Because if you stop hustling---if you pause---you start wondering why you ever thought you wanted all those things."

PAUSING TO LEARN

As I write and as you read this, you are choosing to read this over other things you could be doing. You already have a lot on your plate. So, I am asking you to pause, as Diane was forced to do above. Take time to absorb this new land of leadership. Take time to reset. Learn. Push out of your comfort zone. Take your time. I also want to assure you that what you want most, you already have. You have wonderful gifts within you. You are good enough and smart enough. Sure, you can and will learn more, but you are enough as a person. Most leaders haven't yet learned the people skills inherent in this new leadership model. So you are not behind. Your humanness is the umbilical cord connecting you to humanity, the people with whom you work and live. You are already connected.

> Your humanness is the umbilical cord connecting you to humanity, the people with whom you work and live.

We are interconnected by lives that humble us, bring us to our knees, bring joy and celebration, strengthen our faith and test our faith. It is this ability to be present with others, to seek to understand others, be human and vulnerable with others, admit our mistakes and imperfections, and live with courage that binds us all together. You can lead. You can do leadership. You can learn what you need to learn. There are no perfect leaders. No perfect people. We are beautifully imperfect. You can make a difference in big and small ways. Remember, part of the reset is the new mindset where you are a leader and where you influence others.

At the end of each of the chapters will be suggestions for "intentional pausing" and implementation of the concepts just presented. You will have a starting point for moving forward with each of the practices. Whether you are a parent, supervisor, manager, religious leader, CEO, or academician, the suggestions can be a beginning point or a point of reinforcement for a practice you are already implementing. My goal is that you will conclude after each chapter, "This makes sense, I can do this, I can start right now." I hope you can see why I call each practice essential and non-negotiable as well. My research has been a life of leadership, my observations and practices. I have also consistently learned from the research of others and connected the leaderships lessons from the past into a new leadership model. All the leadership practices included in our journey to a Better Normal leadership are just that: essential and non-negotiable. You will relish them all.

Now, the very good news! Why a Culture of Inspiration is the culture of choice and how you can help create that special culture where you live and work.

Inspiration
Awakens Potential
and New Possibilities,
Increases Approach
Motivation to Strive
for Extraordinary, and
Is The Catalyst for
Leadership for a
Better Normal

CHAPTER THREE

CREATING A CULTURE OF INSPIRATION: THE COMPETITIVE ADVANTAGE

"Your work is going to fill a large part of your life, and the only way to be truly satisfied is to do what you believe is great work. The only way to do great work is to love what you do. If you haven't found it yet, keep looking and don't settle."

— STEVE JOBS

The 7 leadership practices that inspire character, compassion, courage, and the common good create an overall culture of inspiration. We have learned through our discovery of more productive and healthier hybrid work models, new understandings of the inadequacies of "business as usual," and the "great resignation" that people want both their personal and professional life to have greater meaning. The great resignation is the tip of the "Life is too short" iceberg.

A work culture that inspires and enhances life experience is now the culture of choice. Culture is a mix of values, beliefs, and practices that people share and that become the defining aspect of the company, organization, or entity. Most organizations have stated values or guiding principles. However, the litmus test is what employees and associates say in confidence to others. The gold medal culture that attracts, engages, recognizes, and enriches the lives of associates is one that consistently inspires. Gold medal cultures have earned these kinds of responses from the people who work there, "I get to do what I love doing every day. My work is meaningful. Working here inspires me. I know I am making a difference."

A work culture that inspires and enhances life experience is now the culture of choice.

Leaders must learn to create cultures that inspire success and enhance the lives of those with whom they work. Talent seeks thriving cultures.

In the next few pages, we paint a picture of traditional motivation compared to the strongest, most underused, sustaining-motivation of all, inspiration. I want you to see the same clues, the dots, the gifts of the past that I discovered and put together for this new model. The clues, when connected, all lead straight to a culture of inspiration and the culture leaders for a Better Normal must build. But, as Steve Jobs said in his oft quoted speech to Stanford graduates, "You can't connect the dots looking forward. You can only connect them looking backwards. So you have to trust that the dots will somehow connect in your future. You have to trust in something, your gut, destiny, life, karma, whatever, because believing that the dots will connect down the road will give you the confidence to follow your heart, even when it leads you off the well-worn path, and that will make all the difference."

Since I am the "someone" who is writing about the all-encompassing power of leadership inspiration for the

> first time in this context, I do want you to see the
> same evidence I saw in creating this new model.

I want you to feel confident in leading from this new perspective and trust the process of humanizing your leadership. The blinding flash of the obvious for me was that the clues from the past, the dots if you will, told me that we already knew how to create a culture that inspires. Someone needed to identify the ingredients, needed to name it for the powerful force it is, and then capitalize on it through the seven leadership practices that hang together and consistently inspire. So, here's the information you need for either believing you can lead, or changing the way you lead, or thinking about leadership from a totally new perspective. I hope what follows as you continue to read "will give you the confidence you need to follow your heart" to more inspiring leadership.

MOTIVATION AND INSPIRATION: CREATING THE INTERNAL "WANT TO"

Motivation has been long studied, written about, and discussed. The most common question interviewers ask people when they have accomplished something extraordinary is, "Where did your motivation come from?" Or the question to Olympian competitors who train 4 years for one shining moment, "Why do you do this?" The strongest and most powerful motivation comes from within each of us. It is called "internal motivation" as opposed to "external motivation" (the carrot and the stick). Internal motivation is the "want to" as opposed to the "have to" or "must." It jumps past complying to commitment. Commitment and internal motivation sustain effort over long periods of time. We have designated "compliance people" to make sure we are complying with rules and regulations. Leaders want people who are committed, not just complying. We will show the benefits of the inspirational power unleashed by tapping into the internal underutilized potential within each of us. This is when we give our best. This is what sustains us. Inspiration motivates people to go to great lengths, overcome obstacles and barriers, and make great sacrifices to accomplish extraordinary outcomes. I will share later my story of being inspired and reaching my potential in the Wayfinding chapter.

I know I will mention this more than once, but I was a terribly uninspired undergraduate college student except for a few courses where the professor showed some interest in my potential. I was a C + student without a clear purpose. I was motivated to not disappoint by parents and successfully graduate. Call it fear of embarrassment, guilt, or pleasing others, I was not inspired to do my best learning. I was inspired by parties, extracurricular activities, and volunteer work with young people. The big discovery, looking back, was how much I loved interacting with others. Bottom line, academics were a "have to," "ought," and "should" and clearly externally motivated. Relationship skills, the skills that would benefit me most in life and my career, were a "want to," an internal motivation that inspired my best. By the way, I got really inspired in grad school as I started living into my unused potential.

BEGIN WITH THE PROCESS IN MIND

I recall the first 3-day mission-driven team-building workshop that Bob Fisher and I facilitated for Kimberly Clark. We were in a mountain top retreat setting, and it was the second evening. We had designed a process after interviewing each participant on this senior leadership team that we felt would be ideal for accomplishing what this team wanted to accomplish. We were over halfway through the process and still in the disruptive, uncomfortable part of learning new ways to think about teams and what it would take to be a stronger team. Learning and change always create some discomfort and tension in the middle of the learning process. As facilitators, we knew this as natural and expected, but we were still nervous. As the evening session closed and we reviewed the day and our worries, it was the first time I remember looking at my co-facilitator and saying these words out loud. "Hey, we know we have a good process. We just have to trust the process."

Leaders must "trust the process" of building a culture of inspiration. The process is a people process, so it's really about trusting the people you lead. This is where the new leadership perspective begins. Trust people and trust what we know is a process that inspires people. We now know the "process that inspires."

> Trust people and trust what we know is a process that inspires people. We now know the "process that inspires."

You as leader are thinking and acting with two basic assumptions: The first assumption is this.

- People are the most important asset, PERIOD. People are the talented humans we work with every day. All the trends of new open organizations and my research with the leadership gifts of the past affirm and validate this assumption. Maybe I should say the "right people" are the most important asset. This goes with the territory and means the organization has already had the courage to hold their people accountable with determining good and bad fits for the organization. It also means they are recruiting and retaining people who make those around them successful. Recruit talent that fits the culture.
- The second assumption is based on "how" we work together, not on "what" we do together. Certainly "what" and "why" are important, but "How" is about relationships and about the process of acting on assumption number one. Begin with people, begin with how to value and honor that number one asset, and begin with the fact that there is within each of us "discretionary energy," a reservoir of untapped human potential that can only

be reached and sustained through inspiration. "Discretionary" simply means each person choses or volunteers the best thinking, the best ideas, the best work, when inspired. Inspiration is the magic internal motivation, and we now know what leaders can do to inspire others.

The assumptions do not address the bottom-line outcomes or the shared vision that will inspire others. That will come later. The assumptions speak to the "how" we will work and struggle together to accomplish great outcomes. The assumptions are the conditions necessary for success, much like my graduate school learning creed I discuss in the Wayfinding chapter. We will discuss the importance of the other factors, the why, what, and who, that create a synergy of factors. But there is now an abundance of evidence that tells us that the "How" or "the process" is the necessary ingredient for inspiring the best of everyone. Trust the process.

> But there is now an abundance of evidence that tells us that the "How" or "the process" is the necessary ingredient for inspiring the best of everyone.

Each of us can identify times in our lives when we were inspired. You can name those times in your life. You know what it feels like. Only recently has inspiration been researched and translated into meaningful and explosive information. We can thank Todd M. Thrash and Andre J. Elliot, both psychologists, for the research that significantly helped us better understand the concept of inspiration. According to Thrash and Elliot, inspiration has the double-barreled impact of "being inspired" by something and "acting" on that inspiration. Their research, in effect, polished this inspirational diamond in the rough into a shining, attractive, valuable,

> Inspiration has the double-barreled impact of "being inspired" by something and "acting" on that inspiration.

and potent concept. We can see much more clearly the beauty and powerful potential of inspiration.

In short, Thrash and Elliot discovered there are three main aspects of inspiration that we can immediately capitalize on as leaders:

1. Inspiration evokes us to see new possibilities and opens us to new experiences, a real WOW factor,
2. Inspiration has a transcendent quality which allows us to exceed our limitations and expectations to move beyond the ordinary, the real EXTRAORDINARY factor, and
3. Inspiration increases our approach motivation and willingness to tackle tasks we otherwise thought beyond our capabilities. "Approach motivation" is a useful term and may be new to some. The term simply means our "APPROACH" button is activated and we "want to" move toward a task rather than "avoid" it.

Thrash and Elliot also developed the "Inspirational Scale," a measurement of the frequency with which a person experiences inspiration in their daily lives. Inspired people, they found, have several things in common that will bring joy to those wanting to be a more inspiring leader.

Get this. Inspired people report:

- More openness to new experiences.
- Being more absorbed in their tasks.
- Having a stronger desire to master their work.
- Being less competitive with colleagues and thus willing to collaborate.
- Higher levels of internal psychological resources including belief in their own abilities, self-esteem, and optimism.
- Greater levels of spirituality and meaning.
- Viewing themselves as more creative.
- Experiencing more purpose in life and more gratitude.

We see the direct impact of inspiration on self-esteem and confidence, creativity and innovative effort, willingness to cooperate with others, and sustained effort over time. What a gold mine of individual and collective energy. This is the mother lode for releasing discretionary energy and helping make others successful.

And the mother lode of inspiration gold for people and organizations is largely untapped!

Scott Barry Kaufman, scientific director of the Imagination Institute in the Positive Psychology Center at the University of Pennsylvania and author, tells us that "in a culture obsessed with measuring talent, ability, and potential, we often overlook the important role of inspiration in enabling potential." Kaufman goes on to say what a mistake it is to treat inspiration as something elusive, unattainable, supernatural, or divine. The truth of the matter, and what we have minimized for years, is that "inspiration awakens us to new possibilities by allowing us to transcend our ordinary experiences and limitations. Inspiration propels a person from apathy to possibility and transforms the way we perceive our own capabilities."

I love the old saying of someone when asked which was the bigger problem in today's world, ignorance or apathy? The response, "I don't know, and I don't care." With what we now know about the power and potency of inspiration, all of us should be emboldened by the fact that "inspiration propels a person from apathy to possibility and transforms the way we perceive our own capabilities".

Bain & Company partner Eric Garton launched a new research program in 2017 to understand what makes a leader inspirational. They started with a survey of 2,000 people. Their research reinforces what we already know: anyone can become an inspiring leader. However, employee surveys everywhere confirm there are far too few leaders that inspire. More than half of employees believed their leaders were not inspiring or motivating. Even fewer felt that their leaders "fostered engagement or commitment and modeled the culture and values of the corporation." The few inspiring leaders, they found, unlock higher performance through empowerment practices like the seven practices captured here. Note the stark contrast with the outdated practices of "command and control" that we address as toxic and uninspiring.

One of the most intriguing outcomes of the Bain research were the responses of survey recipients when asked what inspired them most about their colleagues. The traits reported clustered into four key behavior patterns:

1. Inspiring colleagues helped "develop inner resources," the internal psychological resources mentioned earlier. I have named this phenomenon the tapping of underutilized potential.
2. Inspiring colleagues helped them "connect with others" through empathy and understanding. I suggest this releases the potential in all and leads to the collaborative mindset that is discussed in a later chapter,
3. Inspiring colleagues stood out by "Setting the tone," included the inspiring traits of openness and unselfishness, an inherent component of creating a culture of inspiration, and
4. The last trait cluster of inspiring colleagues was called "leading the team," which included attention to the vision, greater focus, and servanthood which we include in the chapters on Vision and Urgency.

As you can see, the supportive research for the power of inspiration comes from my colleagues across the county who have devoted their careers to the study of human potential and human behavior. I am connecting the research findings to show the potency of inspiration. It is the answer to our collective observations from people across the country who every day observe what is happening around them at work and in the country and say, "We can do better." Inspiration is the counter for "I quit," the counter to leaders who play on our fears and feed us misinformation. Inspiration calls forth our better angels.

Inspired people are more intrinsically motivated and less extrinsically motivated. Intrinsic motivation is the huge switch from "carrot and stick." Now the spark of motivation comes from within and lights a flame that is sustainable. Kaufman has written beautifully in a Harvard Business Review article entitled "Why Inspiration Matters." Kaufman concludes that "inspiration is the springboard for creativity, facilitates progress toward goals, and increases well-being." As Kaufman concludes his article, he makes these powerful observations. "Another incredibly important, and often overlooked trigger of inspiration is exposure to inspiring managers, role models, and heroes. Think of it. "Exposure to inspiring role models!" Have our collective heads been in the sand about what this means for leadership? These "inspiring role models" are the new Better Normal Leaders! This is you. This is me. This is us.

> "Inspiration is the springboard for creativity, facilitates progress toward goals, and increases well-being."

When leading at Belmont, we were thinking big and acting boldly. We were making really big changes in the status quo of the old Belmont. I always told the team I was leading that whether anyone would ever look back and call our names as the ones who led transformative change at Belmont, we would always know we did and we could be proud. I would openly tell our Board we were living the miracle of Belmont and that I was inspired by what we were doing together. I would never put myself in the hero category, but I do believe I was living into being an inspiring role model. And one of the great "leadership truths" is this: we can all become inspiring role model leaders.

As Gregory Dess and Joseph Picken note in 'Changing Roles: Leadership in the 21st Century,' our competitive global economy requires leaders to shift their focus from efficient management to effective utilization of a company's diversity of resources." Kaufman further notes Dess and Picken's identification of what I am calling the "how" nature of Better Normal Leadership, shifting from a focus on managing people to inspiring and leading people. Do these five shifts to what leaders need to do, noted by Dess and Pickens, sound familiar from our leadership journey so far? You bet. They concluded that the competitive global economy needed leaders who:

- Motivate and inspire with a compelling future vision (vision chapter is coming up),
- Empower people throughout the organization, (our basic assumptions that people are the top asset, and all people can lead),
- Collaborate and share internal knowledge (the collaborative mindset chapter is coming soon),
- Learn from others externally (the leadership gifts from the past and life-long learning), and
- Build a culture that enables creativity (the culture of inspiration).

Listen to Kaufman's gift of wisdom for all leaders as he concludes this article. "To become personally inspired, the best you can do is set up the optimal circumstances for inspiration. As a society, the best we can do is assist in setting up these important circumstances for everyone. An easy first step is simply recognizing the sheer potency of inspiration, and its potential impact on everything we do."

And the easy next step beyond recognizing the potency is to start building the "optimal circumstances" into our organizations as we now know how to do it." Leaders can intentionally create a culture of inspiration.

The implications of the research on inspiration are exciting and empowering. We now recognize the "sheer potency" of inspiration. We don't have to hope for people to get inspired on their own or wait for the right motivational speaker to come around for a temporary booster. What we already know opens new windows and fresh air for a new perspective on leadership. The information we now have on inspiration is so compelling, and as I said earlier, so explosive and far-reaching that being intentional about a culture of inspiration is almost self-evident.

Why wouldn't we want to do everything we could to create an environment that is designed to encourage and evoke the qualities of inspired people, colleagues, and family?

Good grief. What took us so long?

We have some great models to learn from and build on. They have just been waiting for the urgency of this historic moment. We are fortunate to benefit from the work and research of people who have helped us understand that indeed we can all be leaders. It has taken years to debunk the myths of leadership as something only a few were gifted with at birth or that all great leaders were charismatic. And you don't have to be exactly like any other great leader in your field. Your leadership power is in you. There is only one of you. Remember, you are enough. As Mr. Rogers would say to his young listeners, "I like you just the way you are." My grandson and many of you grew up with the Daniel Tiger version of Mr. Rogers. Mr. Rogers was the "soft skills" teacher of his day for children, the "hard skills" adult leaders now must learn. You can learn these skills.

It has been said that Zusha, the great Chassidic Master, as he lay crying on his deathbed was asked by his students, "Rebbe, why are you so sad? After all the mitzvahs and good deeds you have done, you will surely get a great reward in Heaven!" "I'm afraid," said Zusha. "Because when I get to heaven, I know God's not going to ask me 'Why weren't you more like Moses?' or 'Why weren't you more like

King David?' 'But I'm afraid that God will ask, Zusha, why weren't you more like Zusha?"

Being more you. It means that you already have all the potential for leadership within you. You just need a model of leadership that pulls out your best potential and helps you focus that potential in the most powerful way. As you know, there are hundreds of leadership books out there. I will reference several of them that have been most helpful to me in creating this new model. They truly are leadership gifts. But nothing has quite prepared us for leadership for a Better Normal. How do you get from where you are now to where you want to be in this new world demanding a "we can do better" leadership response? The breakthrough comes when we look closely at the leadership clues that have been left for us by brilliant leadership studies prior to 2020. When we connect the clues, the dots of past discoveries about leadership and inspiration, we get to a new discovery that has been right there, almost as if waiting for this time and place: the "individual discretionary energy" potential in each of us and the power of "inspiration" to tap that potential. It is like "new and sustaining motivation is the gift we forgot to open!"

The seven non-negotiable leadership practices are seven practices that hang together, each one an inspirational practice that taps into discretionary energy and the best we have to offer.

The synergistic impact of the seven practices creates the power of this new leadership model for a Better Normal. The extraordinary results come only with implementation of all the practices throughout your family, team, or organization. You will learn them all.

UNDERUTILIZED HUMAN POTENTIAL

This is over simplified but imagine an iceberg and imagine the tip of the iceberg as what you show people. People see only the thoughts, ideas, and behaviors you let them see. There is more to you below the surface, and you may reveal more to a trusted friend or a trusted colleague. Below the surface is the untapped potential. Psychologists and people who study human behavior suggest that we use only a portion of our human potential. Psychologist William James suggested years ago that we use only a small portion of our true potential. The unused human potential is discretionary energy. All of us carry around every day this reservoir of unused discretionary energy, talent, and potential. "Discretionary" simply means we have a choice about sharing our potential with others or using our talents fully at work. We do know that most of us, given the right inspiring environment, exceed our own expectations!

Tip of iceberg
All that others see of you

Unused human potential
Unseen by others
Home of vulnerability

This is what we are seeking to tap into by creating an inspiring culture, knowing that the more you are inspired to give your best, the more aware you will be of what you have to offer. Think back. Haven't you had at least one person in your life who believed in you more than you believed in yourself? I know of two people in my life. My wife, Rubye Lynn, and a graduate school professor at Ohio University, the late Dr. Ed Tremley.

PHYSICAL AND PSYCHOLOGICAL SAFETY

Physical and psychological safety are paramount for a culture of inspiration and reaching the underutilized potential in ourselves and others. The seven non-negotiable leadership practices are intentionally designed to tap into personal and collective unused potential. Abraham Maslow's Hierarchy of Needs, one of the most widely understood and appreciated motivational models, offers another insight into the importance of a culture of inspiration. Take a look at the model below. We want the culture we live and work in to invite personal growth, creating an environment where psychological and self-fulfillment needs are met on a regular basis. Note: motivation increases as needs are met. A term I use synonymously with the Maslow model is "human growth" model. As we will discuss later, most leadership authors in the past have used the term "management model" to discuss how people lead. As you will see, there is a huge difference between a "growth" model of leadership and a "management model." Growth builds internal motivation. Management implies external motivation initiated by managers, supervisors, or the organization.

As we go along, pay close attention to the difference between managing others and growing others, between managing /supervising others and leading others.

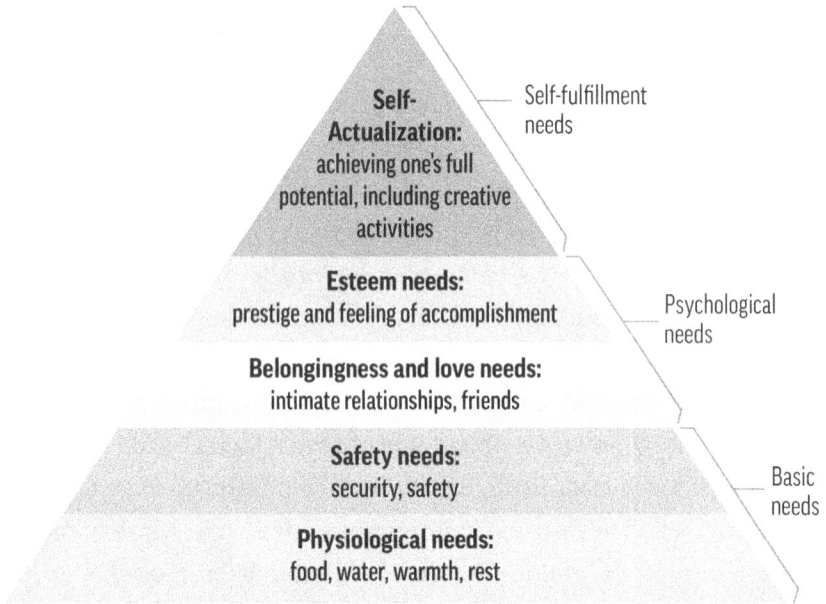

Why not intentionally create a culture designed for people to be physiologically and psychologically safe? Our "leader in me" public schools work hard to create a learning environment as soon as kids walk in the door each morning. School leaders know that many children come from foster homes, abusive homes, homes with not enough food to go around, or little opportunity for clean bodies or clean clothes. Breakfast and lunch are big deals for young learners. Childhood hunger is widespread across the country. And children can't feel psychologically safe without feeling physically safe and secure. Food insecurity dominates the world of hungry children. The Community Eligibility Provision (CEP) is the federal program designed to address this problem, but it needs expanding. Food insecurity only increased during the pandemic. Fortunately, we have examples of leaders in the private sector who are already leading for a better normal, attempting to reinvent CEP into a better system. Tusk Philanthropies, founded by venture capitalist, Bradley Tusk, is stepping up to lobby and act on behalf of this marginalized group of poor and hungry kids. As Tusk and project leader Lisa Quigley discovered, there is a direct relationship between child nutrition and learning. When this basic need, the number one need in Maslow's hierarchy of needs, is met, young learners have the opportunity to thrive. In a recent article penned by Tusk in December 2021, he found that there were 192,580 children facing hunger every year in New Jersey alone. So Tusk is pushing for greater funding to make a real difference in the lives of these children as well as children in other states. That is what better normal leaders do. Make a difference when you realize the systems are broken.

The difference food and nutrition make in the lives of young human beings is life changing, Tusk points out. "CEP is a common-sense way to get food straight into the mouths of children without questions asked, stigma, application forms or poverty tests. Studies have shown that students with greater food security have higher retention and better attendance, graduation rates and academic performance." He goes on to note that during the pandemic, school meals became the norm in New Jersey regardless of income "without the bureaucratic red tape or tedious paperwork," turning another bureaucratic systemic policy failure into a "better normal."

The underlying message to children, "This is a safe and healthy place for you to learn and grow." An even bigger message, "We care about you."

Another billionaire philanthropist, MacKenzie Scott, recently donated $38.8 million to Junior Achievement whose purpose is to inspire and prepare young people to succeed in a global economy. Scott is living up to her promise, the Giving Pledge, signed by many billionaires to donate more than half their wealth. She has focused in the past on funding that would generate more racial and gender equity by donations to historically Black colleges and universities as well as Planned Parenthood Federation of America. Scott has also singled out communities with a habit of removing obstacles for different subsets of people by giving to Boys & Girls Clubs of America and Habitat for Humanity. In short, when children thrive, we all are lifted up. When communities thrive, all boats rise. The Giving Pledge from billionaires is encouraging and inspiring, particularly when the gifts are directed at removing barriers and increasing opportunity for marginalized children and others.

When you create a physically and psychologically safe place for the people you lead, they too will thrive. The challenge for you and all leaders? Be very intentional about creating a culture of inspiration.

LEADERSHIP GIFTS FROM THE PAST

The best-of-the-best leadership from past writers and researchers has been a gold mine of discoveries for me during my career. The discoveries from my life-long pursuit of leading both personal and collective change led to the "mother lode" discovery of the catalytic and explosive impact of a "culture of inspiration." The pre-2020 leadership discoveries gave me great insights on how inspiration taps into our discretionary potential and the leadership practices that consistently inspire. It became a matter of connecting the leadership dots, all gifts from the past, and creating a new leadership model for a Better Normal after 2020.

There are more gifts, more dots, but what follows are ten gifts that significantly influenced me over the past forty years. They led to a great synthesizing after my capstone leadership experience at Belmont University and the events of 2020-2021. These are the pieces of the leadership puzzle that I have seen over the years that inspired some leaders to lead in exceptional ways and inspire others to be successful. As I said earlier, I wanted you to see the same puzzle pieces, the dots, the gifts I saw in creating a new leadership model built solely on what inspires our best.

TEN LEADERSHIP GIFTS FROM THE PAST: THE CATALYST FOR "BETTER NORMAL" LEADERSHIP

Leadership Gift One.

This is hard to believe, but Bill and Vieve Gore actually reinvented leadership in 1958. They answered many of the "why not" questions I am asking now, back in 1958. Why not intentionally create a work culture designed for people to be inspired? Why not design a work environment based on Maslow's hierarchy of needs and the belief that people will give their best in an environment that meets physical, psychological and self-fulfillment needs? The Gores wanted to build a radically different kind of enterprise and thought deeply about the kind of work environment that would best foster innovation and business success. Bill had been strongly influenced by the work of Maslow and McGregor and their work with human potential. Having worked at Dupont, he also had experienced working on small task forces and solving problems more quickly and efficiently when working in small teams. Vieve Gore said, "I think one of the most important things to me, and it was to Bill, is to bet on a person and you trust the person and you believe in them. And if you do that, I don't see how you cannot be successful."

The Gores started with people. They thought right from the beginning that people were the key to success. They asked themselves, "When are people at their best?"

So, they encouraged and invested in personal growth and development, encouraged experimentation and healthy risk-taking, created small collaborative teams, did away with titles, called employees "associates," eliminated us and them, believed that everyone could lead, and that leadership was about making others successful.

2021 CEO of Gore, Jason Field said "Our Enterprise is strongest when we tap into diverse talents and perspectives (human potential) while driving toward a shared vision. We remain committed to nurturing an environment where we help each other grow and push the boundaries of what's possible."

How's this working for the W.L. Gore Company after years of investing in people, self-fulfillment, and tapping into the reservoir of human potential to get the best of everyone? Gore has been recognized over and over as "the world's most innovative company." This different kind of company, intentionally built to inspire the best, has grown significantly and never strayed from its core belief in people. They have been wildly successful internationally with no hierarchy, no bosses, no core business, and a model for an inspiring culture. They were the first to say "boss" and "manager" roles inhibit innovation and creativity. As my friend and long-time Dollar General CEO, Cal Turner, says, "A company led by a "boss" is a company not led."

The implications for leaders for a Better Normal could not be clearer. Amazingly, this gem of how to inspire the best in others for extraordinary results is still waiting to be widely emulated after all these years! More heads still in the sand.

Leadership Gift Two

We have long had a love affair with excellence, greatness, and peak individual and team performance. For me, it began in 1982 with the release of a new book based on extensive research about excellent companies. I got an unexpected preview of this book in the summer of 1981. I had decided to spend my summer learning at Stanford University Graduate School of Business as a part of an Executive Program in Organizational Management. Truth be told, as an educator and a psychologist, I was familiar with the dynamics of personal change and wanted to learn more about organizational change. My experience had already led me to conclude that there were a lot of similarities in the change process, whether it was personal or organizational change. Different languages, but similar process. I soon learned I was right about that. I also learned that I got lucky in my choice of Stanford. It had come down to Stanford and Harvard. So, I couldn't go wrong, right? Unknown to me at the time, the relationship between Stanford and McKinsey & Co., the business management consultant firm headquartered in San Francisco, was strong. Many professors were also McKinsey consultants. The lead presenter in the Executive Program I attended was Tom Peters and we had an opportunity to walk through a body of work he had co-authored and was calling, *Three Yards and a Cloud of Dust*. The working title was out of the playbook of the successful football strategy of Ohio State football at the time. Ohio State football games were actually pretty boring, but Ohio State just kept on winning with a grind-it-out strategy. Peters work was a fascinating study of excellent companies, what they did best day in day out, and what separated these companies from not so excellent companies. We had multiple discussions about the major findings, many after class over a glass of wine from the vineyards near Palo Alto. Not bad for an informal learning environment, right?

Little did I know that this body of knowledge was the soon-to-be released blockbuster bestseller, *In Search of Excellence*. It was the first time for me to have significant real time with an author prior to the release of a book that would immediately become a best seller and have such an enormous impact on business leaders for years to come. In short, the excellent companies were focused on winning, keeping their heads down, sticking to their knitting, caring for each other and the customer, and doggedly repeating the winning formula. "Three yards and a cloud of dust." There is, of course, more to the story.

In short, Peters and Waterman found a number of companies that in 1980 objectively met their rigorous criteria for excellence and they identified 8 characteristics shared by excellent companies. Among their findings were:

- Excellent companies are consumed with staying close to their customer and exceeding their expectations. (Implication for a Better Normal: A broader, more inclusive look at capitalism and all the stakeholders, a significant shift at the time from the obsession with stockholder value alone.)
- Excellent businesses genuinely care about their employees. (Implication for a Better Normal: People are inspired by caring leaders.)
- Values like innovation provide the fuel for successful companies and **inspire** people at every level. (Implication for a Better Normal: When core values and actions align, it is inspiring.)
- Leaders were passionate about their company and people, and much humbler about themselves. (Implication for a Better Normal: It's not about the leader or about a golden parachute, it's about making the company and the people successful. They go together.)

> The mark of "excellence" was introduced into our business language for the first time. In addition, "humbleness" is appreciated on a larger stage and became known as a character trait of great leaders.

Important for our current journey, the excellent companies had leaders that inspired others. Remember Sam Walton and Walmart, one of the excellent companies and excellent leaders? We sought to interview him several times after Peters research made Walton famous. I thought we were pretty darn convincing, but he always said no. "It's not about me. Talk with one of our other leaders. I've already had too much publicity," he said. By the way, Sam was still living in his original home and driving an older pick-up truck when we talked with him. The term "management by walking around" was born and Walton modeled the way by visiting a different Walmart store three days a week, every week. The daily habit included a visit to a competitor's store on the same day. He was putting himself in the shoes of customers and Walmart employees, asking questions and learning. What's it like out there in the real world of day-to-day experience? Humble Sam Walton knew.

Unfortunately, Walmart lost some of the Walton magic as they became more profit-oriented and less people-centered. They have struggled too long with pay equity and benefit packages for associates and part-time employees.

Leadership Gift Three

James Loehr researched and wrote about the mental toughness that we first saw in Arthur Ashe when he beat the highly favored Jimmy Connors in the 1975 Wimbledon finals. Loehr's book, *Mental Toughness Training for* Sports, was the first to document in detail how athletes thought and behaved during a peak performance. Loehr helped everyone understand better what is going on internally, the mind-body connection, during a peak performance. We can all learn about mental toughness from athletes at their best, whether Arthur Ashe or basketball stars Candace Parker and Ja Morant, or golf great Tiger Woods, or tennis legends Serena and Venus Williams and rising star Coco Gauff.

Many successful coaches say as much as 50% of great performance is mental. In short, mental toughness training or athletic excellence training helps athletes learn to use their discretionary energy in a productive fashion, like you are learning to use the leadership practices in this book to inspire others to use their discretionary energy for their best efforts. The key insight from Mental Toughness research: mental toughness is learned through hard work, understanding, and practice, all intentional. Athletes and others who learn the mental part have a remarkable level of performance consistency. They have gained a high degree of control over the process of playing toward the upper range of their capabilities. It is exceptional talent, yes. The real difference maker, however, is the exceptional ability to consistently play to the peak of their talent.

The implications for leaders for a Better Normal are staggering.

What if leaders create the kind of environment where people savor coming to work because they are inspired to work at the upper range of their capabilities? Leaders can be intentional about their own learning and intentional about helping others learn how to think differently and create the right internal conditions for best work efforts.

Non-negotiable mental practices are becoming the norm for athletes that excel just as our non-negotiable leadership practices will become the norm for leaders who truly want to inspire best efforts in others. Naomi Osaka, Michael Phelps, and Simone Biles have helped all of us better understand the importance of mental health and the impact of psychological well-being on performance. We also know this to be true for millions of people across generations who have acknowledged the stress they have experienced from the pandemic alone, the increased sense of isolation, need for greater interaction with others, and the increased overall levels of anxiety and depression.

I am often reminded of the importance of intentionally maximizing a mentally healthy culture when I am asked by my computer to confirm that "I am not a robot." Leaders work with people, human beings. We know that toxic work environments exist where people feel more like robots than real people, often believing their leaders don't care about them as a person. It is a leadership gift for the people you lead to acknowledge the impact of stress and intentionally offer opportunities to learn healthy coping strategies.

Leadership Gift Four

Jim Kouzes and Barry Posner, two Santa Clara business school professors at the time, did something that had not been done before in the study of leadership. They began a different kind of search, a search to discover what ordinary leaders did when they were at their best. In their book, *The Leadership Challenge*, they report that all leaders can identify their personal best leadership experience and write about it through a series of guided questions. The results from thousands studied were the identification of five common characteristics of leadership. In the process, Kouzes and Posner helped demystify leadership more, moving leadership from the pedestal of "you either have it or you don't" to a learned process, open to all.

Concepts relevant to our journey with inspirational leadership:

- Emotion and "heart talk" became more a part of leadership language and practice. (Implications for a Better Normal: a moral compass, ethical and compassionate leadership are the starting points for inspiring leaders.)

> Emotion and "heart talk" became more a part of leadership language and practice.

- Kouzes and Posner underscored a critical component of leadership as "Inspiring Shared Vision" (Implication for the Better Normal: the leadership practice of inspiring shared vision is powerful. Most leaders fail to capitalize on the vision when they fail in the "shared" piece, meaning they haven't taken the time to build ownership. The trick is being intentional about "shared" day after day with everyone in your business, company, organization, or community.)
- Kouzes and Posner created a potent definition of leadership: "Leadership is the *art of mobilizing others to want to struggle for shared aspirations.*"

Leadership Gift Five

Whereas Kouzes and Posner focused their research on peak leadership experiences, I focused my research and writing on peak team experiences. Bob Fisher, good friend, colleague in consulting, and immediate past President of Belmont University, and I wrote about our findings in our co-authored book, *Real Dream Teams.* We captured the seven practices of great teams that emerged consistently from our consulting work and interviews. We asked over 3,000 participants in our workshops to describe their best-ever team experience. Everybody has a best-ever team experience just as most leaders have a best leadership experience. We also interviewed 12 great team leaders from a world-class mountain climber to a Medal of Honor recipient, to a business leader, to a Nobel Prize recipient, to a spiritual leader, to national championship college coaches, to a symphony orchestra director, to a transformative business school Dean. As we discovered, the most outstanding teams were not necessarily the most talented or best resourced. It's all about how teams chose to work with each other. This is the all-important "how."

When we asked people to identify their greatest-ever team experience, what they accomplished and why this team experience was so successful, it was like turning on a light bulb, an aha-type reaction. You can see I really like "Aha" learning moments. As you are reading this, think about your best-ever team experience. This could be any team experience with two or more people requiring collaboration to complete a project or accomplish something that you could not have done successfully without one or more "others." Take two minutes and write down what you accomplished. Then think about the process of the work leading up to the accomplishment. What made it possible? I cannot see your reaction, but I can describe the common reactions from the thousands I have witnessed as they share their team experience with others in a small group: smiles, animation, excitement, energy, and enthusiasm.

Our research on teams at their best provides additional ammunition and insight for Better Normal leadership. Our world, work, communities, and families are interdependent, and we need each other. Big dreams and common missions require collaboration. Each person's role is essential for teams performing at their best and building a trusting culture is essential. The practices of great teams make sense to most everyone. We found, without question, that implementing the best practices is the hard part. This is why "intentional" becomes such a key mantra for inspiring leaders. The implications for new leaders for a Better Normal are many, but the leadership practices that were always identified as most consistently inspiring were clear mission, clear roles and expectations, collaboration, trust and support for each other, and an expectation of success. Great teams don't always win, but they have a mentality of expecting to be successful with each project, game, or team opportunity. Bob Fisher and I had the opportunity to implement best team practices at Belmont University soon after the writing of Real Dream Teams.

> The leadership practices that were always identified as most consistently inspiring were clear mission, clear roles and expectations, collaboration, trust and support for each other, and an expectation of success.

Leadership Gift Six.

As an organization and as a leader trying to create an inspiring culture, people must know you want to understand what they bring to the table, their unique gifts, how they like to work and interact, what motivates and inspires them. High levels of emotional intelligence permeate the most productive workplaces and relationships. Daniel Goldman introduced *Emotional Intelligence* to most people when his book by the same name was released in 1995. Although traditional IQ and academic intelligence are important, Goldman's research found that far more important to success in any profession is emotional intelligence. Emotional intelligence is the capacity for recognizing our own feelings and those of others, for motivating ourselves, and for managing emotions well in ourselves and in our relationships. Goldman's research began to pave the way for what we now know to be true, the soft skills are the hard skills and have a dramatic impact on bottom-line results. In fact, traditional IQ may be important for opening and getting in the door, but once in, it's all about relationships and how you work with others.

> The concept of Emotional Intelligence shines a bright light on affect, feelings, and emotions, signaling for the first time with extensive research that emotional intelligence trumps traditional IQ in most any setting.

The big takeaway for Better Normal leadership is the overwhelming need for leaders to assess their emotional IQ and learn how they can be smarter about the world of feelings, their own feelings and the feelings of their colleagues, friends, and family. It's a whole new world for most leaders, and rarely taught in undergraduate or graduate programs. Emotional Intelligence is learnable and would be one of my first suggestions for the required education and training program for leaders throughout any organization. Emotionally Intelligent leaders are able to see the impact their behavior has on others and work to be appropriate. They admit mistakes, show remorse, and ask for forgiveness. Toxic leaders either are not sensitive enough to realize the impact of their behavior or they intentionally play off the fear and chaos they create with misinformation. They rarely admit mistakes, show no remorse, and consistently blame others.

Leadership Gift Seven

Leading Change was written by John Kotter who I quoted earlier. Kotter was Konosuke Matsushita Professor of Leadership at the Harvard

Business School when his book first appeared in 1995. Kotter's work became a major resource for Bob Fisher and me as senior consultants to the Department of Transportation in their transformational quest to become multi-modal and collaborative in their thinking and acting. In short, they wanted to work like a great transportation team as opposed to separate modal teams. The book *Leading Change* was an outgrowth of the most widely read Harvard Business Review article ever, *Leading Change: Why Transformation Efforts Fail.* This article was based on Kotter's observations of over 100 companies who had tried to make themselves into significantly better competitors. He concluded that a few were successful, a few utter failures, and most tilted toward the "failure" end of the scale. He noted 8 major reasons why the transformational efforts failed. You know what he found to be the number one reason for failure? Listen up. This is powerful and as true today as it was when he wrote it: Not establishing a great enough sense of urgency! This is one of the seeds of inspiration for this book and my focus on "Intentionality."

If you are a book highlighter and want to come back to a statement that supports leadership for a Better Normal and why leadership from the bottom up and top down is so critical, this is the paragraph to highlight, straight from Dr. Kotter.

"The most general lesson to be learned from the more successful cases is that the change process goes through a series of phases that, in total, usually require a considerable length of time. Skipping steps creates only the illusion of speed and never produces a satisfying result." Notice the word "never." I talk about the seven non-negotiable leadership practices that consistently inspire others to engage in best work. Skipping key leadership practices as a leader or not fully investing in inspiring leadership throughout the organization leads to failure and wasted resources. Kotter continues, "A second very general lesson is that critical mistakes in any of the phases can have a devastating impact, slowing momentum and negating hard-won gains. Perhaps because we have relatively little experience in renewing organizations, even very capable people often make at least one big mistake."

After 2020, all leaders face an unprecedented crisis and opportunity.

All leaders stand on a new playing field, forever different.
Urgency and intentionality are even more important, and we
are facing a new reality that no leaders have seen before.

Kotter, writing in 1995, was discussing companies and organizations trying to remake themselves into better competitors in a more challenging market environment. In 2020 and beyond, we still have a challenging and different market environment, but we have the added challenge to be more human, ethical, compassionate, fair, visionary, and collaborative. To be urgent and intentional about leading with these qualities is the process that gives meaning to life at work and home.

Urgency about what is most important and strategic is one big takeaway gift from Kotter. The other is the need to overcommunicate vision and core strategies. According to Kotter, leaders will know they are helping others be successful when everyone from the CEO to the IT folks to the maintenance folks to the receptionists can communicate in their own words the excitement of how they contribute to the vision and mission of the organization. St. Jude Children's Research Hospital in Memphis does this beautifully. You will see this in detail in the next chapter.

Leadership Gift Eight

Over twenty years after *In Search of Excellence*, Jim Collins wrote another block-buster leadership book that resonated with leaders everywhere, *Good to Great.* You have to like the sound of moving from good to great, right? Collins and his research team did exhaustive work with business data that led to the selection of eleven great companies. These companies were selected on one criterion: good to great results on stock returns over a 15-year period. The results were measured on average cumulative stock returns starting from the point of transition (the significant jump in stock returns from past performance) and sustained for 15 straight years. The good to great companies generated cumulative stock returns 7 times the general market in the fifteen years following their transition point. Extraordinary results!

The good to great consequence of Collins' book for me was the discovery of the characteristics of the leaders who led the companies that made the leap from good to great. The similarities of the CEOs, perhaps unintended discoveries but none-the-less fascinating, were the attraction for me. Collins concludes that greatness is largely a matter of the "intentional conscious choice" of those at the top! Remember this. Great leadership is not accidental. It is a conscious choice to create a different normal where you lead. Instructive to our journey to a Better Normal, Collins called the eleven leaders Level 5 Executives, distinguishing them in a hierarchy from Level 3, Competent Managers, and Level 4, Effective Leaders. In summary, the Level 5 Executive "builds enduring greatness through a paradoxical blend of personal humility and professional will." Remember the old line that "it's hard to be humble when you're perfect in every way." Level 5 leaders thrive on the "humility" we saw in Sam Walton. Get this: "They (leaders) channeled their ego needs away from themselves and into the larger goal of building a great company." As I have pointed out earlier, leaders who inspire (and great company leaders did), are "first and foremost for the institution, not themselves." Leadership is not about "me" but inspiring the best in others. As we will discuss later, new open organizations are led at the top by CEOs who are "open" about their role to help make others successful. "Make

> The Level 5 Executive "builds enduring greatness through a paradoxical blend of personal humility and professional will."

others successful" became another leadership gift, a "connecting dot," for the new leadership model for a Better Normal.

Our journey to leadership for a Better Normal is based on a combination of discoveries about peak performing individuals, teams, and leaders as well as those who led the "in search of excellence" and "good to great" companies.

The discoveries are leadership gifts from the past. Along with the ongoing contributions of my humanistic psychology bias, they make a powerful case for people. People really are the greatest assets of any company or organization. We just too rarely act like they are. We too rarely design our work environments around our knowledge of what inspires the best in all of us. But the clues have all been there. The Excellent companies and their CEOs identified by Peters, the Good to Great companies and their CEOs identified by Collins, the mental model of Leading Change as opposed to managing change introduced by Kotter, the leadership practices found by Kouzes and Posner when leaders are at their best, the team-leader practices discovered by Fisher and Thomas in Real Dream Teams, and the practices of peak performing athletes identified by Loehr; all identify a strategic leadership gap between the excellent companies and others, between the good and great companies, between traditional leaders and leaders at their best, between athletes who are mentally tough peak performers and those that are not, and between teams with best-team practices and average teams.

The common threads are there, all gifts, and they lead to an exponentially larger gift when the threads are woven together and the "gift dots" connected: a leadership model fueled with greater intent, urgency, and inspiration, all designed to tap into our reserve of human potential and close the Strategic Leadership Gap between Normal leadership and Better Normal leadership.

Leadership Gift Nine: My Capstone Experience with Leading

You are perhaps wondering how you can write about leadership without having led others, experiencing firsthand what being in the arena feels like and looks like? Although so many of our leadership gifts came from great research of what other leaders did in leading others, I was compelled to write about leadership after 12 years of being in the leadership arena. My last leadership research came from implementing leadership practices with my associates and colleagues every day for 4,380 plus days. On reflection, my career-long learning laboratory with leadership needed a capstone experience to be complete. Then, I needed to experience 2020 and the four powerful forces that converged in that one short year to conclude "We can do better." I want to tell you with some degree of detail about my personal leadership experience since it is a "good to great" experience utilizing the 7 inspiring leadership practices. This experience also allowed me to write with great conviction because I "lived" being a leader.

> My last leadership research came from implementing leadership practices with my associates and colleagues every day for 4,380 plus days.

At any rate, my leadership laboratory had already included a rewarding career of teaching, consulting, counseling, and coaching. And then, and then, Voila! An unbelievable leadership opportunity came along that would allow me to lead, apply, and connect the dots of leadership practices with inspiration and underutilized human potential. In real time. This opportunity and invitation to be a senior leader was attractive and quadrupled in potential since Bob Fisher, my long-time friend, co-consultant with leadership, and co-author of *Real Dream Teams*, was at the heart of the opportunity. Bob and I would be leading together in what would become our best-ever dream team experience.

Ok. It's true. Bob did the hard work of earning the Presidency of Belmont University in Nashville, Tennessee. Two years after he was named President, in 2003, driven by the vision to do something unique and compelling in the academic world and in a city that was on the cusp of becoming a great destination city, I became Vice President for University Advancement at Belmont. Now, it was like, "Can you two guys really lead change, do something transformative, and make a difference like you think you can? Come on! Nashville is the Athens of the South with 18 institutions of higher education. Vanderbilt is literally next door and a stone's throw away. And you envision becoming Nashville's university and making the leap from a good to great university?" Yes, "Let's win championships." This would be our championship. And, yes, we already knew we were at our best when deeply challenged and inspired. We felt this was our moment to lead change, be proactive, urgent, intentional, dream big, and act boldly. Not only at Belmont, but in the larger Nashville community. In addition, and these are big additions, we were very, very fortunate to get the right people on the Belmont bus and very, very fortunate that Belmont happened to be in Nashville, Music City and Healthcare mecca. Location, location, location.

Bob and I had just completed a three-year opportunity as lead consultants with Secretary of Transportation Rodney Slater and his senior cabinet in Washington during the last years of the Clinton presidency. Secretary Slater had led the transformation of the Department of Transportation from a modal thinking and acting department to a multimodal collaborative thinking and acting department. The DOT strategic plan was rated the best in government. Their transformation created a new perspective on "how" to get things done and how to better make transportation decisions for the future. The change Bob Fisher envisioned for Belmont was transformative and I was eager to be a part of accomplishing the emerging new vision. The Belmont transformative vision included a national branding which would move the university from a good regional university to a great university with national and international appeal, enrollment growth, greater diversity and inclusiveness, new facilities, greater educational focus on Nashville's healthcare and music industries, broader educational opportunities, improved and nationally competitive salaries for staff and faculty, and a minimizing of the traditional academic ivory tower mentality. We wanted to leverage the Nashville brand to become Nashville's university. It would take a "good to great commitment" to close the gap between where we were in 2004 and where we wanted to be 15 years later in 2019. As a result, our first strategic planning session was based on Jim Collins' *Good to Great* concepts. We knew it would take real leadership, getting the right people on the bus, confronting the brutal facts about where we were currently and where we wanted to be in the future, a culture of discipline, establishing momentum, and moving the Flywheel faster and faster.

Recall that Collins' *Good to Great* cases were eleven companies that made the leap from good results to great results in stock returns and sustaining those results for 15 years after the transition point. The transition point was the first upward turn in stock performance from market to below market performance and never fall below that upward-turn point again. The 15-years captured by Collins and his team ranged from Philip Morris, 1964-1979, to Fannie Mae, 1984-1999. Regardless of whether these companies have sustained their amazing stock market returns since they made the leap from good to great, the lessons we learned from this research are timeless. In our first strategic planning process at Belmont, we thought "why not" apply the same concepts to a university? The results became extraordinary not so much because of us, but because we were able to practice what we genuinely believed about leadership and what leaders do when they "think big" and inspire and engage others. After all, our colleagues consistently exceeded expectations and were an absolute joy. After the successful hosting of the first-ever Presidential Debate in Tennessee in 2008, the "bring it on" confidence was well established.

For-profit companies, non-profit companies, and institutions of higher education are certainly in different arenas with different measures and definitions for "extraordinary" and "great." When examining the extraordinary results at Belmont from 2004-2019, it is not difficult to conclude that Belmont made the leap from a good university to a great university during this 15-year time frame. I simply don't have comparative data, but we had to be one of the top eleven stories in higher education during that time frame.

The critical commonalities between the for-profit greats and non-profit greats are stunningly similar: big dreams, bold leadership practices that inspire others and tap into discretionary energy/ underutilized potential, and extraordinary results.

Leading at Belmont solidified and confirmed what I knew to be true about leading, and there is no substitute for living what you know and trusting what you know. I will briefly reflect on this capstone personal leadership experience as illustrative of the key leadership concepts I recommend here in our leadership journey. All of us are leaders. The beauty of these leadership concepts, whether you are a parent, manager, senior leader, or CEO; whether you are leading with your family, a non-profit, church, synagogue, mosque, or a for-profit, the basic concepts of leadership are similar and apply to you.

Here is a brief reflection and informative glance at the 2004-2019 Belmont years. We led with what would become the model for this new perspective on leadership. The key indicator for the eleven companies chosen by Jim Collins was stock performance. The key indicator for Belmont was consistently exceeding expectations for the bold financial, branding, new facilities, student success, salary, diversity and inclusion strategic initiatives in the 2005, 2010, 2015, and 2020 strategic plans. Most initiatives and goals were met early. Strategic planning at Belmont was and is an inclusive and campus-wide engagement process of planning that occurs every 5 years. The entire Board of Trustees and all stakeholders were part of the circle of inclusion. Each consensus plan had 7-10 strategic priorities that aligned with the transformative vision and core mission for the university. Accountability goals and objectives in each College and department throughout the university were aligned with the strategic priorities. The vision and strategic plans were and are still the driving forces for change.

BELMONT UNIVERSITY: THE GOOD TO GREAT YEARS

Here's a summary of what happened between 2004 and 2019. Each result below came from intentional strategic initiatives. Each factor is a powerful measurement of success in the higher education world and each criteria reflects a sustaining quality over the fifteen-year period.

- Student enrollment almost tripled and increased each year for 15 years. (From just over 3,000 to over 8,200)
- More than $1 billion was invested in 28 new or renovated buildings and property acquisition. Assets increased for 15 straight years.
- Every new building had an underground parking garage and several had gardens on top, enhancing the beauty, safety, and environment of the campus.
- New Colleges of Pharmacy and Law were established, accredited, and opened in new facilities. Pharmacy and Law Schools are not fully accredited till the first class of students graduate. The bold leap of faith to have new facilities prior to accreditation is very unusual in the academic world.
- Belmont became more intentional about diversity and inclusion. Bridges to Belmont, a full scholarship program for aspiring students of color from Nashville's most underserved high schools, changed the Belmont diversity landscape.

- Two new Vice Presidents were added to the small senior leadership team. A VP for Institutional Effectiveness was significant in helping remove the systemic roadblocks and increase effectiveness. A VP for Spiritual Life, unusual for any university to have at the senior level, showed the commitment to spiritual development and the importance of a moral compass and Ethical Heart.

- Belmont was one of the first higher education institutions in the country to offer Business ethics in the early 1990s. During the Good to Great years at Belmont, Business Ethics was institutionalized through new funding and the creation of the Edward C. Kennedy Center for Business Ethics.

- Schools of Entrepreneurship and Social Entrepreneurship were created and quickly became ranked as top programs nationally. Entrepreneurship became embedded in the Belmont fabric, highly unusual for any academic community.

- Faculty and staff merit salary increases were awarded each year for 15 straight years. Most colleges and universities during this same time frame had no or slight increases, some made salary cuts, and some made staff and faculty cuts.

- Budget increased annually over the 15-years from 60 to over 340 million.

- President Fisher was honored as Nashvillian of the Year and Tennessean of the year, chaired the Nashville Chamber of Commerce Board and the Nashville Convention and Business Bureau Board, all reflecting the vision of being a community partner and Nashville's University. Fisher's leadership is what Jim Collin's called Level 5 leadership.

- Established the first accredited songwriting program in the country, adding a new dimension to one of the top-three ranked Music Business and Entertainment programs in the country. The songwriting program currently attracts over 400 majors from across the country.

- Multiple years of recognition by U.S. News & World Report as a top-10 College or University in the South as well as multi-year recognition for "Innovation as an Institution", enhancing the Belmont brand.
- The Tennessee Healthcare Hall of Fame was created, and the first class of inductees included Danny Thomas, Founder of St. Jude Children's Research Hospital. St. Jude will be featured in several of the following chapters.
- Christmas at Belmont, an annual multi-genre musical performance, became a popular holiday viewing event across the country on National Public Television and the selection to host the first-ever Town Hall Presidential Debate in Tennessee were huge nation-wide image builders.
- Student success increased along with the enrollment including improved average ACT scores, retention rates, and graduation rates.

In addition to the above outcomes over the fifteen years from 2004-2019, three additional "good to great" outcomes occurred in 2020 and 2021, sustaining the extraordinary performance of the past 15 years.

1. In November 2020, Belmont announced a major partnership with Health Corporation of America (HCA), the largest for-profit healthcare and hospital entity in the country, creating a new Medical School at Belmont.
2. A second Town-Hall Presidential Debate was held at Belmont in 2020.
3. In 2021, a world-class, 180 million Fisher Performing Arts Center was completed (named for the retired President and his wife, Judy Fisher). The Fisher Center and what happens within that Center will inspire the best in students, faculty, and the community,

and it will encourage performers and performing-arts lovers from around the globe to come to Belmont University and Music City.

"Leadership is what we used to call it when you saw someone doing something so compelling and exciting that you wanted to be a part of it." — Unknown author

This informal definition of leadership from an unknown author, in part, summarizes what we believed happened at Belmont. There was not a day, with all the headaches and tough decisions that leaders face, that I wasn't fueled by the excitement and challenge of helping create something bigger than myself and bigger than any group of senior leaders. Making a difference was self-reinforcing.

Leading at Belmont and in Nashville became a career, capstone leadership journey for me. I had consulted with over three hundred organizations prior to Belmont, focusing on leadership practices, vision and mission-driven team building, and strategic planning. Personally, implementing leadership practices on a daily basis requires something different than researching or teaching leadership. Here, I was in the arena, not consulting someone else about their arena! It was another leap of faith for me. I planned to stay a max of 5 years. It turns out, this arena was where I wanted to be and exactly where all of us on the Belmont bus chose to be. My 5-year commitment turned into 12-years followed by an additional consulting year to complete my last project, the creation and implementation of the Tennessee Healthcare Hall of Fame.

Belmont became an anomaly in the academic world. We tried to upend expectations for the ivory tower; create an even stronger moral and compassionate compass; engage the Board, faculty, staff, alumni, and current students every five years with a bold vision and challenging strategic initiatives; and then exceed expectations. (From 2003-2021, for example, "exceed expectations" included new Pharmacy,

Law, and Medical Schools plus two Presidential Debates.) The journey was inspiring. Inspiration leads people to exceed expectations. We believed we made the leap from good to great in the academic world with sustained growth, new programming, and significant sustained improvements across the academic spectrum for fifteen years and more. It was not stock growth. It was the growth of human capital. The Belmont leadership experience was an ideal career capstone experience. The experience was the final piece of my leadership puzzle.

The disturbing events of 2020 became the final tipping point, inspiring me to write at a time that was a historic moment for leadership, a time when business, educational and religious leaders are challenged to step up, lead, and advocate for a better normal, better communities, and a better world. The calling became for me, "do the right thing for people." People over politics. People over business as usual. People are the number one asset. Doing good for people is good business. Current leadership practices were inadequate for the challenge and the rising trend of "malignant normality" meant leaders everywhere had to lead differently.

The late Senator Robert Kennedy once said, "Some see things as they are and ask why. I dream things that never were and ask, why not?" We asked "why not" often at Belmont. All we now know about leadership compels me to ask on an even broader scale, "Why not, with the greatest-ever leadership opportunity and over four decades of great research on leadership, create a new perspective on leadership to match this moment. Why not intentionally create a new model with a heart of ethical commitment, character, courage, and compassion. Why not a new model of leadership with a collaborative and selfless mindset, and a culture of inspiration powered by seven existing leadership practices that free untapped human potential? Why not go right to the core of our one humanity and inspire our best?"

Creating a Culture of Inspiration requires an intentional commitment by leaders to a process built on the fundamental beliefs that we do have "one wild and precious life," our one humanity is shared by all, we are interdependent and connected, and people are indeed the most important asset of any enterprise. We honor these assumptions through the process of choices we make in how we care for each other, how we struggle together toward a shared vision, how we communicate with each other, how we make decisions, and how we work. It all begins with the process of how we do things and the choices we intentionally make. We cannot control all the challenges that life gives us, but we can control how we respond. We always have choices. If the "how we interact with each other" process is broken, everything is broken. If we forget we have choices, even in the direst moments, we are trapped. Choice is hope.

> We cannot control all the challenges that life gives us, but we can control how we respond. We always have choices.

Leadership Gift 10: BrenéBrené Brown.

Leaders give hope by assuring people they are free to use their discretionary energy to explore, think more broadly, innovate. Leaders want their colleagues to be courageous and overcome their fears of being who they are. Leaders invite others to be more vulnerable with them, to dig into their untapped potential which is home to their best. As BrenéBrené Brown writes in the opening pages of her book, *The Gifts of Imperfection*, "Courage, compassion, and connection seem like big, lofty ideals. But in reality, they are daily practices that, when exercised enough, become these incredible gifts in our lives. And the good news is that our vulnerabilities are what force us to call on these amazing tools. Because we're human and beautifully imperfect, we get to practice using our tools on a daily basis. In this way, courage, compassion, and connection become

> Leaders give hope by assuring people they are free to use their discretionary energy to explore, think more broadly, innovate.

gifts—the gifts of imperfection." In order to practice these "amazing tools" every day, we do have to create cultures that encourage and reward courage, compassion, and connection. They are essential in a culture of inspiration.

BrenéBrené Brown's research on vulnerability, shame, courage, compassion, and empathy are groundbreaking in nature and become the most recent leadership gift to all aspiring leaders. It is clear that the once considered soft skills of leadership, the relationship skills, are now the "hard skills." Brown's unique research findings add significant and valuable new information for leadership and open organizations. Her work underscores and supports the leadership findings here and all I know to be true about relationship-building. Brown's work was seen first by most readers in 2010 with the book mentioned above and spans an eight-year period till the release of her first book with "lead" in the title, *Dare to Lead,* in 2018.

Brown's work comes at a crucial time when we are also discovering new information about high-performing teams. Only recently have top organizations turned their attention to the characteristics of its highest performing teams, often spending millions of dollars in multiple years seeking the magic answer.

The most significant finding of all stands out like a flashing light in our journey into the power of untapped human potential. The magic ingredient, for children and adults: psychological safety!

More reinforcement for what we discussed earlier with Maslow's hierarchy of needs, learning for children in school and learning for adults in organizations.

From the perspective of a parent, friend, husband, colleague, leader and psychologist, it would be hard to find anything more important in a personal or professional relationship than the knowledge that I would be accepted for who I am: warts, imperfections, crazy ideas, and all. It is safe to be the "Wild and Precious" me. Brené Brown's work is refreshingly humanizing. Her work helps us see differently. It augments and supports richly the culture of inspiration and the need for leaders to create the psychological safety for team members to be vulnerable. Her work is a rare gift that provides hope and courage to leaders and new leadership. We must all dare to lead in this new world if we are to create a better normal.

Peter Senge's *The Fifth Discipline: The Art and Practice of the Learning Organization,* is another gift of significant impact on me as an educator and leader. The takeaway for leaders and organizations is simple: Value learning and growing, individually and collectively. Teach leadership, emotional intelligence, innovation, psychological safety, and relationship skills to everyone. All are key to humanizing leaders and organizations and creating a culture of inspiration.

THE GROWING PAINS OF BECOMING A LEADER

If you are not feeling uncomfortable, anxious, or vulnerable, just a little or maybe a lot, about putting your trust in people and inviting them into an adventure of a lifetime, I would be shocked. You are thinking about getting out of your comfort zone. It is uncomfortable. I have known few people, whether they were thinking about personal change or organizational change, who did not feel uncomfortable, anxious, scared, or all the above. Think of change? Think of leading change and believing that you can inspire others? Think of being more vulnerable yourself and inviting others to be more vulnerable? Think of trusting the process underlying this new perspective on leadership? It takes courage and trust.

Imagine a trapeze. I have often thought about leading change and getting out of a comfort zone to be like this: You am on a trapeze with no net. You are swinging back and forth with your back to a second trapeze controlled by someone else. At some point, the other person will signal you to release your grip, turn around and catch the second trapeze. For a moment you are suspended in space, letting go of the firm grip on one trapeze and trusting a second trapeze to be there for you to get a new grip, a new something to hold on to and keep you from falling. Imagine the moment of truth. Letting go, suspended in air, before grabbing something secure to hold.

This is the "leap of faith." The trapeze leap is scary. So is parachuting out of a plane. So is leadership. Leading change is scary and messy at times. But it is much more exhilarating, challenging, and less fearful, when you believe in what you are doing and trust a proven process. Trust the discomfort of change. It is a natural and normal reaction. It is also very helpful to have other leaders around you who are committed to leadership for a better normal. But, even if you aren't surrounded by other change leaders, you can lead for a Better Normal within your sphere of influence. Whether you lead a small team, a department, a division of a larger organization, you can help create a psychologically safe place for the people you lead to be more vulnerable and creative. Trust you. Trust the change process.

> Letting go, suspended in air, before grabbing something secure to hold. This is the "leap of faith."

CULTURE AS COMPETITIVE ADVANTAGE

No country has more resources than we to lead the changes that will help us thrive in the new world. We are at a leadership fork in the road. The leadership "path less taken" calls us to be brutally honest about the devastation we have seen from virus and man-made systemic pandemics and toxic leadership. Creating a culture of inspiration builds an environment of psychological safety where internal motivation thrives. The strategic leadership gap we discovered can be dramatically closed when change leaders lead with the proven, non-negotiable leadership practices that invite and inspire the best of everyone for a Better Normal.

When Gary Ridge's retirement as CEO of WD-40 was announced, he stated his gratitude for the opportunity to serve for 25 years as "the leader of our amazing tribe of dedicated and passionate people who live our Company's Values every day. Culture is a true competitive advantage, and there are not many companies that have a better culture than the one present at WD-40 Company."

A culture of inspiration can be created anywhere from a St. Jude to a WD-40 to a W. L. Gore and Company to a university to a faith community. Regardless of the product or the service, the organization makes a difference in some way that is compelling, attractive, and important enough to evoke passion in the people who work there. Regardless of the product or the service, every organization can have a "just cause" in their future vision that makes life better for the people who work there, the community they serve, and the environment they live in. Leaders now have the tools to lead, to engage others in leadership, make those around them successful, and make the world a better place.

INVITATION TO IMPLEMENT THE 7 INSPIRING LEADERSHIP PRACTICES

As we close this chapter, I want to shift gears from a straight reading process to suggest a process for deeper learning about the key seven inspiring leadership concepts. Each practice is a practice you can learn or improve. Each practice is inspiring. I suggest a deeper learning process than just reading and underlining key words or sentences because people in workshops consistently report how helpful it is to write and reflect. Writing and reflecting on what you have just read triggers a more active thinking process. We have discovered that thinking "out loud" enhances the learning process. So, what follows is an explanation of what you will see at the end of this chapter and those that follow.

THE LEARNING PROCESS AND OPPORTUNITIES TO LEARN AT THE CLOSE OF EACH CHAPTER

My hope is to activate your curiosity throughout the book to the point that you will want to internalize information as you move through this leadership journey.

Learning is a continuous process of becoming aware of new information, then turning the new information into new understanding, and then finally acting based on the new understanding and new information.

LEARNING PROCESS

Awareness ⟶ Understanding ⟶ New actions

As you respond to learning opportunities in each of the chapters, you will be surprised at the new meaning it brings to the process. You are personalizing your learning and increasing the likelihood that you will tell others about what you are learning and begin to make some changes in your leadership. If you and I were working together during a personal coaching session, I would be asking you to respond in writing often, increasing the likelihood of understanding at a deeper level and taking a new leadership action. I will ask you to be intentional at the end of each chapter related to what you have just read, making a few suggestions for internalizing the concepts of the chapter.

I know you have been inspired in the past. You know what it feels like and how it impacts you. Whether you achieved great individual results or whether you were part of a team, organization, or company that achieved great results, the best individual effort or best collective efforts were necessary and they were inspired. We only offer or volunteer our best over time when inspired. This is

> We only offer or volunteer our best over time when inspired.

a critical point about learning and leading. No one can make us do our best. But we can voluntarily give our best. The difference between compliance and commitment is huge. Sustained commitment is inspired.

BEING INTENTIONAL ABOUT A "CULTURE OF INSPIRATION"

1. I invite you to write down your response to the question, "Who or what has been an inspiration to you in your life and what was the impact of being inspired?" You may think of one specific person or moment of inspiration or a sustained period when you have been inspired. Pick one, write it down, and write the impact of inspiration on you.
2. Identify someone available to you who you respect or admire, someone who acts in inspiring ways. Consider learning from that person and asking that person to share with you their experience with inspiration or being inspired. Note. Even if you think this person might be unavailable to you, I have found that most leaders are flattered you find them inspiring and are pleased to share how they developed the quality of inspiring.
3. I invited you earlier in this chapter to write about your best team experience ever and then to identify the characteristics of the experience that made it your best ever. If you did not do that earlier, add this to your learning now.

Because of the magnitude of what we learned in 2020 and early 2021, we simply can't go back to the old normal. At the same time, we have the greatest opportunity of our lifetime to create cultures of inspiration that call us to right wrongs and more fully live to our potential. Together, we can make a difference and create a Better Normal. Our journey continues with the seven inspiring non-negotiable leadership practices that create the Culture of Inspiration. These practices are compiled from the leadership gifts of the past, reduced to the 7 most inspiring practices under one umbrella of inspiring leadership. These become the Leadership Gifts going forward, the gifts that anyone can open, learn, and lead.

The chart below may help you in seeing the differences between the three leadership models I am highlighting. There are countless organizations called "open organizations" that I will discuss as hopeful examples of "Better Normal" leadership. All organizations, after 2020, simply have to be more conscious of the need to make a difference in the broader community and the world. Hopefully, you can use the chart below to track your progress in becoming an Inspiring "Better Normal" leader.

Intentional Inspiration

	Toxic Malignant Normal		Traditional Bureaucratic Normal		Inspiring Better Normal
Leader Options:	Toxic Malignant Normal	————	Traditional Bureaucratic Normal	————	Inspiring Better Normal
Leads with inspiration	Low Leads with fear, power, and control	————	Medium Intends to lead but lacks new leadership skill sets	————	High Leads to inspire
Acts on the power of underutilized human potential	Low	—————	Medium	—————	High
Believes that people are the most important assets and all can lead	Low	—————	Medium	—————	High
Use their power to make others successful	Low	—————	Medium	—————	High
Empathic with the unique experiences of people coping with structural inequities	Low	—————	Medium	—————	High

Leader Options:	Toxic Malignant Normal	————	Traditional Bureaucratic Normal	————	Inspiring Better Normal
Tells the truth. Builds trust. Engages others in the creation of a shared Moral Compass and Ethical Heart	Low	————————	Medium	————————	High
Leads in instilling a collaborative mindset	Low	————————	Medium	————————	High
Sense of urgency about shared vision, wayfinding, and strategic initiatives	Low	————————	Medium	————————	High
Identifies and recognizes individual and collective work that make a difference	Low	————————	Medium	————————	High
Leads in improving life in the broader community with systemic inequities and the environment	Low	————————	Medium	————————	High
Use their leadership platform to advocate for economic security for all and stewardship of the environment	Low	————————	Medium	————————	High

ABOUT PART TWO AND THE 7 INSPIRING PRACTICES

As I transition to the seven inspiring leadership practices of leaders for a better normal and better world, we have another reminder of our fragile and vulnerable world community. In the opening pages of the book, you will recall the astronauts view of the world from their perspective near the surface of the moon. They thought, from that perspective, that war should be "unthinkable" on this tiny planet. As I write, Russia has invaded Ukraine. Now we see the worst of leadership in the form of a powerful and toxic political leader creating war, the ultimate outcome of lose-lose behavior. Nobody wins. We are also seeing the best of courageous leadership from Ukrainian President Volodymyr Zelensky and leaders from around the world in response to Putin, not only from political leaders but leaders from major corporations as well. We see the courage and compassion, the moral compass of many leaders emerging. War increases urgency for leading with an ethical, compassionate heart, and appreciation of our one humanity.

War increases the urgency of doing what is right. War relegates our "culture wars" to "unthinkable" and trivial.

War is the startling wake-up-call of how important leadership is. It is the humbling and awful reminder of why this moment in history is the greatest leadership opportunity of our lifetime.

The 7 inspiring leadership practices provide hope and inspire the best of everyone. Some of you work remotely, others work in a hybrid model, others work with teammates around the world, and others work in manufacturing or work that requires you to be with colleagues daily. Wherever you are, you can lead from this new and fresh perspective. You can influence the common good wherever we are. People are hungry for more value, purpose, and appreciation.

PART II

THE SEVEN NON-NEGOTIABLE LEADERSHIP PRACTICES THAT INSPIRE OUR BEST

The next seven chapters will continue our leadership journey with the Seven Non-Negotiable Practices that inspire the best in others and create extraordinary results. These are the practices that create a culture of inspiration and build individual and collective success. They have been a lifetime in the making and researched for 40 years.

They get the tag "Non-Negotiable" because they hang together and are synergistic, meaning they are more than the sum of their parts.

I refer to them as "practices" because each is action oriented. The practices are all proactive rather than reactive. As we will see with each practice, each is grossly underused by managers, supervisors, and leaders. Leaving even one practice out of your toolbox negates your work in the other practices and reduces the impact. Recall the Bain research I referred to earlier in the Culture of Inspiration chapter? We discussed the four clusters of inspiring traits they discovered: developing inner resources, connecting with others, setting the tone, and leading the team. Get this. They found that if a leader practiced successfully in only one of these four arenas, that leader would double the chance of being an inspiring leader! Double the chances. Think of what can happen when you embrace inspiration as the key to unlocking human potential and the seven non-negotiable practices of inspiring leaders?

Five of the practices will not sound new to most readers. Two will be new based on the new perspective on leadership post-2020. What is new is that these seven practices are the few that consistently inspire, cluster together, and are synergistic in nature. We know that the most powerful impact comes when leaders intentionally lead with all the practices. Intentionality is core to this new model and all leaders must be intentional together. I also recommend adding the title of leader in some fashion to all managers and supervisors in organizations and companies. Great things happen only when more people know they too are leaders of change. All people can be leaders. If a company commits to the belief that all can lead, a common leadership language can be taught and embedded in the culture. What a great investment.

Chapters four, five, and six, the first three non-negotiable practices that inspire others, form the "How" for this new perspective of leadership for the better normal. Intentionality about leading from an ethical heart, a sense of urgency, and a collaborative mindset define how you will lead. Every other practice is built on this underlying process that fuels all other practices. These three practices clarify and define how people will relate with others and engage others. Chapters seven and eight are the powerful "directional forces" chapters, the vision and wayfinding practices. These are the "Why" and "What" chapters. Why does the enterprise exist and how can we engage our people in the compelling pull of the future? The "wayfinding" chapter helps us with the "what," the strategic steps we need to take to "find our way" from where we are now to where we want to be in the future. Powerful short-term wins are addressed in this chapter as well. In chapter nine, we learn more about the inspiring practice of helping others see how they are "difference-makers" through their individual and team contributions. And finally, in chapter ten, a new leadership practice that jumps out of 2020, the expanded role of new leaders to make a difference related to the newly exposed systemic inequities where they work and live, and act to protect the environment. In short, leaders must lead to level the playing field for those whose life have been made more difficult by unfair practices and policies that have discriminated over time. Current leaders did not create the structural inequities, but they can make them right. Every leader can help make the lives of others better. This is the "just cause" for the common good that is available to any organization.

All clues from the best of the best in leadership and what we have learned in 2020 point to this:

> People are searching for leaders who are hope-givers,
> who care about them as human beings, who want them to
> live and work in an environment that inspires their best,
> and who want them to be able to make a difference.

There are already many inspiring leaders, leaders who are already leading for a better normal, and I will showcase some of them. We simply need more organizations to learn a common leadership language and many more people to lead. We need more organizations to shift from the traditional bureaucratic management style of leading. Toxic leaders are unacceptable anywhere.

My strongest hope is that you will own the practices over time as your own.

SUMMARY

People Are Our Most Valuable Assets. We honor all our stakeholders when we honor first the "One wild and precious life" of each of those we lead.

People and teams can only be **inspired** to volunteer their absolute best effort, and we now know the seven non-negotiable leadership practices that inspire the best in others. We now know how to create a **Culture of Inspiration.**

THE UMBRELLA OF INSPIRING PRACTICES

One. The Ethical Heart: Character, Courage, and Compassion

Two. Urgency: Increasing Intentionality and Reducing Complacency

Three. The Collaborative Mindset: Win-Win Thinking and Acting

Four. Shared Vision: Create Your Own Future or Someone Else Will

Five. Wayfinding: Strategic Initiatives and Short-term Wins

Six. Difference-Making: Recognizing and Celebrating Individual and Collective Contributions

Seven. Empathy into Action: The New Leadership Role to Lead Change for the Common Good

"Leadership Without Ethics Has No Heart And Ethics Without Leadership Has No Legs."

Coach K Center for Ethics
Fuqua Business School
Duke University

CHAPTER FOUR

THE ETHICAL HEART: CHARACTER, COURAGE, AND COMPASSION

"The health of both the leader's and the organization's souls, depends upon staying true to their values."

— MARGARET BENEFIEL, *THE SOUL OF A LEADER*

Who would have thought before 2020 that someone would be writing about a non-negotiable leadership practice calling for leaders to find their moral and compassionate compass? Not only writing about leadership ethics, a moral compass, compassion for people, but declaring this to be the bedrock leadership practice?

Have the moral lessons we learned in kindergarten about "play fair and tell the truth" eroded this much? Has the "handshake" of our grandparents as a trusted commitment to do what we say been forgotten? Are the commonly shared values of every major religion on shaky ground? Are the actions of some powerful political leaders more autocratic than democratic? Is malignant normality a threat to democracy?

Is it really ok to win at the expense of others? Sadly, the answers are trending toward YES to all the above.

Although there have been rumblings for years, in 2020 a massive earthquake of circumstances has shaken us to the core. The magnitude of the earthquake on the humanity scale is the largest in our lifetime. The resulting impact on human ecosystems, how we treat our fellow human beings, and leadership is profound.

The virus pandemic, hybrid work, exposure of systemic human inequities, high profile leaders modeling toxic leadership, and the need for millions more to lead, have added an historic urgency for leaders to view humanity differently and lead differently. And now, the Putin-led war against Ukraine and democracy everywhere. We have been exposed to the worst of leadership, abuse of power, a growing gap between the "haves" and "have nots" in organizations and the country, an overwhelming amount of misinformation, alarming uncertainty about what is true and who to believe. More striking has been the number of powerful leaders across the country and media sources who have been silent or complicit with toxic leaders. Most of all, behaviors that we once thought as cruel, abusive, divisive, and destructive have become normal and judged ok by millions of people. Everyone who leads has three choices about leadership models: Toxic Malignant Normal, Traditional Bureaucratic Normal, and an Inspiring Better Normal.

There have been huge ethical lapses by companies and leaders in the past. We will discuss these lapses more fully later. But, after what we witnessed in 2020, the ethical lapses of the past have been relegated to background noise. Now, the moral compass of leaders is front and center. The Malignant Normality of toxic actions and behaviors generated by hundreds of the country's top leaders is not acceptable. Being dishonest with those you lead is not ok. People need leaders to inspire them to give their best and work collaboratively to accomplish great things.

People want to know that they can trust their leader, that leaders will be honest with them, and that leaders care about them, all of them. It's not only the right thing for leaders to commit to doing, but it is the only way to engage and inspire others.

This first non-negotiable practice is the first leadership practice for a reason. Leaders want to get this right. The other six leadership practices will be useless if this practice is not right.

Leading from an ethical heart with character, courage, and compassion is an inspiring leadership practice. This practice evokes confidence in others by providing the ethical guard rails for aligning actions with clear core values and guiding principles. It builds on the values we learned in kindergarten, churches, temples, mosques, and synagogues. It builds on what we learned from spiritual leaders and practices. It reinforces our basic humanity and humanness. It assures that the leader is committed to doing the right thing and doing it with compassion. It centers us. It offers the hope of equity and fairness. It helps build trust in the process of how we work together. The practice of the ethical heart provides the framework for decision making. Another useful way of thinking about this concept of character is thinking about a "moral compass."

On January 8, 2021, I came back to this chapter, two days after the President of the United States of America encouraged his supporters to march down Pennsylvania Avenue and storm the capitol. The last time anything like this happened was 1814, it was the British who did the "storming", and it was the War of 1812. This time, the President's own colleagues were in the House and Senate chambers to receive and confirm the electoral college votes. Speaker of the House Pelosi and Vice President Pence were particularly in danger because of their unique responsibilities on this day. Their lives were threatened, and they were within seconds of being harmed. Some in the mob wanted to kill them. Crimes against the police, others, and the nation's capital were committed. People died. The President watched it all unfold on television and, from all the available information, did nothing to stop the attack, never once initiating any action to help protect his endangered colleagues or the capitol.

THE FATAL EMBRACE OF MALIGNANT NORMAL LEADERS

It has been two days since this happened. As an author, I know how unusual this is. In the middle of drafting this book and chapter on ethics, moral compass, and compassion, a monster event happens that sadly provides another rational for this leadership practice. I had to take a "timeout" before writing, to balance my objectivity with my immediate emotional disbelief, outrage, and sadness. Prior to the unbelievable and unthinkable assault on the capitol and our country's congressmen, congresswomen and senators, seen across the world by millions of people whose faith in America as the shining light of democracy dimmed, I was already passionate about leadership for a Better Normal. I had already confirmed from a career of leadership that the moral and compassionate compass for leaders was a bedrock leadership practice. Non-negotiable. I had already written that if this bedrock practice is not right, nothing would be right. I had never witnessed any American leader betray and endanger people he should be leading and protecting. My sense of urgency has only intensified. Since this is a book on leadership, we are looking at this event and the actions of a powerful President, the leader of the free world, through the lens of leadership, rational thinking, and compassion for fellow human beings.

You may recall the movie "Black Hawk Down?" Peggy Noonan, a 2017 Pulitzer Prize Award recipient for Commentary, captures a scene from this movie that resonates for this moment. She writes, "The movie is about the Battle of the Bakaara Market in Mogadishu, Somalia, in October 1993. In the scene, the actor Tom Sizemore, playing your basic tough-guy U.S. Army Ranger colonel, is in charge of a small convoy of Humvees trying to make its way back to base under heavy gun and rocket fire. The colonel stops the convoy, takes in some wounded, tears a dead driver out of a driver's seat, and barks at a bleeding sergeant who's standing in shock nearby:

> **Colonel**: Get into that truck and drive.
> **Sergeant**: But I'm shot, Colonel.
> **Colonel**: Everybody's shot, get in and drive.

On 1.6.2021, we all got shot.

Democracy and decency got shot. Leadership got shot. Now, the only way we can recovery and heal is to be brutally honest about what we now know about the reality of 1.6.2021. A President's leadership directly impacts other leaders and the leadership narrative. How does this abuse of power affect the leadership boundaries for other political leaders? How do responsible business, religious, academic, and political leaders respond to misinformation and lead to protect the people they lead? How did this happen and how can we learn from this event to assure something similar doesn't happen again? There was nothing normal about this.

What we witnessed and what the world witnessed is an epitome example of what happens when Malignant Normality goes unchallenged. A malignancy spreads. Let me define Malignant Normality again. Malignant Normality occurs when behaviors we once thought of as unacceptable, unfair, cruel, dehumanizing, and destructive become acceptable, normalized, and glossed over. When the behaviors are justified or accepted by many people, the malignancy spreads more quickly. In retrospect, what happened was predictable based on the long-standing patterns of behaviors of this President. It is the result of a dangerous man who continues to show little or no compassion, empathy, or remorse. From numerous audio recordings, videos, and observations, he sadly appeared to be incapable of empathy, remorse, or understanding of the consequences of his words and actions. It appeared from multiple observable and documented evidence that the leader of the free world had no guard rails or a moral compass. Even worse, he was encouraged by the silence and compliance of many other political leaders, business leaders across the country, news agencies, social media, conspiracy theorists, as well as the millions of decent people who truly believed in him because they never heard the truth from any of their media sources. "He is the President. Why would he lie to me?" "If it's on the news, it must be true."

And sadly, mainly because of misinformation, millions of good people have been silent and compliant, giving permission for the trend toward malignant normality. As Malala Yousafzai, the Pakistani activist for female education and youngest ever Nobel Prize laureate, reminded, "We realize the importance of our voice when we are silenced." Instead of trying to justify and excuse the events and actions that led to January 6, 2021, leaders must find their voice, be honest about what happened in order to heal and build back better. It is stark because none of us can imagine a leader of any successful organization, company, democracy, or enterprise leading with those behaviors. I write about this in this book on leadership at this moment in history because it reveals so much about our human frailty, the seductive lure of power and control, winning at the expense of the more vulnerable, and the urgent need for a multitude of leaders to lead for a better normal.

THE PUZZLING DISCONNECT: SHARED CORE VALUES, BUT DEHUMANIZING BEHAVIORS

Personally, I am puzzled by this gut punch to our ethical principles and core values that we say we believe in. We are the "Liberty and justice for all," "One nation under God," "Law and order," and "All people are created equal" country. In addition, millions of us seek out a mosque, synagogue, church, or temple for moral and spiritual guidance. All major religions share the common values and beliefs of honesty and truth-telling, loving God and neighbors, doing no harm, striving to do good, taking care of the poor and vulnerable. Former President Jimmy Carter wrote with growing concern about America's moral crisis in his book, *Our Endangered Values,* saying "All major religious faiths are shaped by prophetic mandates to do justice, love mercy, protect and care for widows and orphans, and exemplify God's compassion for the poor and victimized." Familiar guiding values come from the Golden Rule, The Ten Commandments, The Native American Ten Commandments which leads with "Treat the earth and all that dwell thereon with respect," and Mahatma Gandhi's Seven Social Sins, to mention just a few.

> All major religions share the common values and beliefs of honesty and truth-telling, loving God and neighbors, doing no harm, striving to do good, taking care of the poor and vulnerable.

There are many spiritual leaders that we draw strength from. Gandi is one. He was an Indian lawyer, political ethicist, and espoused and lived non-violence as the method for advocating for social justice. He led the successful campaign for India's independence, inspiring movements for freedom and civil rights the world over. Gandhi summed up his guiding value principles as "social sins" and they are as relevant for this historic moment as they were 75 years ago. Gandhi's social sins are:

1. Politics without principles,
2. Wealth without work,
3. Pleasure without conscience,
4. Knowledge without character,
5. Commerce without morality,
6. Science without humanity, and
7. Worship without sacrifice.

As with Martin Luther King, Jr., Mother Teresa, and Nelson Mandela, non-violence was non-negotiable. Gandhi's non-violent actions against injustice were called Satyagraha in Hindu and are translated as pleas for truth, and truth is always on the side of justice. Martin Luther King, Jr. would say later that "Christ gave us the goals and Mahatma Gandhi the tactics" to respond to injustice, live ethically, and honor our one humanity.

There really are few people who would say they disagree in principle with shared religious or spiritual values and beliefs. Most people would agree with the concept of living ethically. But acting on what we say we believe has been difficult. We have had a great and painful awakening. We have seen the results of Malignant Normality and what happens when we rationalize our core values away. We have seen the normal systemic inequities along with its double standards. We don't need more information, more gut punches to tell us that this is not who we are.

As I am writing this chapter, I yearn for more of Parker Palmer's voice when he wrote *Healing the Heart of Democracy: The Courage to Create a Politics Worthy of the Human Spirit*. Palmer wrote in 2011, already despairing about our heart, the ethical heart of "we the people". In his opening pages he writes, "As our distrust of 'the other' beyond our borders hardened and we began making aliens of each other (a "we" that included me), I fell into a spiral of outrage and despair. How did we forget that our differences are among our most valuable assets? What happened to "we have nothing to fear but fear itself"? When will we learn that violence in the long run creates at least as many problems as it solves? Why do we not value life, every life, no matter whose or where? Or understand that the measure of national greatness is not only how successful the strong can be but how well we support the weak?"

Then, Palmer asks the big question, "And where have "We the People" gone—we who have the power to reclaim democracy for its highest purposes, unless we allow ourselves to be divided and conquered by the enemy within and among us?"

In short, it is up to us as the new leaders for this new world to guard and protect our colleagues and neighbors. The heart of democracy is directly related to the heart of leaders and organizational life.

One encouraging example of what business and religious leaders must do came recently from an unlikely source, the Chief Executive of the Women's Tennis Association, Steve Simon. And get this. Simon's decision could cost the WTA over one billion dollars in revenue. Here's the position he took after WTA Chinese tennis star, Peng Shuai, accused former vice premier Zhang Gaoli of forcing her into a sexual relationship. Peng's posts were immediately shuttered, and she disappeared for over two weeks. No satisfactory explanation came from Chinese officials or from Peng. So Simon stood up for her, immediately. He ordered tennis tournaments suspended in China until he saw proof that Peng "is free, safe and not subject to censorship, coercion and intimidation." Note the contrast of this action with the inaction of the three official organizations that failed to protect our women gymnasts. In a CNN interview, Simon spoke about his rationale.

"There are too many times in our world today when we get into issues like this and we let business, politics, money dictate what's right and what's wrong," Simon said. "We have to start, as a world, making decisions that are based on right and wrong, period."

The massive trove of articles known as the Uber Files that exposed the unethical behavior at the top of the Uber organization came from one man: Mark MacGann, Uber's former top lobbyist and the face of the company in Europe during Uber's international expansion. MacGann was an unusual but courageous whistleblower in that the files revealed his own complicit behavior, at times, with the very corporate behavior he now exposes and condemns. He explained in an interview with the Guardian why he decided to come forward. In addition to being harassed online and in person and worrying about the safety of his family, he said he was motivated by his responsibility for what had happened and wanted to make amends. "We had actually sold people a lie. How can you have a clear conscience if you don't stand up and own your contribution to how people are being treated today?" he reflected. MacGann blamed the corporate culture and urged others to learn from the Uber mistakes.

It's a people-over-profit decision. Business as usual is not ok. The consequences of malignant normality and toxic leadership has disastrous consequences. Enough-is-enough. This is about character. This is about courageous and compassionate leadership. This is about doing the right thing and aligning action with core right and wrong values.

Your goal, with this leadership practice is to be explicit about the guiding principles of your leadership. Guiding principles identify the priority values for your leadership at work and home. In the following chapters on urgency and collaboration, we will discuss more the importance of identifying and clarifying your personal top values. Your priority values are your values in any environment. What you most believe in doesn't change from one location to the other. The ideal scenario is that the guiding principles in your work environment, the collective values of the organization, allow you to honor your personal values. Personal values are what you own as sacred to you. Guiding principles form the collective guard rails for ethical behavior in an organization, family, or team.

> Guiding principles form the collective guard rails for ethical behavior in an organization, family, or team.

Almost every company struggles with business ethics related to pay equity, economic security for all employees, harassment, hiring practices, health insurance, day care services, maternity leave, and transparency in decision-making. Some organizations struggle with honesty in accounting, short-cuts that maximize quarterly profits and hurt employees, what to do about waste products and other issues that have negative environmental impact, or how to encourage people to vote and make it easy for them to do so. Obviously, there are a myriad of ethical issues that leaders need to address intentionally.

I want to share a few examples of how leaders and organizations have struggled to align their vision, mission, and strategies with their core values. In each case, we discover people challenging business as usual, the current normal. Later in the chapter, I want to invite you to consider how you will lead now that we have all been exposed to glaring systemic inequities and the alarming Malignant Normality. I want you to hear the voices of those who have coped with long-standing double standards that have made their lives more difficult. You will be surprised at how many there are. Again, these who struggle are us.

This is a challenging chapter to write, simply because facing the truth is hard. But we are suffering as a country today because so many leaders have not had the courage to speak the truth. So, please stay with me through this difficult chapter as I write about our neighbors and colleagues, those you lead, your family. They deserve to not only be understood but valued and appreciated. They deserve to know how to separate truth from fiction. When we show we care and understand, we will build a new kind of trust, learn so much more, and find better solutions together. This is the foundation chapter in our journey to inspiring leadership. Seek first to lead with the Ethical heart: Character, courage, and compassion. The Ethical Heart is home to your "moral compass." This is the foundation for trust building and psychological safety.

> When we show we care and understand, we will build a new kind of trust, learn so much more, and find better solutions together.

LEADING WITH A MORAL COMPASS

In a long visit with Father Theodore Hesburgh a few years ago on his campus, we spoke mostly about his experiences as a 35-year leader of Notre Dame University. He had led the university from a football school to a first-rate university, led in the civil rights movement, and significantly influenced higher education. Interestingly, he was so widely respected that he received 150 honorary doctorate degrees over his career! That is a Guinness Book of Records little known fact! Because of his bold leadership on many fronts, we searched for some of the secrets behind his overall leadership effectiveness. What did he do that helped him stand up for his moral principles time and time again? "Well, it is really important that you lead based on what is morally the right thing to do. Being tentative is not good. It's a bit like doing battle. The trumpet call cannot be unclear!" So, as leaders, in our struggle to do what is right with all we have learned in the past months, our trumpet call to do what is right must be clear.

I have been impressed with individuals and organizations that have done some deep dives into what they will do with their one wild and precious life and the lives of those around them. Real soul searching, if you will, into what they value most and the difference they want to make as a person and in leading others. I know we are dealing with some heavy stuff here, but I appreciated Jeff Keane's cartoon touch in Family Circus on January 7, 2021, right after the horrific day at the capitol.

VISUALIZE DOLLY TELLING JEFFY

"Conscience is when God sends a text to your head."

A lot of people and leaders have been struggling with their conscience and more so with their response to those texts!

The following "Aha" experience captures the wakeup call of one young man in 2020 that might be like the discovery process we all are going through related to the truth of the Malignant Normal and the unintended marginalizing and minimizing of others. The struggle of this young professional basketball player to do what is right is the struggle we all must have to be more intentional about doing what is right. It is late August 2020. The Milwaukee Bucks are scheduled for a National Basketball Association (NBA) playoff game. Jacob Blake, a Black man, had recently been killed in Kenosha, Wisconsin, just south of Milwaukee. Blake was shot multiple times in the back by police. We are in the locker room just prior to the scheduled starting time. Listen in as Milwaukee Bucks forward, Kyle Korver, talks about his team's emotional discussion moments before they are to leave the locker room for the game. Korver described how assistant coach Darvin Ham was in tears following the shooting, and then how teammates George Hill and Sterling Brown were the first to express not wanting to play, and the rest of the team following their lead. Korver said, "I just sat there with tears running down my face, and I was looking at my jersey that says, 'Black Lives Matter,' and I'm like, 'What are we doing?' Then, one teammate, George Hill, decided he wasn't going to play . . . . We all just sat there and were like, 'We're all with you."

Kover, speaking later at his alma mater, Creighton University, shares why he felt his role was necessary and important. "It's always interesting for me as a white man in these spaces. What to do? How do I help as a white man? What do I say as a white man in this space?" Kyle then expressed his poignant "Aha" experience, "You know what you do? You stand with the marginalized. And when you can, you amplify their voice, and you listen to their thoughts, and you listen to their ideas, and then you find your way to help out."

After January 6, 2021, I would add this about our response to leaders who have helped create a Malignant Normal environment. To paraphrase Kyle Kover:

"You know what you do? You stand against the leaders who create and enable a Malignant Normal or leaders who are content to get back to normal, you amplify the voices of those harmed, you speak the truth, you challenge the people around you to think about our common moral compass, and you find ways to help out."

This first inspiring leadership practice, The Ethical Heart, is an underused but highly inspiring practice that after 2020 rises to the top of the non-negotiable inspiring practices. The four powerful forces that converged in 2020 to create the greatest leadership challenge of our lifetime reveal a huge gap between "business as usual" and a "Better Normal." And now, a fifth unimaginable force has been added with a former President leading in a threat to his own colleagues and to the country. To be honest, leadership in response to Covid 19, to broken systemic issues, to malignant-normal leaders had already been weak, uninspiring, and often silent and complicit. As a result, The Ethical Heart has catapulted to the top of inspiring leadership practices.

> **Given the circumstances, leaders now must be much more intentional about values, business ethics, earning trust, and speaking up for their people.**

As Kyle Korver looked down at the "Black Lives Matter" basketball jersey he was wearing when he made his decision to align his actions with what he believed, leaders for a Better Normal must do the same. What would be the value message on your jersey that you want to lean into?

I may be confirming what you already know about me, but I do believe there is a spiritual dimension to inspiration and leadership. In fact, as mentioned earlier, when we explore the values of major religions, there are just so many spiritual values we all share. And there are so many spiritual leaders who have written powerful 21st century lessons based on the teaching of Buddha, Jesus, Muhammad, and Confucius. The reason I mention this now is that I want to reinforce how important it is for the new cadre of leaders for the Better Normal to align their leadership practices with the values common to all humankind. This is the time. These common beliefs we all share spiritually must directly impact how we live and work with each other.

These beliefs, I think, are the heart of our moral compass and how we intend to live, work, and lead. They form the hope for accepting the interdependence of our fragile world and the vulnerable of our one humanity.

Arthur Brooks, a Harvard Professor, PhD social scientist, bestselling author, speaks about his spirituality and his view as a Christian about the oneness of humanity and how we should treat others who have had less opportunity. He speaks directly to the practice of the Ethical Heart. Brooks talks about the unity of all life and all individuals. His Buddhist monk friends told him to think of the unity concept as a stand of aspen trees. The trees are not a bunch, they are one organism, the largest living organism. So you go to Aspen, Colorado, it's one tree. "It's that I exist, you exist . . . but we don't exist autonomously of each other in a real, moral way." Brooks goes on to quote from the Biblical scriptures found in Matthew 25, "As you did for the least of these my brothers and sisters, you did for me." He suggests that what Christ was "really talking about was the cosmic unity of all people to each other and all people to God . . . He's saying the poor? They're me. They're you. That cosmic unity is incredibly important for understanding that it's not just alleviation of poverty because poverty is uncomfortable, alleviation of poverty because we can, because we are rich. But because they are us. And all we are doing is that we're being one with each other."

Brooks' monk colleagues were talking about their concept of emptiness when they asked him to think about Aspen trees as an example of one humanity, cosmic unity. Brooks suggests we think of our one unity to each other and God by thinking of Jesus's admonition to think about our brothers and sisters as our brothers and sisters. Women, men, Black, Brown, White, Indigenous, LBGTQ. "They are me. They are you."

Putting these beliefs into practice is always the more difficult part. Therefore, we certainly will need other core values like courage and determination in order to trust and follow our moral compass and live ethically as new leaders. The new policies and practices for a Better Normal must be aligned with our moral compass, compassion, and the creation of a psychologically safe environment in which to work and live. The most important thing I learned as a child about a moral compass was in kindergarten. It was a simple little phrase and question, "What would Jesus do?" This little four-word question was like the Mary Oliver question in how it made me think as a child. At the time, I never asked the "What would Jesus do?" question out loud with playmates or friends. I couldn't quite rap my tiny arms around speaking to others about this moral imperative. But this was clearly a "sandbox" moral compass for me. Now, as an adult leader, I have to wrap my bigger arms around my values and ask you to do the same. So, I invite you in this chapter to think about the roots of your moral compass and the values you want to turn into guiding principles for your leadership. I am suggesting throughout this leading non-negotiable practice chapter that we must get this right. This is the foundation of our credibility and leadership.

> I am suggesting throughout this leading non-negotiable practice chapter that we must get this right. This is the foundation of our credibility and leadership.

"Leadership without ethics has no heart and ethics without leadership has no legs," – Coach K Center on Leadership & Ethics (COLE)

Thanks to the Fuqua Business School for making a distinctive mark on leadership education with academic centers that focus on Leadership and Ethics, Social Entrepreneurship, and Entrepreneurship and Innovation. Fortunately, they are joining a number of innovative programs that are beginning to place more emphasis on character, inclusiveness, equity, and diversity. Sanyin Siang, Executive Director of the Coach K Center, says that current leaders can't just think of what is good for the organization, "Today, they also have to bear the responsibility of societal stewardship. The society has ramifications for what is happening in our organization, and our organization has ramifications for what is happening in society. There is this interdependence." COLE's mission is to empower leaders of consequence to change the world through knowledge and connections. I particularly like their philosophy of "Leadership without ethics has no heart and ethics without leadership has no legs." They bet the farm on character, "entrepreneurial leaders of exceptional character, ethically grounded and possessed of a global mindset. These leaders will inspire their followers to meet and exceed an organizations' goals through actions that are, at one and the same time, highly productive and highly ethical, while continuously serving the best interests of all the organizations' stakeholders. We call these remarkable individuals 'Leaders of Consequence.' The distinguishing features of the program are character, leaders of consequence, and living a life of significance. There is not a mention of power, control, ego, how to pack a golden parachute, getting what you want, or normal leadership. It's about serving others and making a difference. It is not surprising that Mike Krzyzewski is co-founder of this innovative leadership program. After all, his basketball program has been the most sought-after program by the nation's top high school players for decades. Why? Most players would say they chose Duke to fine tune their potential pro-level basketball skills, learn at a great academic University, and most importantly, learn life lessons from a coach committed to helping players become better people. Coach K is the winningest basketball coach in college history for a reason. He just surpassed my favorite coach of all time, Tennessee's Pat Summit.

> The distinguishing features of the program are character, leaders of consequence, and living a life of significance.

Just before going to press, I learned of a new program established at my former University that will incorporate Coach Rick Byrd principles of integrity, character, and leadership into new academic curriculum across the campus. Byrd was heavily influenced by the iconic UCLA Coach character, John Wooden, who we featured in our Real Dream Teams book. Byrd just retired from Belmont after 33 years as head basketball coach and after being inducted into the National Basketball Hall of Fame and receiving the John R. Wooden Legends of Coaching Award. How invested was Byrd in helping make his athletes true student-athletes and learning the bigger lessons for success in life? Since 2001, Belmont men's basketball leads the nation in Academic All-American selections with 18. In addition, in the NCAA Division 1 era, every Belmont player who completed eligibility under Byrd's mentorship earned his degree, with only two scholarship student-athletes transferring out over his final 15 years. Coach Byrd helped create the Belmont culture of inspiration and was a rich part of what I have called the "good to great" years at Belmont. It never hurt that his good golfing pal Vince Gill sat directly behind the Belmont bench and cheered him on at most home games. By the way, Vince once ran the length of the court yelling at a referee for what he thought was a lousy call. The ref blew his whistle, stopped the game, walked over to Vince and told him to cool it. Then he said to Gill, "I'm probably the only one in this gym that bought your last CD."

This section would be incomplete without the mention of another woman I was privileged to work with at Belmont, legendary Betty Wiseman. Betty became known across America last year as Belmont Betty for her enthusiastic support of Belmont women's basketball during March Madness as many Americans heard for the first time about her amazing trailblazing career in women's basketball. Betty pioneered the way for integrated women's basketball in the south in 1968 at the height of the civil rights movement when she became the first women's basketball coach at Belmont. "All I saw were talented women players that just wanted an opportunity," said Coach

Wiseman. Incidentally, Pat Summit was an early camper in Betty's popular summer basketball camps. Always an advocate for women and equity in sports, Betty's example was a forerunner for Title IX 4 years later, opening the door of opportunity for women athletes to succeed in most all sports. The Jostens-Berenson Lifetime Achievement Award is just one of many recognitions that have honored Betty's lifetime of helping create something better than the norm of the day.

Coach K, Coach Summit, Coach Byrd, and Coach Wiseman were cut from the same cloth, and between the four, have had enormous impact on future coaches, the game of basketball, and the lives of their players. They always have led with heart, passion, compassion, and a moral compass. And they have been models of leadership that challenge us all to be our best selves.

The Ethical Heart is about intentionally leading with a moral compass, compassion, and honesty. All relationships are built on trust. Psychological safety comes from trust. It is hard and necessary work. As a leader, you are inviting people into a trusting relationship, and you want people you live with or work with to know what you stand for. You want people that you lead to know they can count on guiding value principles that will guide decision-making and policies. You want people you lead to know you care about them as human beings. You want them to be successful. This practice is the intentional starting point.

> The Ethical Heart is about intentionally leading with a moral compass, compassion, and honesty.

I am not sure where the "marble jar" concept of building trust originated, but I do know that Brené Brown provides a great example of the concept from a conversation with her daughter, shared in "Dare to Lead." Based on my leadership experience, the marble jar is a great visual for understanding trust. Trustworthy behaviors earn marbles. Untrustworthy behaviors take marbles out of the jar. We can probably count on one hand our marble jar friends. When I was a practicing psychologist, I saw a lot of people who were desperate to find someone to talk to that they could trust. Trust with a client, friend, co-worker, or family member is similar and is built over time, not in one grand moment or several dramatic encounters. Trust is many small responses over time, and each time you are trustworthy with someone, you get a marble in that person's marble jar. For my counseling clients, they had to learn to trust me if they were to share honestly the thoughts, feelings, and narratives related to the depression and anxiety that brought them to me in the first place. I had to earn their confidence and protect what they told me. So, there were not too many quick solutions. I needed to be a full marble-jar person in their life for them to feel understood, listened to, and unconditionally accepted. Only then would they become more aware, gain new insights, and have the strength and confidence to act in healthier and healing ways. The healing solutions were always within them. They had to discover the solutions in a psychologically safe space.

My wife, two daughters, and I talked within our family a lot about honesty, fairness, and kindness during the growing up years of our now adult daughters. We worked to live out our beliefs and values at home, school, work, and in the community. In terms of this leadership journey, I write about this process as aligning behaviors with core values and guiding principles. Our family tried to stay grounded and consistent. We were blessed by how we treated each other. Both daughters had marble-jar friends and quickly grew to know who they could trust and who was not trustworthy. We saw those values mature in the lives of our daughters and how they aligned their behavior based on those values. I must admit, to this day, both daughters give their mom and me grief about not spending a little more time helping them understand that not everyone played by the same rules we did!! "Mom and Dad, not everybody plays fair!" Even though not everybody plays fair or works with compassion or acts with kindness, I am proud that these patterns of behavior are still non-negotiable with our adult daughters. We can't control how others behave, but we can control how we respond. We always have choices!

LINKING ACTIONS TO CORE VALUES

As we move toward operationalizing the practice of The Ethical Heart, I want you to consider doing what Harvard Business School graduates have been doing since 2002. Harvard MBA graduates have been asked the Mary Oliver question just prior to graduation. It all started when Tony Deifell, Harvard M.B.A. '02, asked that simple question of his fellow graduates. "Tell me, what is it you plan to do with your one wild and precious life?" According to Katie Koch, a Harvard Staff writer, Deifell's "inquiry produced surprisingly deep insights into the hope, dreams, and motivations of his graduating class----and created a tradition, the HBS Portrait Project, that's still going strong."

> **The simple question evoked a more personal reflective response of how many lives they hope to influence and how they plan to honor their most personal core values.**

"It's not enough to make money; it's how you make money," Deifell said. He hoped to inspire a way to think of professional ethics as a way of matching one's behaviors and actions to one's most personal core values. "It's about putting a stake in the ground and living in a purposeful way."

What follows is how Tony Deitfell answered the question, "Tell me, what is it you plan to do with your one wild and precious life?"

"I used to teach photography to blind and visually impaired students. One student made photographs of the cracked sidewalks at the school and sent them to the superintendent as "proof" of the damage. She included a letter asking for them to be fixed. 'Since you are sighted,' she wrote, 'you may not notice these cracks. They are a big problem since my walking cane gets stuck.'

Deitfell continues, "I want to notice all the cracks in my world— the prejudice I still have about cultures I don't understand, the arrogance that I know anything with certainty, and the privilege I have by virtue of my skin color, gender, and Harvard education. Sometimes the cracks seem small and easy to overlook—saying people's names incorrectly, not giving thanks before a meal, forgetting my mom's birthday (she's said that was a big crack), and being too judgmental of others. Sometimes the cracks are obvious—if I pay attention. My calling in life is to use my skills as a media artist, entrepreneur, and leader to help everyone notice the cracks, because there are many."

Four years later, Deitfell reflected on the power of the Portrait Project and his original answer to the Mary Oliver question. "After writing my essay, the 'Cracked Sidewalk' became a pivotal metaphor that helped me define my calling in the world . . . it had a very concrete impact on how I live my life. The concrete impact translates into being CEO and Co-Founder of The Muse Factory/Awesome Box, a company that brings together friends and family to share photos and messages custom-printed into a box set of beautiful cards as a gift to tell someone how awesome they are. "What a wonderful way to make someone feel like the most awesome person in the world! It was so personal and one of the best gifts I've ever received. I cried on the first card. Now I have a lifetime gift," shared one of the Awesome Box recipients.

Tony is also Founder and Chief Evangelist of WDYDWYD (Why Do You Do What You Do), a spin-off of Mary Oliver's question for the Portrait Project. This becomes a great question for every leader of any team to ask all those on the team. It can be a meaningful part of the visioning process which we will discuss later. In short, Tony creates both a process and product that inspires others to imagine possible futures and then act to move in a new direction, much like this new model of leadership.

Tony Deitfell hoped to inspire a way to think of professional ethics as a way of matching one's behaviors and actions to one's most personal core values. The leadership practice of The Ethical Heart is designed to help leaders think differently and inspire a way to think of professional ethics as a way of matching collective behaviors and actions to collective core values. As he says, "It's about putting a stake in the ground and living in a purposeful way." Think about you and those you lead "putting a stake in the ground to **work** in a purposeful way." Every day! So, as you consider using the Mary Oliver question with your colleagues and those you lead, be intentional. Invest the time to do this. It will be an amazing process to introduce your new leadership practices and how you plan to lead. It will take time. It will also be a high-payoff investment. Keep visualizing the following as we move through our journey together.

Alignment

Collective Values–Guiding Principles
Moral Compass and Compassion

Strategies–Actions
Decisions–Policies

In Brené Brown's most recent heavily researched book, *Atlas of the Heart: Mapping Meaningful Connection and the Language of Human Experience*, Brown writes, "In my most recent research on courage and leadership, the ability to embrace vulnerability emerged as the prerequisite for all of the daring leadership behaviors. If we can't handle uncertainty, risk, and emotional exposure in a way that aligns with our values and furthers our organizational goals, we can't lead." Let those words soak in for a minute.

The WD-40 company that I mentioned earlier, yes, the same WD-40 company that is the solution to most squeaky wheels, put their values out front declaring, "We live, breathe and play by our values. Everyday." The Chairman, CEO, and tribal leader at the time of this writing is Garry Ridge. Tribal is the WD-40 term for "community" and he bluntly says that the core values are "the rock" the company stands on. Listen closely to their statement of values as it is an ideal illustration of a company that aligns everything with its values. "Our company values support our vision, shape our culture and guide us as we apply our own philosophies and judgments to our work life. We live, breathe and play by our values every day. Our values grant us freedom so we can each make autonomous decisions, yet still act as one. We recognize life is full of conflicts when it comes to living values. Sometimes you can't honor two values at the same time. That's why our values are force-ranked, and our first value is more important than all others: At WD 40 Company, we do the right thing." Hear the freedom that comes with clear values and guardrails. Values make it easier to make critical decisions. And as Brown noted above, "vulnerability has emerged as the prerequisite for all of the daring leadership behaviors" like aligning actions with values, daring to do the right thing.

The WD-40 Company also values being a learning organization and looks for "learning moments" to spark continuing improvement of individuals and teams. Their culture is self-sustaining because they intentionally create a culture "where people enjoy a sense of belonging and purpose." Recall Maslow's Hierarchy of Needs where belonging and purpose become the launching pad for self-actualization, creativity, and innovation?

VULNERABILITY AND TRUST: WHOSE ROPE ARE YOU WILLING TO HOOK INTO?

Lou Whitaker led the first all-American climbing team to the summit of Mt. Everest. Lou's brother Jim, also a climber, was on another climbing team that went to the summit of Everest. Jim stood at the summit. Lou did not, but he helped others on his team be successful in reaching the summit. Lou and Jim are both extraordinarily successful climbers with different stories. We liked Lou's story of helping get others to the top of the mountain and are convinced that leaders for a Better Normal will be ones who help get others to the summit of their potential. Thus, when we interviewed Lou a few years ago, we asked about his unique process of picking a climbing team. He was quite clear in his response. "I pick the first team member. The two of us then pick the third member, then the three of us pick the fourth member. We repeat this process, all picked making the next selection till our team is complete." "That is interesting," we replied, "but why do you pick your team that way?" Whitaker looked a little perplexed, like you should know this, but told us that all serious mountain climbers have experience with a lot of other climbers. They each have a list of the best climbers with which they have worked. So, it gets harder as you go along because there are more choices, but that brings strength to the final team. Here was the gem of wisdom and why Whittaker used this kind of selection process. "Well, when you're climbing mountains, you better well trust and believe in every person whose rope you hook into." Here's a clip from *Real Dreams Teams*. "When Lou Whittaker's mountain climbing teams encountered danger in the form of ice and snow, strong winds, or the steepness of the slope, their response was to tie themselves together with climbing ropes. In so doing, they committed themselves to support the safety of their teammates, even to the point of risking their own lives to save others. If a person lower down the mountain than you falls, the risk of them causing you to fall is not as great because they would not have time to gather momentum before the slack in the line is gone. However, if a teammate at a higher elevation falls, the risk to the supporter is much greater, more difficult to break their fall. Whittaker says that it is a sobering process to decide "whose rope am I willing to hook into?"

After 2020, everyone has to decide the kind of organization they are willing to hook into, the kind of leader they can trust and follow.

This is why culture is so important and why people are now choosing cultures to work within. Cultures tell people whether or not it is a psychologically safe place to work. For some time, all of us have known that millennials and Gen Zers have a passion for making a difference and want to work with organizations committed to making a difference in the broader community. It is now more obvious that it will be hard for anyone to lead effectively without the leadership practice that aligns everything with core values and commitment to doing what is right. Companies like WD-40 and other organizations that are already leading for a better normal will attract the best and brightest talent because of their values, how they work, live, and play as a community or tribe. Better Normal organizations distinguish themselves quickly.

In addition to using the Mary Oliver question as you implement the practice of the Ethical Heart: Character, Courage, and Compassion, I want to share another concrete example of "Guiding Principles" and how one of the most successful brands in the country used their guiding principles to leap from "great" to even "greater." I want to share the non-negotiable practices that led me to a Better Normal at the beginning of my leadership career. Finally, I want to take you inside the strategic planning process of a faith community as they grappled with clarifying their core values and how to live those values in a rapidly changing world. (As we know, many faith communities have had trouble aligning their practices with core beliefs and have often not stood with what they say they believe.) Upending expectations and new discovery is not a new concept, far from it. But the leadership crisis and opportunity after 2020 and early 2021, makes "Better Normal" leadership and "practices that inspire" mandatory and non-negotiable for leaders going forward.

ST. JUDE CHILDREN'S RESEARCH HOSPITAL

If you aren't already a fan of St. Jude Children's Research Hospital in Memphis or one of the millions of people who donate to St. Jude each year, prepare yourself to become a fan and donor. St. Jude may be the most recognizable brand in America, a brand built on prayers for a miracle and cures for childhood cancers.

Founded by Danny Thomas in 1962, St. Jude is a story of miracles. It all began when Thomas (then Amos Jacobs) prayed to St. Jude Thaddeus, apostle of Christ and patron of hopeless causes. His prayer came as he was making a major career decision. He prayed, "Show me my way in life and I will build you a shrine." Amos Jacobs did indeed find his way, changed his name to Danny Thomas and kept his promise to Saint Jude. Danny Thomas declared on the day that St. Jude Children's Research Hospital opened its doors on February 4, 1962, that "no child should die in the dawn of life." That would have been Danny Thomas' core value statement based on his miracle "Aha" experience. At the time, only 20% of childhood cancers in this country were cured and for acute lymphoblastic leukemia (ALL)—the most common form of childhood cancer—only 4% of children would live. St. Jude researchers and world-class doctors set out with a focus of improving cancer cure rates in America. And improve the cure rates they did. Get this. From 1962 to 2018 the cure rate for childhood cancers in this country went from roughly 20% to over 80%! For ALL, an even bigger cure rate of 96%.

During this same time, St. Jude lived out another value of Danny Thomas. He believed that parents "should not have to worry about anything but their sick child" when they came to St. Jude. That belief translated into a commitment to parents that there would be no direct treatment cost associated with their St. Jude experience. Each year the fundraising arm of St. Jude Research Hospital, ALSAC, raises enough money from over 10 million donors and multiple grants to cover the annual operating costs of roughly 1.4 billion and to cover the promise made by Danny Thomas years ago. ALSAC (American Lebanese Syrian Associated Charities) is led by inspiring President and CEO, Richard C. Shadyac, Jr. So, raising over 1.4 billion dollars is not a misprint. Just one of the many fundraising events each year, the annual St. Jude Memphis Marathon, attracts thousands of runners from across the country.

To demonstrate the power of core beliefs and guiding principles owned collaboratively throughout an organization, the above St. Jude story gets bigger and bolder. The founder's belief that "no child should die in the dawn of life" has been so ingrained in the culture of inspiration at St. Jude that in 2018 the vision of "no child" would leap beyond America to the world. No child meant no child, period. "Winning" for St. Jude was redefined to mean no child in the world should die in the dawn of life. Although St. Jude had a 25-year history of humanitarian efforts with partners around the world, this normal was not good enough. CEO Downing and other senior leaders wrestled with their core values and the alarming early deaths of so many children with cancer around the world, particularly in third world countries. They concluded they had to significantly broaden the scope and scale of their reach. A Better Normal for their research knowledge and protocols could reach children around the globe. As a result, St. Jude Global was launched in May of 2018. This expanded vision and new initiative will ensure that every child with cancer and other catastrophic diseases around the world will have access to quality care and treatment. (More later on the early results of the Global Initiative.) For this to come to fruition, another core value shines brightly, the willingness to "share intellectual property" in the form of "curing medical protocols." How rare and how encouraging to our fragile world and to people beyond where we work and live. St. Jude provides a shining example of the positive impact of sharing brain power, intellectual capital, and resources to help others and inspire those helping make it happen. They are reinventing leadership in the world of medicine and medical research.

St. Jude Children's Research Hospital in Memphis is a model for living into values through seven guiding principles. Each year, Summer Freeman, leader of Executive Communication, told me, "We set up an internet site and ask employees to nominate coworkers who reflect one of the values. From hundreds of submissions, we narrow down the candidates to about 40 shining examples." St. Jude not only has identified their seven Guiding Principles, more importantly they operationalized them by showing all the employees what each Guiding Principle "looks like" in real life! Summer continued, "The honorees and their stories of living out one of the principles are celebrated each year and featured in a booklet that is distributed to all faculty and staff." The value statements serve as guiding principles for St. Jude employees in daily decision making, regardless of the person's role. Employees don't have to guess what a guiding principle means. They learn what it means from stories, stories from fellow employees who see another employee living the guiding value principle in real time. The opening page of the book with 40 stories reads like this.

"AT ST. JUDE, WE ARE DRIVEN BY A SET OF CORE VALUES. These principles help guide us in our behaviors and decisions, ultimately empowering every employee to deliver on our mission." More than 5,000 people work at St. Jude—individuals of many ages, races, backgrounds and talents. Some are passionate about discovery. Others are focused on healing. Still others excel in administrative or support roles. What unites and motivates them every day?

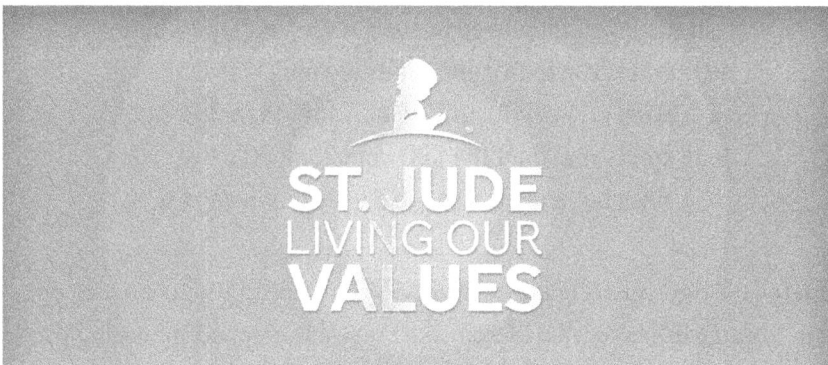

"It is our mission: Finding cures. Saving children.

To fulfill our lofty goals, we adhere to seven core values that are simple, yet profound:

1. Always recognize that advancing treatment for children with catastrophic diseases is at the center of everything we do.
2. Do what is right; take ownership of what you do.
3. Work with purpose and urgency—your efforts matter.
4. Embrace the challenge to create a new tomorrow.
5. Work collaboratively and help others to succeed.
6. Always be respectful of your coworkers, our patients and their families, and visitors to our campus.
7. Make the most of St. Jude resources and be mindful of those who provided them."

The really big leadership news from St. Jude is how they leverage their powerful vision, mission, and values/guiding principles, helping every person in this over 5,000-person team see how their role connects to "no child should die in the dawn of life," "finding cures and saving lives," and creating an environment of inspiration for children and their families. Dr. Downing, St. Jude CEO, leads and models the way.

> In the 2020 Employee Survey, in the midst of Covid 19, great uncertainty and fear, Downing was lauded as a trusted and comforting voice. More than 95% of St. Jude employees said the CEO communicates the vision, mission, and strategy in a way that inspires.

Here is a rigorous researcher and MD by training who now is rigorous about leading with different skill sets. He stepped up and chose to be intentional about his leadership during difficult times with a particular focus on communicating regularly via institution-wide emails, videos, and a blog. In addition, he reinforced the sense of "we are all in this together" through community-building activities. The Ethical Heart, the collective moral compass and compassion of the organization, permeates St. Jude and is led by the CEO. This is leadership for a Better Normal, and leaders at every level of any organization can do this (those of you who still have titles as bosses, managers, and supervisors as well as those of you have not thought of yourself as a leader).

The Ethical Heart of Change leads the way as an intentional and non-negotiable leadership practice. Being deliberate and transparent about how you as leader intend to lead in relationships and policymaking drives the creation of the Culture of Inspiration. You, as a leader, are saying up front with every colleague with whom you work or family member with whom you live, "Our moral compass and values will guide our life together and decisions we make. We plan to always strive to do the right thing and live and work based on what we value."

If your leadership is focused on your family, you will want to find the time to have a family discussion about values important to the family. Honesty, curiosity, love, and fairness are worth talking about. I will share a list of core values you may use later in the chapter. Work and life outside work in the new world will blend as new leaders will need to live their values and follow their moral compass with colleagues, family, and friends.

In a world where we have become more divisive, mean-spirited, cruel, and where winning at the expense of others could become a deadly malignant normality, leaders must be clear about norms and expectations, what is acceptable and what is not.

You will recall some worse case scenarios when there was no internal control system or moral compass at the top of the organization. Do these names and scandals sound familiar: Enron 2001, Freddie Mac 2003, Lehman Brothers 2008, and Bernie Madoff, 2008? These were ethical train wrecks and led to sweeping congressional action in the form of the Sarbanes-Oxley Act and new regulatory requirements. Even Sarbanes-Oxley did not prevent the multiple ethics breaches of Wells-Fargo revealed first in 2018. On January 6, 2021, we witnessed another ethical train wreck. Faith Communities have had their own worse case scenarios related to ethics and leadership, most recently the summer 2022 bombshell report from the Southern Baptist Convention detailing decades of sexual abuse and inaction. The unethical behaviors that enabled the above debacles have never made companies, families, or communities stronger or better.

We will show that there is a way of living, working, leading that significantly improves outcomes, job satisfaction, inspires the best of everybody, and contributes to the common good. The leader can model the way and lead with the bone-deep values and a moral compass that support high individual and collective performance and superior outcomes. The practice of the Ethical Heart is the practice of leading ethically with heart, courage, and compassion. And yes, it connects beautifully with accountability and responsibility.

Leaders simply don't have to leave core values, heart, compassion, and respect behind when they have hard conversations about job expectations, fairness in decision-making and being accountable.

There are respectful, compassionate, and ethical ways to deal with tough conversations, including the conversation with a toxic leader colleague who must change behavior or leave.

Paul Ingram, Kravis Professor of Business at Columbia Business School, has focused for over ten years on the importance of values in an organization and the specific values that individuals hold. Working on the premise that values are the internal control system, Ingram suggests that when faced with a crisis we rarely have time to explore options with any depth. Leaders need to be able to rely on their core values. Knowing one's values explicitly from having gone through a values identification process allows leaders to make clear, more informed, and satisfying decisions. Most importantly, intentionally identified values guide us to discerning ethical and moral implications in our decision making. Our values evoke our best selves and become our moral compass.

You recall W. L. Gore & Associates mentioned earlier, the company often recognized as the most innovative company on the globe. As we mentioned, the founders were very influenced by humanistic psychology and creating a work environment that would inspire personal growth and self-actualization. Gore credits its long-term success to its unique working environment fueled by the guiding principles of Freedom, Fairness, Commitment, and Waterline. "With these principles as our foundation, we unleash the innate potential that our founders saw in all individuals. When we do this well, we open new possibilities for ourselves, our fellow Associates, our Enterprise and our customers----and pave the way for innovations that will break new ground and contribute to the greater good of society."

> The founders were very influenced by humanistic psychology and creating a work environment that would inspire personal growth and self-actualization.

The Gore Company provides one of the best models of a "Better Normal" and the creation of a "culture of inspiration." Alicia, from the Medical Products Division, sums it up well, "It's not just another job. It's not just another career path. It really is a vehicle for personal growth." Do you hear the connection between great work and personal growth? Alicia is saying I don't have to leave my personal world at the door when I come to work. As I grow because of my intentionally designed work environment, there is a positive impact on personal life and family life. What other company do you know that has no core business but to create the future? They have been praised for product and organizational innovation. Founded in 1958, they have been envied for years for "what" they do, but the big opportunity, which few have capitalized on, is "how" they do it. It's the biggest clue that inspired me and is a magnet for all the other clues that led to this book. The "how" is of course the organizational structure that allows the values-driven process to work: freedom to talk at any time with anyone in the organization; enormous amount of time working every day on what you love to do and do best; no bureaucracy and no boss to interfere with work; promise of fairness and inclusiveness; and a beautiful process of making and keeping commitments to each other.

As we journey along with the number one practice of leadership, the Ethical Heart, I have long been concerned with the moral and compassionate compass of faith communities, the last place we should be looking for those not living into their core values. They should be models of ethical influence, but many have not been. We already know that Sunday morning is the most segregated few moments in the country and that faith communities have often talked the talk but not walked the talk of their values. Now, just like the rest of the world, these millions of people are searching or should be searching for a "Better Normal." These are good people who want to make a difference but have not, at least not to the degree of leading to the healing of our broken systems, reducing systemic inequalities and inequities, as well as stewarding and nurturing the environment. We already know we need more leaders everywhere. We need communities of faith to lead in helping all those leaders in their communities to lead from their core values and an ethical heart. They are perfectly positioned for this challenge.

Since so many people relate to spiritual development or a faith community as the source of their core values, I want to share a personal experience with a community of faith that has a long tradition as a caring urban church in Nashville. When Rubye Lynn and I joined that church in 2003, despite their long humanitarian and reconciling history, they had already started an intentional process of discernment to become even better people and seek a "Better Normal." West End United Methodist Church grew as Nashville grew, purposefully choosing not to join the earlier urban and white flight trend to the suburbs. As a result of white flight and as late as 1991, Nashville was a ghost town. Fortunately, strong political and community leadership recommitted to the city. Now we see a city transformed and nationally recognized as a place to live, work, and play. West End's recommitment to stay and be a part of something better is a portion of the Nashville story.

It Is somewhat unusual for communities of faith to take a deep dive into strategic planning, but that's what had happened in 2002 led by Senior Pastor, Tom Laney, and later fully implemented under the leadership of Michael Williams and Carol Cavin-Dillion. The thinking process, in summary, centered around the idea that if we are committed to being a vibrant and robust church in this space with so many neighbors in need around us and so many ministry opportunities, we need to do better. We need to discern and create a more relevant vision, mission, and set of beliefs that will inspire us to make a difference in our urban setting. We need to also confirm our core values and then act on them. We need to make a bigger difference.

Get this. Over 750 people participated in the discernment process of listening to each other and their community neighbors around them. A new and powerful vision emerged, one that reminded me of my little moral compass from kindergarten, "What would Jesus do?" The new vision for West End United Methodist was "We believe that West End is called by God to be and become The LOVING LIGHT OF CHRIST: Connecting, Transforming." The mission therefore became, "Called to Live the Light, the loving light of Christ so that lives and communities are transformed by God's grace." So, for me and others that easily translated into "What does Live the Light look like in my relationships with others, how I treat others, how I make decisions, and how I live the light?" To answer this question, we needed to be more specific and identify the core values or bedrock beliefs that told people what "Live the Loving Light" looked like, similar to what St. Jude did with their Guiding Value Principles.

ALIGNING DAILY ACTIONS AND DECISIONS WITH CORE VALUES.

This is where the rubber meets the road. Personal and organizational future visions are one of the true norths, telling us where we are going. We will talk about vision in an upcoming chapter. Vision is a powerful directional force, but even more powerful is the internal directional force, the moral compass. How did St. Jude make the leap to a global vision? They kept examining their moral compass, their guiding principles and what "no child" dying in the prime of life meant. How did West End Church mentioned above get to the new service initiatives like the anti-racist covenant? They kept examining their bedrock beliefs and challenging what they would do if they lived more fully into those beliefs, like the belief that God loves everyone unconditionally.

Values, by definition, are what matters most to us. And we know that most people have never clearly identified the two or three values that are most important to them. Most organizations are not adamant about their core values. Usually when you hear from a business leader, "it was just a business decision," or from a political leader, "it's just politics," you are hearing the BS rationalization for a questionable decision that was not good for the people affected. To be clear, values are values whether personal or organizational. We have one set of values. So I challenge you to name them, clarify your values. Core values are non-negotiable. Our values give us courage in tough times, with hard conversations, and difficult decisions. Values give us the courage to not be silent or complicit with toxic behaviors and toxic people. The emerging small army of Better Normal leaders have already made time to clarify their values and the values of those around them. See Exhibit D, the List of Values. If you haven't done this, listened to yourself and to your colleagues, this

> Core values are non-negotiable. Our values give us courage in tough times, with hard conversations, and difficult decisions.

exercise will be a gift. You will have a gift, a moral compass, that will guide you in aligning your actions, policies, decisions, and strategic actions with your moral compass.

Here's a part of a note I wrote to my two adult daughters after I participated in the process that led to the bedrock beliefs of my faith community at the time. I explaining to them, in part, the impact on me of discerning and confirming core beliefs with others.

"Dear Elizabeth and Stephanie,

This little note is a result of a "family and spiritual moment" of the morning, a morning when your mom left for Memphis to be with Mama D and help out for a couple of days and I went to early church at West End.

The service featured two things, an infant baptism and a sermon on one of the bedrock beliefs we created/affirmed as a congregation over the past several months at West End. I really have "owned" the beliefs we confirmed through a series of small group discussions:

1) God loves everyone unconditionally. (Being more intentional about the "everyone," meaning "reconciling" and loving all of God's children.)
2) God calls us to be in a community of faith.
3) God calls us to love and serve others.
4) God is with us; we are not alone.
5) We believe in the forgiveness of sins.
6) Jesus, the human face of God, is our teacher.
7) Prayer connects us to God's transforming presence and power.

At any rate, these are certainly very close to what I can affirm as basic beliefs for me after going through an activity with others, all of us trying to discern what our life experiences had led us to believe. Stephanie, you asked me a few years ago about what

I really believed after all this time devoted to "church activities and church going." I don't think I gave a very thoughtful response at the time. So, part of this, I guess is the answer to your question."

I share a portion of the letter I wrote to my daughters years ago as a way of sharing my journey with participation in an intentional strategic planning process of one community of faith and its impact on me. I had led many similar processes with businesses and organizations, but never participated as a member of a faith community that wanted to be more intentional about making a difference and living out the beliefs and values they professed. Most important, the intentional deep dive into vision, mission, and bedrock beliefs for this one community has led to multiple new ministries, now well over forty-five relevant new ways to serve others in underserved neighborhoods around the church. The new ministries relate directly to the vision of becoming the loving light of Christ, connecting in meaningful ways with others and transforming lives.

At this writing, in early 2021, they have already actively responded to one of the broken systems revealed fully in 2020 with an Anti-Racism Covenant that details specific commitments and actions that are anti-racist. They recognized that people of faith have for years said, "we are not racist." Now they are being intentional about taking actions that are anti-racist. What a shift from saying, "I didn't create all these problems and broken systems. Why should I have to help fix them? Seeing the face of Jesus or God in all people? This is hard stuff and means there are so many tough conversations that I must embrace." People at West End are saying "yes" to all the above. (The Anti-racism Covenant that West End members developed is included as an appendix.)

I want to mention another intentional faith-based initiative in which West End United Methodist and Belmont University in Nashville are currently engaged. I spent significant time at both institutions when living in Nashville, so I have a small stake in what both are continuing to do to provide moral and ethical leadership, creating what I am calling leadership for a Better Normal and better community. Working with The Center for Healthy Churches, Belmont sought to identify churches that were working to be relevant, creative, and responsive to the communities around them. In other words, are there churches that not only gather, like most church congregations do on Sunday, but scatter throughout the week to make a difference in the lives of people around them. Are there churches that practice what they preach? If so, what are they doing? So many churches are not thriving because they only "gather." The Center for Healthy Churches is a mission-driven consulting group that focuses on helping congregations and clergy find new life and energy in the 21st century through a clearer and more compelling vision for the future. Instead of avoiding hard conversations and complex issues, clergy and congregations are taught to seek out solutions, explore opportunities for growth, and learn how to make a real difference in the lives of the congregation and the community. Belmont wanted to lead in strengthening local congregations in their efforts to thrive within their discrete contextual settings. In the summer of 2019, they did a focused study of 12 thriving congregations in Dallas, Philadelphia, Charlotte, Nashville, and Richmond. At the same time, Belmont began enlisting local congregations in the urban core of Nashville to partner with them to explore what it meant to be a thriving congregation. Belmont sought a grant through their Curb Center for Faith Leadership and the Lilly Foundation awarded a grant of $1 million to support the Thriving Congregations Initiative for 5 years. There are now 18 churches engaged in a collaborative partnership to support each other in learning how to thrive in the new world where doing good, serving others, and making a difference must be more intentional. Many good people, many well intended people, will need to lead.

I also would say to other faith communities who want to be more intentional about living into the values they profess, to deeply consider where your moral and compassionate compass leads you in making more of a difference in the community around you. Faith communities are many. Be bold and courageous in living out what you believe. So many people are hungry for you to lead, do what is right, and practice what you preach. I pass a church sign almost every day that reads, "Lord, make us instruments of your peace." I am thinking the Higher Power might encourage us to modify this often-used prayer to a prayer of affirmation, "Lord, we commit to being instruments of your peace." Like, step up and be what you pray for. Live the peace you pray for. I encourage you to visit the West End United Methodist Church in Nashville web site and be inspired.

LEADERS ARE THE ENGINEERS OF THEIR OWN TRAINS, AND THE LEADER'S MORAL COMPASS ASSURES STAYING ON THE TRACKS.

The astronaut perspective of a fragile world and the reality of 2020 is revolutionary. As we discovered during the pandemic, we are all in this together. In America, we are witnessing with shock the exposure of glaring healthcare disparities between the poor and the rich, between people of color and others, between those with health insurance and those without. We are seeing first-hand the impact of mass incarceration and the disparity in the justice system between the rich and powerful vs. the poor and vulnerable. We are seeing intentional policies that protect guns over children and youth. We are seeing the many broken systems that for years have favored those white and wealthy. I am white, but not wealthy. Multiple discoveries in my adult life and career have led me to acknowledge that I am unfairly privileged by my gender, race, and opportunities. It's in the water. It's in the system. I am part of the system. I am not proud of that, but I acknowledge it. Only then can I learn from it. Now I can be part of the solution.

When I reflect on my high school years, I spent hours most every day with a basketball, football, or baseball in my hands. I was the point guard, quarterback, and shortstop on those teams and got a fair share of recognition for being a decent athlete. However, my little school system was still segregated at the time. I was a fairly clueless, naïve, innocent, and happy young guy. I never thought till after I graduated from high school that perhaps the best quarterback, point guard, and shortstop in the county were being bused 90 miles roundtrip each day from Smithville to the Black high school in Lebanon. And this story is just the tip of the iceberg of what I have learned about a system that made opportunities easier for me and more difficult for others.

We are all now learning how the broken systems perpetuate the staggering vulnerability of millions of Americans. The current reality of where we are vs. where we are fully capable of being in the future creates a gap that is stunning. These are solvable human issues with pandemic impact, and it is up to inspiring leaders to create solutions.

The great organizations of the future will be intentional about their moral compass and willingness to seek solutions for man-made and systemic pandemics like racism, erosion of the environment, gender inequities, and affordable healthcare. As a leader in almost any organization, 70% or more of your colleagues could be marginalized by systemic issues, will have lived their entire life in systems with a double standard, and thus all of us are negatively impacted. As a leader, if you want to reach your potential and want your colleagues to reach their potential, you must say, "I know this to be true, that systems are broken and unfair. I may not understand exactly how each of you have coped with this fact, but I know the system has made it more difficult for you. I am committed to working with you to make our systems fair and equitable." Leaders for a Better Normal can't immediately fix the broken systems, but they must acknowledge first that they understand and are committed to working with all their colleagues to make the systems better. There is a new just and inspiring cause for any leader in any organization. This is your promise as leader. If some of your people are marginalized, all

> This is your promise as leader. If some of your people are marginalized, all your people are.

your people are. Think of the message that organizations send when they are clear about their core values, guiding principles, and offer a working culture that inspires and a space where all people belong and have purpose.

As we have discussed leadership gifts from the past that led to some of my epiphanies, leaders have the opportunity every day to connect people to each other and create transformative, caring workplaces. As we will discover in a later chapter, the number of people who have not had one positive interaction with their manager or boss in a full year is staggering. The isolation that so many workers feel is depressing. People are wired for and thrive on connection. We can do this. You can help people connect and you can connect with others every day by simply being concerned. Connecting and caring is another "hard skill." If you aren't doing this now as a leader, start surprising your colleagues!

Mountain climber Lou Whittaker, who I referenced before, told us something very significant from his leadership experience of leading the first-ever all-American team to the top of Mt. Everest. We asked him, very intentionally, had his feet actually been on the summit. Honestly, he looked at us like, "Don't you guys get it?" Here is his wisdom that is a blinding flash of the obvious. "If any of the team gets to the top, all of us get to the top." It's like if you are a team and the team wins, hell, we all win. Get it." And we were the ones writing about what separates Real Dream Teams from all the other teams. And that is the beauty about learning from others. If we are curious and open to learning as leaders, we will be open to follow what we discover. In the case of the marginalized people you lead, if they lose, you lose. If they get to the top, you get to the top and you all win. Win-win.

This is why leading with an ethical heart of character, courage, and the common good is the number one leader commitment. It is practice of doing what is right. Better than Normal leaders have empathy and compassion for others. If there are no guard rails and guiding principles/values to guide leadership behavior, the train and the engineer are surely lost.

FINDING HOPE AND COURAGE WHEN OUR WORST SELVES HAVE BEEN EXPOSED

We are the wealthiest, most powerful country in the world. Yet, we are ugly Americans in many ways. Our state of the union demands more from all of us, particularly those who lead, educate, and parent. When I finally realized my career path was leading me toward the study of human behavior and psychology, I hoped I might make a difference in the world and that human behavior would change for the better during my lifetime. I hoped we would be able to share the world's resources, to live from the abundance theory rather than the scarcity theory, to think and act more globally and from the perspective of one humanity, and that we would lead more from our democratic principles of equality, justice, and our better angels. We are not where I hoped we would be, but I am still hopeful.

I am hopeful because leaders, educators, teachers, ministers, rabbis, priests, and parents can be more intentional about the precious lives that look to them for inspiration to lean into their best selves and make a difference with their lives. There are multiple beautiful examples of people and companies at their best during the pandemic.

The healthcare professions have led the way with their response to Covid-19. People in the healthcare professions have responded so compassionately, professionally, and tirelessly because their professions are professions with a moral compass. When you chose the medical and nursing professions, you chose the moral and compassionate compass that goes with it. The oath for a physician is some form of the Hippocratic Oath and for a nurse, some form of the Nightingale Oath. The decisions and practices of the medical profession flow directly from the oaths and values of the various healthcare professions, providing if you will, guiding principles for daily work. As a result, they have never given up, even when countless people have refused to protect themselves and others by wearing masks, social distancing, and vaccinations. They have been committed to serve those in need and living their oath commitment to do so.

Thousands of people have become more aware of and responsive to "food insecurity" issues that are systemic and exacerbated during the pandemic. Contributions to food banks have risen and, in most cases, met the challenge of an increased demand. Hundreds of companies have become more aware and responsive to systemic racism by creating strategic actions designed to change policies that are racist to anti-racist. Millions of Americans are finding their voice for equality and justice for all of humanity. The challenge, of course, will be sustaining these early commitments.

As Tony Deitfell found through the HBS Portrait Project, becoming aware of "the cracks in the sidewalk" was life-changing for him. We are hopefully witnessing a transformation of how we respond to "the cracks in the systems" as we see them so vividly exposed. The exposed needs of people pained and hurt by a pandemic have evoked inspiring responses. Now we have seen the long-standing patterns of inequity that touch the heart of change, our common spiritual values, and I am hopeful that leaders will lead with strong "enough is enough" responses and level the "field of dreams and hope" for all.

These are all examples of "America, the beautiful," connecting core spiritual values with meaningful actions and the implications for leadership and the Better Normal are clear. New leaders must be clear about their personal "oath" to serve their colleagues and lead from the core organizational values, family values, and/or personal values. I mentioned earlier that leaders are "hope-givers" and search for ways to bring hope to their colleagues. I, along with countless others, found hope and inspiration for a Better Normal through the poem written and read at the Presidential inauguration on January 20, 2021. The young poet laureate was 22-year-old Amanda Gorman who said, "What I really aspire to do in the poem is to be able to use my words to envision a way in which our country can still come together and can still heal."

Part of our new discoveries about leadership is how important clear guiding principles and values are and how important it is for us "to be brave enough to be the light." I often use moral compass, core values, and guiding principles as interchangeable concepts, all intentionally designed to guide decision-making. Guiding Principles are like the rudder on a ship. They are foundational reference points that leaders can openly discuss with others when making decisions. All good organizations today have clear guidance about discrimination of any kind. This means, after 2020, that all leaders must be more courageous and intentional about eliminating policies and practices that perpetuate systems that favor some over others. "Making progress" is simply not good enough for the new Better Normal. We must lead differently. And this is why this non-negotiable leadership practice is the lead practice. We need rudders. We need more light.

I would never have dreamed before 2020 that three or four historic forces would merge in one year to pull back the curtain revealing the brutal reality of a common enemy in Covid-19, a significant and undeniable number of marginalized people, and the negative impact of traditional bureaucratic leaders. I would never have dreamed of the devastating impact of leaders who have created and enabled a new trend of Malignant Normality, attempting to normalize dehumanizing behaviors that threaten our very democracy. Finally, I would never have dreamed that leading with an ethical heart would be the headline for a book on leadership, but it is.

THE MORAL IMPERATIVE TO DO THE BEST YOU CAN FOR THOSE YOU'RE LEADING

Leaders have a wealth of untapped resources available for responding to these unprecedented times and to the greatest leadership opportunity in our history. The first leadership practice of the Ethical Heart draws on the untapped potential of more intentionally and thought-fully aligning organizational behaviors with core collective values of the organization. The value resources we need are right in front of us. They start with the shared values that cross all spiritual and religious time zones, forged through the centuries as the ethical heart of one humanity, just waiting for us to live into them more fully and inspire the best of our God-given "wild and precious lives."

BEING INTENTIONAL WITH THE LEADERSHIP PRACTICE OF THE ETHICAL HEART

1. We have discussed the critical need for leaders to be intentional about their leadership. Since every leader needs a starting point for inviting colleagues to become a part of a special work environment, I suggest you and those you lead respond to and discuss the Mary Oliver question, *"Tell me, what is it you plan to do with your one wild and precious life?"* It helps to share how the Harvard University folks use this in their MBA program. Harvard always adds a bit of credibility, right? Ask your colleagues to think about and write their response to the question and then devote time to the active listening of each person's response in a team meeting. If you have a large team, you will want to break the group into smaller groups of 7-10. It has been my experience that afterwards, individuals are eager to hear the response of other colleagues not in their small group. It is important for every leader in the organization to share her or his response and devote time to listening to those colleagues in the leader's sphere of influence. The Harvard Portrait Project, with the Mary Oliver question as the focus, is a competitive recruiting advantage for the Harvard MBA program. Using this with your team will be a powerful statement for those with whom you work. It creates the opportunity for an intentional invitation to work with a leader who values the "one wild and precious life" of each of the leader's colleagues. You can

further underscore your intent to create a psychologically safe environment where decisions are guided by the most important guiding value principles of the organization. Guiding principles are just what they say, a guide to how we think and act.

2. What Guiding Principles, like those of St. Jude, might you create (or already exist) that reflect what you/organization value most and want to guide decision-making across your team, organization, or family? See Exhibit D for a List of Values. Most individuals and most organizations have never named or clarified core values. Your individual and organizational moral compass is your internal guidance system. This is urgent work. Do it now!! Use the List of Values intentionally. You can't align your actions with your values if you haven't clarified your values.

3. Identify those in your leadership scope of influence who are in systemically marginalized groups like women and Black and Brown colleagues. They have lived with a double standard all their lives. Spend time with them and listen to their stories. Then, honor what you hear. This is a broadening of your role as leader and necessary given the reality of 2020.

A word to leaders: As you begin to be more intentional about leading for a Better Normal, I would suggest doing a lot of active listening and learning from those around you. Hearing your colleagues answer the Mary Oliver question, clarifying values and discussing guiding principles, and listening to stories of "feeling marginalized" by double standards. All of these exercises will be fresh and amazing new information for you and your colleagues. Treat this as new information. You are not creating a new problem by talking and listening. You are simply allowing for the unspoken to be spoken, listened to and appreciated for what it is. This listening process will not only lead to stronger ethical underpinnings for decision-making, but you will also learn and better understand your organizational community or family. In the process you will also be creating greater psychological safety for everyone. All of us want a culture of safety and inspiration. Remember the experience of the WD-40 Company and St. Jude Children's Research Hospital. Values free people to be their best. Cultures of inspiration are freeing where individual and collective efforts exceed expectations.

Urgency is the Fuel For The Greatest Leadership Opportunity of a Lifetime

CHAPTER FIVE

SENSE OF URGENCY: INCREASING INTENTIONAL LEADERSHIP, AND REDUCING COMPLACENCY

I t was Sunday, April 14, 1912. By 10 p.m. at least seven wireless warnings about ice had reached the Titanic. Although officers anticipated reaching the ice field by 9:30 p.m., the ship pushed on through the night at 22 knots, the un-slackened and normal speed. The last warning came about 11 p.m. from the ship California, less than ten miles away. 'Say old man, we are stuck here, surrounded by ice.' From the Titanic came these words, 'Shut up, shut up. Keep out. I am talking to Cape Race. You are jamming my signals.' At 11:40 p.m. the inevitable happened. An iceberg was hit. Two and one-half hours later, the Titanic sank. Hundreds perished."

In 2020 we received multiple warnings about current leadership practices. We have yet to listen. We have not yet taken dramatic action to change course. The four huge icebergs are still there. Based on what we now know, Titanic results are likely if we don't increase the urgency about how we lead. Normal urgency is deadly.

As we discovered in Chapter 3, the best of the best leadership practices and studies lead to inspiration as the common thread to exceptional performances and outcomes. A culture of inspiration is the culture of choice for long-term sustained performance that exceeds expectations. Urgency is the second practice of leaders who inspire the best of everyone. Overall, urgency about the very nature and narrative of leadership is needed in response to the new world landscape. The challenges of current reality outlined in chapter one and further noted below form the backdrop for why we need to reinvent leadership. It is a leadership opportunity that any person can seize.

I want to share something that was written in 2015 by Gary Hammel. Hammel is one of the most powerful voices for new leadership. He is a London Business School professor, director of the Management Lab, and the most reprinted author in Harvard Business Review history. From Hammel's foreword to the Jim Whitehurst book, *Open Organizations,* listen closely to his words and the case he makes for a dramatically new leadership narrative and the rationale for the quick demise of "bureaucratic normal" and traditional management models of leadership. "The human capabilities that are most critical to success---the ones that can help your organizations become more resilient, more creative, and more, well, awesome—are precisely the ones that can't be 'managed.' While you can compel financially dependent employees to be obedient and diligent, and can recruit the most intellectually capable, you can't command initiative, creativity, or passion. These human capabilities are quite literally, gifts. Every day employees choose whether to bring them to work or leave them at home." Initiative, creativity, and passion are tucked away in that reservoir of "discretionary capabilities and energy" just waiting to be inspired!

These are words from 2015. Leaders haven't listened very well. Unfortunately, there has been no quick demise of "Bureaucratic Normal" and not much has changed in leadership circles in the last few years despite all the new evidence. Plus, we have seen a rise in "Malignant Normal" leadership and the malignant normality that silent and complicit leaders, and a lot of good people have made possible. Hammel is making the case for reinventing leadership. He correctly and wisely identifies the "post bureaucratic" traits of the new open organizations, like "strategy making will be a dynamic, companywide conversation" and "individuals will compete to make a difference, not to climb a pyramid." Note that none of the traits can be managed. We will make the case here that all of them can be led and the upcoming chapters continue to point the way to how to lead. All of the human capabilities that Hammel identifies as most critical for success in the future depend on human beings. And human beings at their best are only inspired by leaders with relationship skills, people skills, and emotional intelligence. We know that leaders can only inspire others to bring their human capabilities to work.

It is post 2020. Leading organizational thinkers and consultants, leaders for open organizations, and world class business professors and authors like Hammel have made powerful cases for change.

The words quoted above are strong and compelling, but those words and hundreds of leadership books have not been enough to significantly change wide-spread leadership behavior.

We have the thinking, we have the leadership wisdom, but we are lacking in the pace of leadership acceptance and the number of change leaders. The pace is like pushing a boulder up a hill. Incremental and slow is not enough. Obviously, we need greater urgency about leadership and the totally new world after 2020-2021. We need less management and more leadership. We need thousands of new leaders to lead for a better normal. Just imagine the potential.

THE URGENCY ASSUMPTIONS IN THE WORLD OF PANDEMICS, HYBRID WORK ARRANGEMENTS, ECONOMIC INSECURITIES, HUMAN INEQUITIES, AND INADEQUATE MANAGEMENT MODELS

- Normal is the enemy of better normal. Leaders must bring a new perspective to the new world that is forever different.
- Leadership is broken and must be reinvented and transformed.
- All of us are leaders: We need more people to understand how they can make a difference and lead within their sphere of influence.
- All humanity is "wild and precious:" Leaders must be intentional about leading from a different mindset.
- Compassion, kindness, psychological safety, and "courage to be" help define the leadership mindset.
- Toxic, malignant normality is unacceptable. Leaders silent and complicit with malignant normality cannot lead.
- Traditional bureaucratic normal leadership is inadequate.
- Only Inspiration: Understand, believe, and act on the fact that only inspired people chose to give their best thinking, collaborative acting, and create sustainable, extraordinary results.
- Moral Compass: The leader's moral and ethical compass is the heart of inspiring leadership. Organizations, for profit and non-profit, business and religious, can be difference-makers with compelling future visions for their work.
- Fact: We know what inspires people, and leaders can learn to inspire themselves and others.
- Fact: We train people for every job in the organization and company except leadership. Most people are promoted into leadership positions, given a new title, and set up to fail.
- Fact: We need many more leaders throughout every organization who share a common leadership language and shared leadership practices that inspire others.

- Fact: Leaders for a better normal must lead in addressing and reducing the systemic inequities in the organization and the community.
- Traditional leaders and toxic leaders do not inspire others. Current toxic leaders must be willing to change their behavior or leave. Bureaucratic leaders must be trained to be leaders for a better normal and drive leadership deeper into the organization. Only leaders who inspire others can create the better normal at this historic time.

Imagine how urgency would change with this scenario.

Imagine every person in the organization being invited to lead by doing what's right, doing all they can to improve their work and align their work with the guiding principles and the most important strategic initiatives, and do all they can to make those they work with more successful.

Of course, also imagine that all people learn, as soon as they come on board, what "right" and business ethics look like, learn how they will have opportunities to improve their work skills, learn exactly what the guiding principles and/or core values are, learn about the vision, mission, and strategic initiatives of the organization and how they contribute, and understand that they are encouraged to make suggestions for improving the work process and encouraged to give feedback to colleagues to help make them more successful.

Wow. If this happens, as it does in open organizations and Better Normal-led companies, of course it makes a difference. Of course it creates a culture of inspiration. Of course it increases personal ownership and commitment. Now everyone has a sense of what is most important and how they can make a difference. Of course it increases urgency, urgency for the right things.

With so many things and so many issues on the plate of any leader, the leadership practice of urgency is about bringing focus to the most important AND most urgent priorities. Of course, this means great planning and hard conversations. It also means urgency about the right things. I introduce urgency now, hoping that along with the leadership practices of The Ethical Heart and The Collaborative Mindset, you will have the process practices, the "how we will work together" practices, which assure you get good information, make good strategic decisions, and inspire your people to own and live out the strategic priorities.

Urgency is elevated to the second most critical of the seven non-negotiable practices of inspiring leaders because of the magnitude of the issues exposed in 2020. There are systemic failures everywhere and the tip of the sphere is leadership. Where are the leaders? How did this happen? The most common response to any new discovery of a systemic issue raising its ugly head is, "We are obviously very concerned about this issue, we are doing a thorough investigation, and will do everything we can to make sure it doesn't happen again." And then it happens again. There is simply no time to waste in turning the exposed leadership inadequacies into the greatest leadership opportunity of our lifetime.

Urgency as a leadership practice burst into our awareness in 1995 through the work of John Kotter, then Professor of Leadership at the Harvard Business School. In his book *Leading Change*, mentioned earlier when we discussed the Culture of Inspiration, Kotter shifted the leadership conversation from managing change to leading change and leading with urgency.

At the time of Kotter's writing in 1995 and based on his vast experience with organizational change, he wrote about the leadership changes that he thought would be necessary for the rapidly changing global business environment of the 21st century. Kotter writes, "major change efforts have helped some organizations adapt significantly to shifting conditions, have improved the competitive standing of others, and have positioned a few for a far better future. But in too many situations the improvements have been disappointing, and the carnage has been appalling, with wasted resources and burned-out, scared, or frustrated employees . . . a significant amount of the waste and anguish we've witnessed in the past decade is avoidable."

Kotter concluded that people trying to lead transformational change made a number of mistakes but, "By far the biggest mistake people make when trying to change organizations is to plunge ahead without establishing a high enough sense of urgency in fellow managers and employees. The error is fatal because transformations always fail to achieve their objectives when complacency levels are high."

Here we are, over 25 years later, with still bigger challenges. We not only are not being urgent enough, but we are still managing change instead of leading change.

The brutal reality of 2020 has added and exposed a new perspective on human fragileness and the crying need for leadership for a better normal. Leaders now must broaden the scope of urgency that Kotter wrote about near the turn of the century to reflect the current new insights, understandings, and actions needed to vigorously respond to the impact of what we learned from 2016-2021. In summary:

We still have a rapidly changing and highly competitive global business environment. We still have far too many leaders and managers across the board who are complacent about or don't understand their work priorities. Therefore, complacency and "business as usual" is the carryover sense of urgency from the old normal. (Urgency 1)

Now we know that several systemic inequities at work affect quality of life and economic security for most working people. Roughly 70% of working Americans have experienced and suffered from systemic inequities and less opportunity. (Urgency 2)

Now we know that some powerful political leaders, and those complicit with them, have modeled toxic and destructive leadership practices, creating a malignant normality leadership option that diminishes the lives of all people and particularly marginalized people. (Urgency 3)

The leadership void: Now we know there are far too few leaders throughout most organizations and that supervisors and managers are not trained to be leaders. We need more leaders and a common leadership language for all. (Urgency 4)

Now we know that the "hard skills" of leadership are those that inspire others including the relationship skills of empathy, compassion, courage, assertiveness, emotional intelligence, and win-win collaboration. In traditional Bureaucratic leadership, these skills have been considered the soft, touchy feely, non-rational skills, and have not been appreciated or utilized to their potential. (Urgency 5)

In short, we have five strong cases for urgency: the sense of urgency needed to move the organization or team toward the future vision and top mission-driven strategic initiatives in any normal year plus the four new urgent mandates revealed by the events of 2020 and early 2021.

What this means is upping the urgency and reducing the complacency in these five areas, dramatically increasing leader intentionality and the number of leaders.

It does not mean the old "tyranny of the urgent" and moving from one fire to the next. It does not mean the sky is falling and we are doomed. It does mean that we now have enough information about the fact that you can't accomplish strategic priorities in a culture of complacency, period. And, as Kotter and other observers of leadership needs in 2020 and beyond, we simply need many more leaders in every sector.

As with normal being the enemy of the "better normal," complacency is the enemy of urgency. A sense of urgency is inherent in transformational change, so thinking and acting with an urgent mentality has been integral to my past consulting work and my leadership at

Belmont University. Prior to Belmont, when my consulting group worked with leaders on strategic change, the lead question we asked to trigger "urgent thinking and acting" was, "What will happen if nothing changes in the next 3 years, and you continue to operate as you are operating today?" The response to the "no change" question was predictable and immediately bothersome to participating leaders. Here's a sample of responses from the past.

As with normal being the enemy of the "better normal," complacency is the enemy of urgency.

If we don't change:

- We might not be in business.
- We will be much less competitive.
- Some of our best people would leave.
- We will not be able to sustain our organization and we will lose customers.
- We will become outdated and be so far behind we could never catch up.
- I can't imagine the outcome of no change.
- We would all be out of a job.
- We would cease to exist.
- No change is out of the question.

No change is out of the question. How would you answer this question where you work?

As people seriously consider what would happen if they continued with "a business as usual" or "no change" strategy, lights begin to come on related to the changes needed to become or remain robust and competitive. We never worked with any organization or company that didn't begin to feel more urgent about their long-term plans, in effect admitting that their normal would not be acceptable going forward. For example, at the U.S. Department of Transportation (DOT) where we worked as senior consultants, the problems with modal solutions instead of multi-modal transportation solutions were obvious. The government systems which they inherited encouraged them to be turf protective and silo oriented. Highway, rail, airways, and the other modes of transportation were funded separately, served a different set of constituents, competed for resources, and rarely were intentional about working together. These were all bright, well-intended leaders in each transportation mode. They discovered, however, that they were too far along in their planning on a highway or rail or airway initiative before they started talking to each other about a seamless transportation solution that would better meet the needs of their millions of traveling customers. "No change" was not an option. Urgency grew.

For example, the budget process had always been a competitive process within DOT, all vying for a portion of one pot of money. In the past, each mode of transportation within DOT had strategically determined their own priorities and the modal priorities had been in competition with each other. With a new sense of urgency about multimodal thinking and acting, two key processes reflected the new urgency and new motto of Working Together Better. First, the overall DOT strategy plan was voted best in government and the budget process, for the first time, was done with a focus on the top priorities of the total Department of Transportation. Recall, this is a Secretary of Transportation who is a political appointee working to inspire modal leaders, long-time civil servants, who have worked for both Democratic and Republican Presidents. They, like Secretary Slater, worked for the American people but they came to their positions differently. In essence, Working Better Together could not be mandated, it had to be inspired. And Secretary Slater was front and center in inspiring others and leading change. He left a meeting with then Prime Minister Tony Blair and other government leaders to be front and center for the first vision-driven team-building session with all the modal leaders. For three years, he was always a front-row leader, no cell phone, no walking in and out of the meetings, and fully present. One Department of Transportation was the driving vision.

Change and urgency about change, therefore, is non-negotiable for any person, parent, leader, company, or organization that wants the best and wants to improve in any way. You can see the value, so after you see the value, how do you lead change? Since the enemy of change is resistance and complacency, the next step is brutal honesty about the pockets of resistance and complacency. I will use the term "brutal honesty" often in the next few chapters simply because you have to identify the real sources of complacency. Some of my colleagues like the term "naked truth." At any rate, no system or process is spared. No elephants left in the room.

There are guidelines to how you go about identifying the roadblocks and points of complacency. Recall that you are building a culture of inspiration starting with the ethical and compassionate heart. So, we are intentionally seeking to honor all the stakeholders and create a psychologically safe environment for honesty and truth-telling. Leaders do this by being clear about the necessity of exposing roadblocks to "urgency" without blaming and finger pointing. We are going after the flaws in the system, not flaws in people. People are a separate issue. As always, accountability is a critical part of the system. If people aren't being held accountable, then identify "lack of accountability" as a roadblock. Our behaviors, actions, and policies have consequences.

> We are going after the flaws in the system, not flaws in people.

I have already referenced John Kotter's excellent book, *Leading Change*. Six years later, I was asked to review, critique, and write a recommendation for another Kotter book entitled *The Heart of Change*. This was a book of inspiring stories from people who led change by dramatic appeals for change that touched the heart and emotions of people. The manuscript was a delight to read and critique, becoming part of my own inspiration for authoring this book years later. The stories were all about inspiring people to act and change their behavior. I want to share one of my favorite stories from that book, a story written by Jon Stegner. This is how he got the attention of senior leaders with an unorthodox, non-analytical appeal. Jon was not a senior leader, nor did he have great resources available to him. Jon saw what he thought was an ineffective and costly system, found his leader "with-in," and decided how he could make a difference.

In Jon's large organization, he felt there was a systemic problem with the entire purchasing process and that the company had a chance to save up to 1 billion dollars over a five-year period. That's a bunch of money. His problem was how to get the attention of the top leaders who he thought were basically unaware. How could he help them be "brutally honest" without pissing off the very people he wanted to see "the truth?" He asked a summer intern to do some research on just one purchased item, gloves, to keep it simple. All the plants used gloves, and everyone could relate to that item. The summer intern came back after the research and reported that their factories were purchasing 424 different kinds of gloves! The same glove could cost $5 at one factory and $17 at another. And the company bought lots of gloves. Jon asked the intern to gather a sample of each of the 424 gloves, put the price on each pair, and sort by the different divisions of the company. Remember, gloves were just one of many items purchased using the same process. So gloves were just the tip of the iceberg.

Here's the brilliant part of this story. They invited the various division heads to a board room with an expensive wooden table where they usually saw neatly stacked piles of "important" papers. Instead, they saw 424 pairs of gloves, separated by divisions within the company, with all the different prices. Rarely speechless, these leaders were speechless. It was like, "do we really do this?" "Yes, we do." The gloves became a roadshow and went to every division. With a little more student research of what competitors were doing, a mandate for change came quickly. The "gloves on the boardroom table" story became a rich part of company history.

Pretty dramatic, huh? Highly creative and designed to touch emotions. Shocking people into action if you will. No way to dismiss the power of this simple presentation and no way to stay complacent about the purchasing process. Urgency became critical and a lot of new, saved money became available for better use. Note that the research was done by student interns and the initiative begun by someone outside the realm of senior leadership, a clever leader who found an inexpensive way to bring urgency to a big problem. I particularly liked the "how," the process used to get to the dramatic presentation. No blaming or finger pointing or name-calling, just a creative way to demonstrate a systemic company issue in an undeniable format.

For "gloves on the boardroom table" stories to become the norm rather than the exception, leaders at all levels in the organization must see themselves as leaders, not just managers or supervisors. Better yet why not empower everyone to find the leader with-in? Why not train everyone as a "what-if" thinker in a psychologically safe environment? Everyone can be a change leader, constantly thinking of ways to improve the process.

Most of us know about Curious George, the good little monkey who was always curious, getting into good trouble, and always escaping danger just in time. Curious George books have been around since 1941 and so beloved by children the world over that the books have never been out of print. As we parents know, children have a delightful inquisitive nature, much to learn, and curious about most everything. The best of pre-K, kindergarten and elementary education is built on that natural inclination to ask questions, explore, and learn. So, in our home, we have the books along with a stuffed and cuddly Curious George in our grandson's room. We have all learned from this little guy. George gives us permission to constantly reinforce learning, curiosity, wonderment, questioning, observations, and discovery when we see those qualities in our grandson. It is common for us to figuratively ask Curious George to join us when gathered for a family dinner.

"What is something new you learned this week?" We all have our turn at answering the question.

In a culture of inspiration, urgency to discover your personal and collective best is the order of the day. We want a room full of "Curious George" people when we create, plan, make decisions, and implement. People and organizations with big dreams seek out new information and any ethically sound resource to move toward the dream. Curious behavior is rewarded and celebrated. Want an innovative and creative environment? Make it safe to be curious and innovative. Want some great information about the critical art of rethinking and reinventing? Read *Think Again* by Adam Grant. Grant does an amazing job with a deeper dive into challenging assumptions, any assumptions, and why a better normal culture cultivates the ability of everyone to rethink and reinvent. In addition, he writes informatively about the necessity of "psychological safety" for the rethinking process to thrive.

> In a culture of inspiration, urgency to discover your personal and collective best is the order of the day.

If you have read closely, you already know my bias against the terms "manager" and "supervisor" simply because, by definition, they suggest that people need more supervision and managing and are less capable of making good decisions without more help. The terms also limit managers and supervisors, suggesting they are not expected to lead. So, for "gloves" creativity, innovativeness, and emotional impact to emerge, we need more urgency and leadership throughout the enterprise.

URGENCY KILLERS

I want to challenge common phrases I have heard over and over, phrases many of us have uttered before. I call them urgency killers because they kill innovation and creative thought immediately. "That is way too big for my pay level" or "That's what the guys who make the big bucks get paid to figure out." or "All we can do is push this up to senior leaders, and good luck with that." Other killers are "That's not the way we do it here" or "That's not our responsibility." "We are no worse than anybody else" gets a blue ribbon for a killer response. There are just tons of good ideas that never get heard in tradition-al work environments. Without Jon Stegner, think of the millions of dollars of waste that would have continued because of a flawed purchasing process.

Bold leaders for a Better Normal, then, are urgent about inspir-ing their team to close the gap between where they are now and where they want to be in 3 years. Leaders want everyone to think and act as Jon did.

> **Leaders get smarter by listening to the people who do the work every day. They see the obstacles and roadblocks better than anyone.**

Overcoming roadblocks and being better able to serve customers, serve clients, serve patients, serve people in your congregation, cre-ate better products, be more profitable, and moving toward the vision is inspiring.

Bob Fisher and I consulted with senior leaders at one Nucor Steel plant and several Kimberly Clark facilities during their Good to Great years. Their stories are captured beautifully in Jim Collins' outstanding book, *Good to Great,* mentioned earlier. What Nucor Steel, Kimberly Clark, and the nine other featured companies discovered, according to Collins, was that doing only what you are good at only makes you good. If you wanted to be great, you needed to focus solely on what you could potentially do better than others with whom you were com-peting. Think about this concept. What can you potentially do better than your competition? This is what needs urgency. Otherwise, you will just be ok or good. Collins used the term Hedgehog to describe the laser focus, discipline, and commitment of the great companies to a simple concept used as a frame of reference for all decisions. A company or organization's Hedgehog concept comes "from a deep understanding about the intersection of three circles" derived from the following three questions:

1. What can you be best in the world (your world) at?
2. What drives your economy engine?
3. What are you deeply passionate about?

According to Collin's, Nucor Steel answered these questions as follows:

"Best at? Creating the culture and technology to produce low-cost steel.

Economic engine? Profit per ton of finished steel.

Passion? For eliminating class distinctions and creating an egalitarian meritocracy that aligns management, labor, and financial interests."

What Nucor Steel did strategically and what we experienced in our visits to their Blytheville, Arkansas, facility, translates nicely to entities of any size in any sector of business, profit or non-profit, religious or secular. Nucor Steel is an excellent example of equity, fairness, transparency, and inspired people. They have been urgent, disciplined, and focused. Lessons for any leader:

- Live your Hedgehog concept with disciplined actions and policies consistent with your Hedgehog concept.
- Put your people first.
- Eliminate hierarchies, titles, and privilege which create "us and them" mentality.
- Take care of those you lead with benefits and perks.
- Share profits with people in profitable years.

- Leaders take more cuts than others in recession years.
- Status and authority come from the demonstrated ability to lead others.

Consider this, within your scope of influence. Consider the three questions noted above about what your team can be best at doing, your economic engine, and what you are deeply passionate about? This is powerful stuff. And any team can create a version of these basis questions, especially what you can be best at doing and what is your passion. As a leader, you are responsible within your scope of influence for inspiring practices. Urgency connects directly to the strategic priorities. The chapters on strategic direction are coming up. All the leadership practices that inspire are interconnected. At the core, I am asking you to stay curious, learn from what others have experienced, and believe that you can translate any success of others into something meaningful for your leadership wherever you are.

The second leadership gift from the past that I wrote about in the previous chapter was Tom Peter's and Bob Waterman's research that led to *In Search of Excellence* in 1982. At the time, they began their writing with two chapters devoted to "new theory," making the case in one chapter that there was much more to management than the rational, do it by-the-numbers style of management which had been dominant. In a second chapter, they wrote about motivation waiting to happen and that the excellent companies paid more attention to their people and what motivated them. But motivation, as we discuss in this book, was not currently a focus and was "waiting to happen" when they wrote in 1982. You should know about motivation, they thought, but the really important stuff would be in the eight chapters that discuss in depth the eight characteristics that the excellent companies had in common. Here's the big deal from their advice in 1982 about the two chapters that talked about the people skills and heart of managing, the non-rational part of management. Well, they wrote, this is good to know, but it's ok to skim over these chapters to get to the real findings, the hard stuff. We want you to be aware of the human side of this, but it's not what you need to understand most. Note that these are not quotes from their book but my interpretation.

Two decades later, in 2003, Peters and Waterman reissued their book with a new introduction and their tune has changed related to the importance of the human issues. It's not okay twenty-one years later to skim over what they called the non-rational, human part of management. "Management systems that treat people as 'factors of production,' as cogs in an industrial machine, are inherently de-motivating." This is what I call normal, traditional bureaucratic leadership, and it is uninspiring. Then Peters reminds us in 2003 that "people are wonderfully different and complex," and that "leaders need to set people free to help, not try to harness them." And here's the kicker. "The hardest thing to manage is the 'soft stuff,' especially culture. Yet without serious attention to the so-called soft stuff, leaders will fail." There's not much wiggle room. "Leaders will fail." The old "soft stuff" is now the hard stuff. We need stronger leadership focus and more leaders. I am confident that Peters and Waterman, if writing again in 2020, would be even more explicit about the value of the "soft stuff" and why leaders will fail otherwise. When I write about "if this isn't right, nothing will be right," the soft stuff is what I am talking about. It is the "how" part. The relationship skills. Remember, "you will fail" otherwise.

Whether you are an established leader or new leader, I believe answering the question, "What will happen and where will we be in 3 years if we don't change anything?" is a potent exercise for you and the people you lead. It is enormously helpful in identifying the biggest change issues and challenges. Used in conjunction with a traditional SWOT (Our Strengths, Weaknesses, Opportunities, Threats) analysis where you are brutally honest about current

> "What will happen and where will we be in 3 years if we don't change anything?" is a potent exercise for you and the people you lead.

reality, any leader will find the process helpful in finding roadblocks and pockets of complacency that need greater attention and urgency.

I also encourage you to be urgent in discovering your "hedgehog" since this will drive your sense of urgency. The thoughtful answers to the three questions posed by Collings should be the core of the hard questions you ask in strategic planning.

I write knowing that I encourage a lot of shared learning when planning and being intentional as a leader at the end of each chapter. I know that many leaders would prefer that another person facilitate the shared learning experiences I suggest, giving the leader a chance to participate along with colleagues. The facilitator could come from within the organization or could be an outside consultant-facilitator. The important thing is doing it. Learning together is the important thing, developing some common understandings as well as some new ways to communicate between and among colleagues. While leading at Belmont University, I facilitated some new learning experiences, I invited a consultant to come in at other times, and with systemic issues, we had a helpful and strong Vice President of Institutional Effectiveness, Dr. Paula Gill, that engaged all the stakeholders in the work of change and the work of owning and implementing the new changes. Get this. She engaged and challenged all the stakeholders. Good facilitators do this. Change is never any one leader's responsibility or only senior leaders' responsibility. For change to stick, the problem must be seen, accepted, and owned by all the stakeholders.

Big change, transformative change, extraordinary outcomes happen because a high percentage of people "get it" and can openly talk about it. Inspiring a change process can be and should be a fun learning experience.

People are very proud to be a part of major change done right. Leaders are life-long learners and reward learning with the people they lead. Paula was there every Saturday for several Saturday mornings, along with me and my team, when we implemented a transformative change in our Advancement process. The process we changed was one we inherited but we wasted zero time on blaming those who came before us. It was a roadblock to our getting better and it needed to be improved. And the extra work on Saturday morning made us a better team. We did it together.

Another leadership insight from the past came from Peter Senge and the gift of thinking about your organization or company as a "learning organization." It's hard to imagine leadership without seeing it as a continuous process of learning and growing. Complacency or incremental change or "that's the way we have always done it" are the normal. This is why you and your colleagues need to be comfortable with "urgent talk" which helps create the culture of inspiration. After you have decided that "no change" is crazy talk and unacceptable, urgent talk becomes part of the culture, an exciting and inspiring part of the culture.

> **When strategic planning is done right, top priorities pop out, vision and mission are confirmed or changed, and it becomes obvious that to reach your future destinations within a given time frame, everybody must discover and learn.**

There will be short-term wins to celebrate and short-term mistakes to learn from. This is the environment inspiring leaders invite. This is the culture you recruit others to join and be a part of. Your place is no normal place to work. You will keep learning, you will keep growing, and it will be exciting and fun/enjoyable!

Leadership and parenting are not that different. A family is a small learning team with parent leaders. New leaders and new parents are in the same boat. How in the hell do we do this? Why should we have to guess our way through this important undertaking? Sure, we have learned from other leaders and other parents, but we don't want to screw this up, right? So, there's some urgency here to get it as close to right as possible. As parents, my wife and I knew we wanted and had to be learners. No complacency here. And we also wanted our girls to learn, be able to make choices, use their brain. Families are small leadership laboratories, in the sense that good parents and good leaders believe that what they are doing is important and urgent. Rubye Lynn and I right away agreed we needed to be on the same page and be consistent with our two girls. No good cop, bad cop. We had shared responsibility here. Rubye Lynn was a child development major as an undergraduate and I a psychology major. She knew a heck of a lot more about children than I did, but we both knew enough to think through the discipline aspect of parenting.

The "discipline talk" for parents is like the "urgent talk" for leaders in many ways. We want good things to come from holding ourselves accountable in both arenas. We thought of discipline more in terms of accountability, accountability to each other. Children never needed to be punished. They often needed to learn new behaviors just like their parents. We wanted to learn and grow as a family, play by the same rules, and see being accountable as something that strengthened the relationship. If we could do that as parents, we felt we were on the right track. Accountability should be a relationship-builder, not a relationship damager. Shaming and belittling are harmful whether at home or work. Why would we want our children to be afraid of us? Good grief. Parents and children share in being accountable to each other. If our girls needed to tell us where they were and when they would be home, we owed them the same commitment. They would call us if they were running late, we would do the same. They would call us if they ended up in a car driven by someone who had been drinking. We would drive to get them no matter the place or hour. We also agreed that seatbelts were non-negotiable. Non-negotiable situations like this had a sense of urgency.

I recall a bitterly cold night with blowing snow and interstate travel ill advised, personally making the decision to not take the last motel room available and drive on from Memphis to Little Rock after dark. We started our trip from my little hometown near Nashville. The weather was getting worse, not better. The interstate officially closed minutes after my decision. Fortunately, we did make it home, but it was a flawed decision. My decision could have had tragic consequences. Afterwards, I apologized to my wife and young daughters. We did what the U.S. Army would call an "After Action Review." "I said, I made a mistake. That drive was too dangerous. Too many bad things could have happened. Let's talk this over, review what happened and see what would have been a better decision. What can I and we learn from this? It was clear my ego got in the way, and it was clear I dominated the decision." You know what I was saying to myself when I said, "Let's go on." I was thinking, 'I know how to drive in this kind of weather. We can do it.' I had not listened well to my family or the weather advisories. We talked about the consequences of becoming stranded without enough warm clothes and blankets. What about the impact of other drivers out there who had made equally bad decisions? How could we talk more openly about the options we had before making a decision? It was a humbling experience. It was also scary to talk about it, but we learned from it. The point is, I learned a lot about me and all of us learned about the value of listening more fully to each other. The pros of getting home to our warm beds and meeting my need to "be in control" and "we should be able to do this" needs did not at all outweigh the real risk factors.

We also learned a lesson about the value of being vulnerable and acknowledging what was really going on. Honestly, I had not realized until this incident how strong those unconscious assumptions of my being in control were and how much they could interfere with my decision making. What a valuable lesson, and one of the many valuable lessons that would help me pay close attention to the emerging new research on vulnerability and its impact on leadership. Leaders and parents can learn much about the armor they use to protect themselves and the negative impact it has on making decisions and deciding what is urgent. Getting home was not urgent on that snowy evening. Staying safe was urgent.

Our various armors are mostly unconscious; perfectionism, self-doubt, anxiety as a way-of-life, "not enough," need to be in control. We learned our armors in childhood and they became the way we perceive the world. Armors minimize our ability to be more authentic and live more fully. Most of us have had to do battle (no pun intended) with one or more armors as I have. As we seek more individual and collective creativity, innovation, entrepreneurship, and better decision-making, we would be wise to be more urgent about reducing the armors most of us carry around with us daily. Your armors and those of your colleagues work directly against a culture of inspiration and best thinking and acting. "Darn it. One more thing we have to be intentional about."

> We learned our armors in childhood and they became the way we perceive the world. Armors minimize our ability to be more authentic and live more fully.

It's hard to let go of an armor or any behavior if you are unaware of it. We keep going to the armor because we think it protects us and we have used it for so long. The good news is we have more resources than ever to help us discover the armors we use to protect us. More good news. Really good things happen when we, for example, let go of the armor of having to "be perfect"! We can join the one humanity of beautifully imperfect people. No one is perfect.

We learned in the fall of 2021 about a young Kentucky University football player, J.J. Weaver, who was born with 6 functional fingers on his right hand. A picture of his hand went viral on social media as ESPN did a special story on him. The secret was out. An elementary teacher learned about this and invited Weaver to speak to her diverse elementary class about his uniqueness. Weaver did speak, pointing out how different and unique each child is and how they should be proud of being different. He now uses his platform and his "imperfection" to inspire children and young people to celebrate their differences.

There are hundreds of stories emerging about the power of vulnerability. We already know that the leader's willingness to be appropriately vulnerable and create a psychologically safe environment for others to be vulnerable is a leading component of great teams. Always remember, it takes courage to listen. It takes courage to be vulnerable and share your imperfection, to admit a mistake, to say "I don't know," and to share your own moments of anxiety and depression. As I mentioned earlier, you and I are beautifully imperfect and share this common trait of being human. This is the tie that binds.

> We already know that the leader's willingness to be appropriately vulnerable and create a psychologically safe environment for others to be vulnerable is a leading component of great teams.

More good news, we don't have to reinvent the wheel on vulnerability education and learning. As I mentioned earlier, there are many leadership gifts available to us and I will reference them repeatedly. Brené Brown, who I have already mentioned often, leads the pack related to recent research and writing related to vulnerability, empathy, courage, and shame. In fact, her TED talk, *The Power of Vulnerability*, is one of the top five most-watched TED talks in the world, with over 35 million views. It's an easy find. Go to TED talks and Brené Brown. Take a quick 30-minute break and look at it. Right now. You will be inspired to learn more.

One quick testimonial for Brown's work. I was impressed with the unique praise she received from Ed Catmull, President of Pixar and Walt Disney Animation Studios for Brown's work with his team on vulnerability. "Brené visited Pixar to talk with our filmmakers. Her message was important, as movies are best when they come from a place of vulnerability, when the people who make them encounter setbacks and are forced to overcome them, when they are willing to have their asses handed to them. It is easy to sit back and talk about the values of a safe and meaningful culture, but extraordinarily difficult to pull it off. You don't achieve good culture without constant attention, without an environment of safety, courage, and vulnerability. These are hard skills, but they are teachable skills." He then recommends starting with Brown's *Dare to Lead* book.

For leaders for a better normal and inspiring the best in all of us, we need less complacency and greater urgency for increased empathy (the path to accepting and understanding others), elimination of shame and reduced protective armor (inhibitors to learning and growth), and increased courage to share our one wild and precious life, talents, thoughts and feelings with those around us. This will be entirely new learning for most organizations. It simply is not done extensively. Even if a few leaders in any organization have invested in learning about their own protective armor, how to gain the courage to be more vulnerable, and how to be more empathic, all leaders need to learn these "hard skills" to maximize positive impact on the organization. And, on your bottom line. These are powerful new skills for most people. We have learned to armor up. Armor up is the knee-jerk response to feeling vulnerable and we have to unlearn it to be our best.

Psychological safety is the foundation for increased willingness to be vulnerable and honest about armors, our "gifts of imperfection."

After 2020, there are four "better normal" urgencies that leaders have to elevate to the same degree of urgency as any "normal" transformational effort. These go beyond addressing the normal complacency in most organizations that John Kotter wrote so well about in his two books, *Leading Change* and *The Heart of Change*.

For a better normal, leaders must treat with urgency the exposed systemic inequities, marginalized people, toxic and bureaucratic leaders within the system, and the need for many more inspiring leaders with a common leadership language.

The systemic inequities include the uneven playing field between white, black, and brown people, gender inequities in pay and promotion, and inequities between stockholders and stakeholders. Intentional leadership to address this urgency means doing your homework, standing with those who are marginalized, making their voices heard, and developing action plans to address any policies and practices that contribute to the marginalizing. Work to assure equal pay and more leadership opportunities for women and be accountable for eliminating the barriers and policies that create the unequal playing field. Work to become anti-racist and be accountable for measuring progress to eliminate racist policies and behaviors. Leaders for the better normal develop and execute strategic plans to address the reality of discriminating practices. Remember Parker Palmer's *Healing the Heart of Democracy* messages from 2011 now extend to "healing the heart of leaders and organizations."

We train people to be better at their jobs. Whether you are an accountant, information technologist, project manager, chief financial officer, lawyer, or programmer, you regularly keep up and learn best practices. Continuing education is the norm. Good organizations train and grow their people to constantly be better at what they do. Then, we promote the best of the best to be leaders, but we don't train people in leadership skills. These seven non-negotiable leadership skills are learnable and teachable. Leadership practices are like mental muscles as with other jobs, they get stronger with use. But we don't teach leaders to be leaders. And we don't teach managers and supervisors how to be leaders. Management skills and leadership skills are two different sets of skills.

> Good organizations train and grow their people to constantly be better at what they do. Then, we promote the best of the best to be leaders, but we don't train people in leadership skills.

So, wake up out there. Why not share the basic leadership language with all people with the expectation that all have a leader with-in, and all are expected to lead? This will up the urgency and reduce complacency.

As a related item to urgency in leadership development and training, think about how different we are generationally. For example, Millennials, your colleagues born roughly between 1982-2000 and numbering over 75 million, are often described with these terms: entitled, naïve, tecno-savvy, impatient, and want to make a difference quickly. They bring so much to the table and are beautifully talented. They like working in teams and tend to be collaborative. However, they grew up spending far more time with technology than they did with peers. Leaving their phone turned off during a meal and in a meeting is tough and for many almost impossible. Many would say their I-phones and laptops are addictive. In short, they have far more high-tech skills than they have high-touch skills. They clearly have different skill sets than I have. I need their tech skills and they need more relationship skills. Most Millennials will work in jobs that need high-touch, strong relationships, and trust. Relationships and trust develop over time with multiple interactions that require patience.

Where do millennials and their older generations of colleagues learn the relationship skills? Where do most people learn these valuable tools that spark creativity, innovation, learning, and inspiration? The point is, they don't. Not in any systematic way.

Not in college. Not in most grad schools. Not on the job.

Inherent in this new leadership model are the following beliefs:

1. Everyone is capable of leading,
2. We need all people who have others to lead, manage, or supervise to know how to lead, how to inspire others, and how to create

a psychologically safe environment that encourages innovation, creativity, and sensitivity to broader systemic inequities, and

3. We need significantly more education and training related to all the above leadership needs. Those companies that invest in becoming a learning organization are rewarded with increased motivation, job satisfaction, enhanced teamwork and productivity, and increased ROI (return on investment). These new "hard skills" are a part of the needed, common language of leadership.

As to the last point, as you think about more education and training in relationship skills for you and your team, consider a trusted colleague in Human Relations or an outside consultant. Ideally, you could find someone who is capable of teaching a variety of skills sets and someone who could build trust with your folks over time. When I was coaching and consulting, I found the most rewarding consultations to be ongoing when I had a chance to develop a relationship with the organization. Do your homework. Make sure the person or consulting firm you chose is a good fit for your culture. The key always is talk to others who have used the consultant or consultants before and get estimates of their fees. You want to have the kind of relationship with your consultant that will allow you to be consistent in creating a leadership package that will permeate throughout the organization or the group you lead.

In the mid-80s, CEO Don Tyson and his senior team at Tyson Foods began the implementation of a growth strategy with the intent of doubling in size and becoming the world's largest fully integrated producer, processor, and marketer of poultry-based food products. To achieve this ambitious vision meant numerous acquisitions with the right fit for the vision. It was a daunting task with multiple challenges. One of the strategic challenges was the integration of cultures and the people within the various cultures. The people in each acquired company had been competitors with Tyson Foods. Now they would be on the same team with a larger vision for the future. They would be collaborating with each other, working together. The people in charge of company training wanted to be strategic and get in front of the acquisition challenge.

They asked me and my consulting partner and friend, Bob Fisher, to design and implement a 3-day Tyson mission-driven team-building program for multiple teams of people. These would be teams of men and women, half from Tyson Foods and half from one of the acquired new companies, coming together in groups of 16-20 and meeting each other for the first time. Obviously, it was tougher for those coming from the newly acquired company. They were now wearing the Tyson logo and Tyson hats. It felt strange to everybody. But there could be no second-class citizens. It was the beginning of new relationships and trust levels were low. Marble jars of trust were empty. After all, they were all in the same boat now and they needed to start rowing in the same direction. From a rational standpoint, being on the same page made sense. But as Ed Catmull says above, "you don't achieve good culture without constant attention, without an environment of safety, courage, and vulnerability."

We tried to humanize the process as quickly as possible and find something in common to which they could all relate. These were former competitors who now needed to be on the same team. So much of what they did on a day-to-day basis was work in teams, not in isolation. This is true for most organizations and companies today. Team performance is critical. So, we asked a very simple question that became the key research question for our later book about highly effective teams. It is like the question that Kouses and Posner used in their research for their book, *The Leadership Challenge.* Whereas Kouses and Posner asked, "Tell Us About Your Best-Ever Leadership Experience" to discover what leaders do at their best, our question was, "What was your best-ever team experience?" Our instructions were simple. "Tell us a time when you had to work closely with one or more people to accomplish something you could never have accomplished as well by yourself. It could be a family, sports, religious, company-organization, civic, or volunteer team experience that required several days or more to complete the project or accomplish the objective." Of course, we got team stories from all over the place. Interestingly enough, work experiences did not dominate, and we discovered early on that working together, being collaborative, was not the norm. We also discovered that every person had a best-ever team experience of some kind. We had people write the experience on a worksheet in order to think about it in more depth and reflect on what was successfully accomplished and what characteristics stood out most as to what made this experience so successful.

As each person in a new group of 15-20 people shared their best-ever team experience and the key factors that made the experience successful, it would be their first real knowledge of each other on a level playing field. Whether the best-ever team experience was a successful school team championship, community group development effort, major work project, a cancer recovery group, or a family pulling together to overcome a challenge, the stories were high ownership, blood-sweat-and-tear stories that exceeded expectations. As I mentioned earlier, the exercise always brought high energy, laughter, and strong emotions. For many, it was the first time to talk about the best-ever team experience in a group. Most of all, the stories revealed so much of what they had in common. It was the start of becoming more a part of a team and a new company, a new Tyson Foods.

Highly effective teams, better leadership, greater innovation, and better normal are not accidental. They are intentional and they are urgent in the post-2020 era.

The leaders of the post-2020 era must be a new wave of learning leaders who dare to 'lead the way' in inviting others to share their best. Most people want to make a difference, want to find hope, compassion, meaning, and joy in their lives at home, work, and play. They want to be more authentic, connect with the people around them, be better and grow.

And, if people are invited by leaders into a psychologically safe and compassionate environment where trust is built, personal and collective aspirations nurtured, and urgency exists for things that matter, people and families and organizations will flourish.

In most organizations, there is a wealth of underutilized human potential waiting to be inspired. Each of your colleagues has a reservoir of discretionary energy and potential waiting to be discovered. This is new territory for most leaders. After 2020, we are leaders in a new frontier intending to level the playing field, hear every voice, and make a difference. We are inviting our colleagues and associates on a journey to be human, to honor the "one wild and precious life" that each of us brings to the table, to connect, to learn from each other, and to do good work together.

THE FIVE URGENCY HOT BUTTONS THAT MATTER

1. Urgency about the compelling vision, critical mission, and the top strategic priorities. A "Hedgehog" focus and determination.
2. Urgency about systemic inequities and the impact on marginalized women, Black and Brown people, your organization, and the community. This is a just cause just waiting to inspire any organization.

> This is a just cause just waiting to inspire any organization.

3. Urgency about current toxic "malignant normality" leaders in the organization who can't or won't change.
4. Urgency about expectations for more people to lead throughout the organization or throughout the leader's sphere of influence.
5. Urgency about organization-wide education for leading change and creating a culture of inspiration with a common leadership language.

Increasing urgency and reducing complacency has always been necessary for transformational change, always a hot button. Big change fails otherwise. The last four urgency hot buttons emerged suddenly in 2020 in response to the brutal realities of the year, creating the biggest leadership crisis and opportunity in our lifetime. The leadership landscape has been forever altered. Some organizations have been successful with creating the urgency needed for transformational change. Because of the recent revelations of the new better normal urgencies, the jury is still out on how organizations and leaders will respond to the latter four. If the response is not intentional and urgent, however, the outcomes cannot be good. Somebody powerful is not listening. Somebody in control is not paying attention.

> *Transformational change in any year creates competitive advantages for those who succeed. Equally so, leaders who successfully address the latter four urgencies will create competitive advantage.*

Why? Success means you are aware, you have listened, you have understood, and you have had the courage to lead based on what you know to be true. You have helped the people you lead know you have a sense of urgency about doing the right thing. You have created a psychologically safe environment. You have earned the trust of most people. If your strategic priorities are designed to create competitive advantage, you will likely have created several advantages: happier and satisfied associates, greater productivity, increased profit, a more attractive place to work and competitive advantage in recruiting and retaining talented people. People see what you are doing, and they want to be a part.

BEING INTENTIONAL WITH THE LEADERSHIP PRACTICE OF URGENCY: ACTION STEPS

Intentional sounds like homework, right? Well, yes. It is extra work beyond reading. It is the only way I know for you to develop the new leadership muscles that will drive your success as a leader. It is the only way I know to "become" a lifelong learner and have a greater impact on others, at work and at home. Becoming is growing. The action steps below and after the following chapters do require an extra investment of time. After all, you are on a rethinking and reinventing leadership journey. Look at this as an invitation to an adventure with unimaginable outcomes.

1. Two chapters from now, we will journey to the land of vision. Vision is why you do what you do. Vision can and should be compelling and attractive. Everything you do as a leader connects to the vision of where you want to be in the future and the strategies you chose to reach the vision. Given the five urgencies, you know you will be working beneath your potential if you don't address them directly and acknowledge them with those you lead. I have found that talking individually with people prior to meeting in small groups most helpful. This is a listening exercise for you as leader. You want to hear what others think about bringing more urgency to each of the urgency hot spots.

2. Listen to Brené Brown's TED talk on vulnerability. Then, consider listening and discussing with your closest associates. Also consider reading Brown's *The Gifts of Imperfections* as a further dive into the relationship between vulnerability and psychological safety.

3. As you read this, I realize you might be thinking that you want to coordinate your efforts with other leaders or with the person who leads your work. You may also want to save the issue of "urgency" until after you have addressed the "no change" question with your team or people you lead. Recall that I discussed this early in this chapter as a great starting point for identifying roadblocks that people see in the process of becoming even better at what you do. "What if nothing changes in how we do things and how we work together in the next 2-3 years?" After people respond to this question, you can begin to identify the systemic or organizational

issues that most need to change. Remember that you are focusing on roadblocks to improving and moving toward the compelling vision, not using this as an exercise to finger point or judge colleagues. You want to be urgent about the top 5-7 strategic priorities in your strategic plan.

4. The leadership gifts from the past that will greatly enhance your journey with the first three leadership practices may come from unlikely sources for traditional leaders. If you are intrigued by this adventure we are on and willing to dig deeper into these core leadership practices, I want to reference three people who can be great learning companions to you in solidifying the hardest practices of leadership. I have referenced Brené Brown's groundbreaking work already. Another learning companion who has helped thousands of people with their process of becoming more fully human is Tara Brach. Check out her books, *Radical Acceptance* and *Radical Compassion.* In addition, be aware of Krista Tippett's insights in *Becoming Wise.* Tippett resonates with me as she has spent her life committed to listening to others and sharing what she learned. "I listen for wisdom and beauty, and for voices not shouting to be heard," Tippett says. She has listened for years to hundreds of voices not shouting to be heard as host of the public radio program and podcast *On Being.* As a learning leader, parent, or teacher, The Ethical Heart, Creating Urgency, and the Collaborative Mindset, form the foundation of inspiring leadership. Each chapter provides insights on the process of "how we will work together" and are the new "hard skill" chapters. These practices invite you to embrace the relationship aspect of leadership, opening the door to a new perspective on leadership and the richness of our shared humanity.

5. I have referenced Jim Collins *Good to Great* book several times already. Because I have personal experience with both Nucor Steel and Kimberly Clark, two of the companies included in this book, I know I am partial to them. But if you want to dig

deeper into the Hedgehog concept and the power of knowing your passion, economic engine, and the potential of being the best in your world at what you do, read this book and discuss with your colleagues.

Collins' description of the culture differences between Nucor and Bethlehem Steel, for example, is one of the best examples I have seen of major culture differences in the same industry. Nucor is an example of Better Normal leadership, being urgent about their Hedgehog, and creating a culture that inspires the best in others. The Bethlehem Steel Collins describes showcases the worst of Bureaucratic Normal leadership and a culture of us and them, the haves and have nots. They never answered the question "What will happen if we don't change anything in the next 3-5 years?" They never successfully confronted the changes needed to survive in a globally competitive steel industry and never found their "Hedgehog." They were never urgent about being urgent, until it was too late. Bethlehem Steel declared bankruptcy in 2001 with final dissolution in 2003.

We
Are
Family

CHAPTER SIX

THE COLLABORATIVE MINDSET: WIN-WIN THINKING AND ACTING

"My model for business is The Beatles. They were four guys who kept each other's kind of negative tendencies in check. They balanced each other and the total was greater than the sum of its parts. That's how I see business: great things in business are never done by one person. They're done by a team of people."

– STEVE JOBS

Recall the image of the earth from the moon. This book began with the amazingly insightful message from moon-traveling astronauts. They shared a common perspective of the earth as a tiny living planet with one human race floating through space. They saw a fragile world where war should be unthinkable. Fighting cruelty and hate with more cruelty and hate would be unsustainable. The astronaut earth view is a powerful visual image of our interdependence, connectedness, and humanness, as well as our vulnerability. We share one humanity. We are social beings, wired for living and working together. Pretty simple concept, but we have done our darndest to make it hard.

The Collaborative Mindset is the third non-negotiable practice of leaders who inspire the best in others. It is the "no man is an island" concept, the "It takes a village" mindset. Sister Sledge's song "We are family" is dancing in my head right now. I'm also hearing Michael Jackson's "We Are The World," written and recorded for famine relief efforts in Ethiopia. We all have our own special reminders of our oneness with the world, our dreams of a beloved community, our hopes for greater unity, and our knowledge of abundance. It is a simple concept. And we have done an amazing job of not living into the collaborative mindset of seeking solutions that benefit the common good. The hundreds of broken systems and policies that continue to marginalize millions of people is evidence enough that leaders have failed and leadership itself is broken. This chapter is devoted to a leadership practice crucial to the success of leaders for a better normal. No leader is successful without others. The best leaders earn their status by helping others be successful and collaborating to make things better.

Donald Peterson was CEO of Ford Motor Company from 1985-1989 and was named CEO of the Year by Chief Executive magazine in 1989. Petersen was best known for his response to a simple question he posed to a Ford car designer. He asked the designer if he was proud of the design he was working on. Surprisingly, the designer said "no." Ah, the beauty of seeking feedback from those who do the work every day. This "no" response led to an amazing transformation of "how" the Ford design team worked within the team and with other teams. Petersen asked the Ford design team to design vehicles they would be proud to buy and park in their own driveways! For this to happen, the design team had to be more open with each other and had to be able to talk more quickly with engineering, marketing, sales, manufacturing people without working up and down every existing silo. So, they made a dramatic shift from a more traditional model of bureaucratic silos within the organization to an inclusive, collaborative, and team-oriented model. The outcome? The wildly successful design of the Ford Tarus and Mercury Sable, providing the motivation and profit to carry Ford into the next decade and beyond.

The Petersen story is a testimony to being curious, asking questions, and listening to what you hear. One simple question. "Are you proud of what you've designed?" And then you start asking more questions. "Why is that?" And then you discover that the whole system is closed, uncollaborative, and silo-driven. Nothing win-win going on.

We talked with Petersen as part of our research for Real Dream Teams since his shift in leadership philosophy to a team-oriented model underscored the best of a Real Dream Team. Now, Petersen's leadership falls into the Better Normal leadership category. The vision for Ford Tarus and Mercury Sable and the collaborative work it took to reach the vision were better than the norm for Ford. As we sat with Petersen and discussed his and Ford's success at a critical moment in Ford history, he suddenly invited us over to a little display important to him. He had a point he wanted to make about his leadership style and why he was successful. He then asked, "What do you see?" Bob answered, "A turtle on a fencepost." Petersen then made his point. "Remember this. If you ever see a turtle on a fencepost, you know it didn't get there by itself."

LEARNING TO CHANNEL COMPETITIVE SPIRIT TO FUEL COLLABORATION

Winning and competition are deeply ingrained in American culture. Even as I write the opening words of this chapter, I feel the tension between connectedness-humanness-togetherness and, on the other hand, competition. Winning and competing seem a bit like apple pie and motherhood. Of course, that is what we learned growing up. Competing and winning are our default, go-to responses. Choosing to collaborate, then, is not an easy choice. It is like a continuous tug of war between competition and collaboration. We love competition, but the results are in on the tug of war in families, businesses, politics, and relationships: collaboration gets the nod every time.

In truth, both competition and collaboration have a place in our lives. What is necessary is how we define winning and how we use our competitive spirit. This is another time when . . . we better get it right.

In today's world with multiple shared aspirations for all humans and a fragile, vulnerable world, a collaborative mindset truly is non-negotiable. In families, companies, and organizations, collaboration is non-negotiable. So, let's wrestle for a moment with "how we define winning."

Former UCLA basketball coach, John Wooden, was the first team leader Bob Fisher and I thought about when we started interviewing world-class leaders for our *Real Dream Teams* research. It also happened to be the easiest interview to schedule. We simply picked up the phone and called his home phone listing in Bel Air, California. Pretty naïve beginning, right? Well, guess who answered the phone in a couple of rings? The man himself. He quickly invited us to his home for the interview, which was an unexpected gesture and said so much about him as a person. He discussed his famous pyramid of success in detail, and it was a delightful interview.

Wooden shared a powerful story about his first in-depth discussion with Kareem Abdul-Jabbar (Lou Alcindor), just the two of them at court side in Pauley Pavilion on the UCLA campus. Abdul-Jabbar was the best big man UCLA had ever recruited. Wooden described in detail two strategies for Kareem's playing days at UCLA. "I told him that we had two choices for the years that he would be playing for UCLA. (Note that freshmen could not play their first year at this time, so his career would be only three years.) First, I could design an offense that would make him one of the greatest scorers in the history of college basketball. However, if we played to focus on his scoring, we probably would not win national championships. The second choice was to use a strategy that would emphasize his rebounding, defense, shot blocking, and passing as well as his scoring ability. He would also be playing with other talented players, and we would focus on becoming the best team possible. With this approach I was confident that we could win championships. I had to tell him also that with the team approach, he would not be chasing an NCAA individual scoring record. When I presented him with these alternatives, Kareem listened intently. I finally asked him to take as long as he needed to think about which option he preferred. I thought he would at least take a few minutes to think about the options. Instead, he responded quickly. 'That's easy, Coach---let's win championships!' He was one of the most unselfish players that I ever coached." And win championships they did, each of the years Abdul-Jabbar was there. In fact, during the Wooden era, UCLA won 10 national championships in a 12-year period. At the same time UCLA was winning team championships, another college player and his coach decided to define "winning" differently. This player would become the all-time leading scorer in NCAA history. The name? Pete Maravich at LSU. It was great fun to watch Maravich play. He led the nation in scoring for three straight years, averaging 44 points a game. However, LSU never played one game in the NCAA tournament during Maravich's career. There were no team championships.

Every leader, every team, and every organization can decide what "winning" means for them. We like winning. I don't shy away from using the term "winning" because we get to define what that means. Since so many people are inclined to think of working independently, completing tasks independently of others, leaders must be intentional in helping their colleagues understand the importance of collaboration and working together toward shared goals and shared aspirations. The concept of win-win collaboration is so crucial to organizational success that we often began our mission-driven team building sessions with an exercise called "Win As Much As You Can." The activity is deliberately designed to evoke the tug of war between competition and collaboration. Individuals and teams basically had to decide whether "You" meant winning as an individual or "You" meant winning as a team. All the people participating in the activity worked together every day in some way. As the exercise began, the knee-jerk response was consistently "compete" against others. In the compete scenario, someone always wins, and someone always loses. The activity was also designed to provide opportunities for discussion about another option where everyone could win. They had the "Kareem choice." Do I want to win for me, or do I want us to win? What is the championship? Most groups, after much discussion, could see the advantages of working together in order for all to win. After all, this training was about teams working together! The phenomenon was the knee-jerk response to compete, to win at the expense of others. In this activity, win-lose or lose-lose actions were zero sum outcomes. Participants in this exercise would remember this insightful exercise years later.

I recall a senior team of eight leaders where one team member chose himself over the team in the last round, winning the most individual points at the expense of his teammates. They had already discussed and promised they would define winning as a team win prior to the final choice. His teammates felt betrayed. They never let him forget what he did, even 10 years later! This activity was a simulated learning experience with little real consequences. But the feelings evoked temporarily, like feeling betrayed were real. You can bet the discussion which followed this simulation was lively and insightful. Participants could readily identify current unproductive and hurtful work experiences where they felt someone, or the system, won at their expense.

Most organizations have winners and losers unfortunately. The huge lesson for reinventing leadership is the awareness of how many people believe the system is winning at their expense. Now we know that the number of people who fall into the loser category of systemic inequities is in the millions.

THE KNEE-JERK CHALLENGE TO COMPETE

The leadership opportunity for leaders in any enterprise is the challenge of "knee-jerk." It is the gut-level, automatic response to compete, even when competing with your own teammates is counterproductive to the vision, mission, and strategic priorities. It is one of the reasons transformative change efforts fail. There is too much complacency and not enough urgency about defining what winning is and too little urgency and accountability related to the collaboration it takes to win together.

There are three essential terms that need to be a part of the common leadership language for this non-negotiable leadership practice. The terms originated in game theory and zero-sum outcomes.

> The leadership opportunity for leaders in any enterprise is the challenge of "knee-jerk." It is the gut-level, automatic response to compete, even when competing with your own teammates is counterproductive to the vision, mission, and strategic priorities.

1. Win-Win: The Collaborative Mindset. People work together to accomplish goals and missions that are bigger than any one person or role. The working assumption is we need each other to be successful and we work to make others around us successful. The work is interdependent. All energies are directed at the goal, mission, and progress toward the vision. Systemic inequities can be addressed in a win-win environment. Trust levels are high. People are inspired.

2. Win-Lose: Some win at the expense of others. The sum is zero and the loses equal the wins. Energy is wasted by people pulling in different directions. Strategic priorities and systemic issues are not fully addressed. Marginalized people continue to be marginalized. Discretionary energies are not fully tapped. The potential of the

individual, teams, and organization is not realized. Losers are much more aware of the negative impact of losing than are the winners. Often those who are winning at the expense of others are unaware of the full impact of the behaviors, practices, or policies that minimize, hurt, or make work more difficult for others. Winners may have good intentions, but negative impact is still there.

3. Lose-Lose: This is a nobody wins scenario. The most counterproductive of the three scenarios and the result of people losing over long time periods. At its worst, lose-lose will be the result of an unchecked growth in "malignant normal" leadership, misinformation, and conspiracy theories. The war in Ukraine is lose-lose. Only Putin and those most loyal to him perceive the war as a win while millions suffer, and democracy everywhere is threatened.

> **To move from our natural inclination to compete, it is critical for families, organizations, and people who need to work together to accomplish a common goal to determine first what "winning" means for them. This means actively talking about what success looks like and then reinforcing it when it happens.**

I was inspired by the spontaneous win-win that came at the end of the Tokyo Olympics high jump competition between Italy's Gianmarco Tamberi and Mutaz Barshim of Qatar. Both had cleared the same height, neither had a failed attempt until each failed three times at the 2.39-metre mark. So, they ended up tied. When the two talked with the Olympic official, the official first offered a "jump-off," meaning they would continue competing till one won and one lost. Then, the surprising, eloquent, and inspiring solution came from the mouth of Barshim in response to the "jump-off" offer. "Can we have two golds?" asked Barshim. The official nodded and the two competitors nodded in agreement. The friends clasped hands, embraced, and jumped with joy. Barshim explained that this went far beyond trying to break your opponent emotionally. He said, "This is beyond sport. This is the message we deliver to the young generation." It is a message for all of us. The pot of gold has enough gold for all. Think of abundance rather than scarcity. A new and magical definition of "winning." And we all have the power to define what winning means for us and those we lead. And please substitute "success" for "winning" if the term winning itself doesn't resonate for you. Define "success." Define what your championship looks like.

In most organizations and most families, working together and collaborating should be at a premium. It simply doesn't make sense in a highly interdependent family or organization to win at the expense of others. I will use the term "Win-Win thinking and acting" and "collaborative thinking and acting" interchangeably. With Win-Win/ collaborative behaving we are working to find common ground. We are working to find how we can best work together toward a mutually beneficial goal, mission, or vision. Another way of thinking about it is using the many talents of various people and various teams to reach an eloquent solution

---

If we define our championship well, we can determine the interdependencies and how best to use our talents and resources. Remember, don't take cooperation for granted. Leaders must teach it, name it, and reward it. Be intentional.

Win-Lose behavior immediately creates problems for families, teams, and organizations where people depend on others and need each other to be successful. Why? We have all felt the sting of someone or others winning at our expense. It doesn't make any difference whether the intent to win at our expense exists or not. When it happens, it hurts, and it creates anger and misunderstanding. It is dysfunctional. In the last chapter we addressed the new "urgency" of systemic inequities revealed boldly and sadly in 2020. Systemic inequities are win-lose to the core. Some are winning at the expense of others. Some are privileged at the expense of others. The people who experience the pain the most are always those who are marginalized, on the losing end of win-lose. As mentioned in the last chapter, Bethlehem Steel, institutionalized privilege and hierarchy, systems that reeked of leaders winning at the expense of the people who did the real work of creating steel. This was a great example of systemic inequities. Win-lose turned into lose-lose as most stakeholders eventually lost. The new normal era challenges us to call out the unfairness of win-lose behavior, actions, and policies by their name: dysfunctional, unfair, and not good for business or people.

Serena Williams made a rare public statement about systemic inequities in March 2021 while defending and advocating for her friend Meghan Markle. Meghan and Prince Harry had just been interviewed by Opry Winfrey about the pressures they had faced as part of the Royal Family, including racism. Serena said, "I know first-hand the sexism and racism institutions and the media use to vilify women and people of color, to minimize us, to break us down and demonize us." As Rebecca Solnit says in one of her essays, "Once we call it by name, we can start having a real conversation about our priorities and values. Because the revolt against brutality begins with a revolt against the language that hides that brutality."

The Win-Win collaborative mindset can create a new language for any relationship and for any organization. It is the language of eloquence, fairness, equity, and our one humanity.

No privilege and no caste system. We really are all in this together. Contrast Win-Win with Win-Lose, where some are winning at the expense of another or others. The final option is Lose-Lose, where everyone loses. "I may not win, but I'll be damned if you are going to." The latter behavior is evident today in the worst of partisan politics, nobody wins, and many are hurt.

The challenge is this: Winning at the expense of others has so become a part of the fabric of American competitive culture that it has become institutionalized and systemic in traditional bureaucratic entities. To be intentional about changing the Win-Lose and Lose-Lose patterns of behavior may be a bigger battle than you think. Behavior change is tough, even when it rationally makes total sense for the greater good. Have you ever personally tried to change a long-standing pattern of behavior? Have you ever attempted to change the culture of your team, home, or organization? It's hard, whether it's personal change or organizational change. The dynamics are similar. Change creates discomfort. Discomfort yells internally, "Go back to what's comfortable. Now!" So, remember this as you attempt to learn new leadership skills and practices. Uncomfortable is normal. No discomfort, no change. Expect and welcome the tension of learning and growing.

MY PERSONAL STRUGGLE WITH OVER-PLEASING AND WHAT PEOPLE THINK OF ME

I grew up in a small town where, like the *Cheers* bar in Boston, "everybody knows your name." They not only knew your name, but they also knew your behavior and any perceived bad behavior at school got to your parents before you got home from school. News travels fast in small towns. It was like everyone was the preacher's kid. Being "good" and polite was heavily rewarded. An occasional "shit" from my grandmother, who lived with us, was tolerated, but not from me.

I was a pretty compliant, polite, play-by-the-rules, "awe shucks" kind-of-guy. I wanted to be friends with everyone. Getting along with and pleasing others was my strength, I thought. I knew how to listen, be empathic, build relationships, and make friends. But there was a big downsize, too. I could and did live my values, but I couldn't speak my values. What people thought was more important than what I thought. It was more difficult for me to make decisions and disagree. I had lots of opinions and beliefs that I couldn't verbalize unless I already knew I was in a safe, like-minded situation. If there was any hint of conflict, I would be the one to say, "I'm sorry" or "my fault." Hey, I had all these people to please, to get permission to be me. In short, my strength became a weakness because of my fear that someone wouldn't like me or be pleased with me. So, one of my armors was over-pleasing.

Only years later, as I was digging deeper into a career centered around human behavior, did I discover one of the "fear triggers" that captured what would happen if I weren't always the good guy. It actually turned out to be pretty funny. I discovered the "repressed culprit" during a high school class reunion. We were talking about the things we remembered about each other. The themes for me were corny jokes, over saying "I'm sorry," sports stories, and water balloons. When asked, "why did you never get in trouble?" what spontaneously popped out for the first time was "The Permanent Record." A friend said, "What the hell was that?" Then another, "Oh, I remember!" The ominous "Permanent Record" was the worst thing that could possibly happen to you. It was worse than being sent to the principal's office or being suspended from school. No one ever saw a permanent record, but it was the last threat made by a teacher or the principal to stop undesired behavior. It started in elementary school and when we talked more about it, many of my classmates remembered it. "You don't want this on your permanent record, do you?" It was hilarious and revealing. The funny part, looking back, it was like this unsaintly deed on the permanent record would be the first thing St. Peter would see at the Pearly Gates, and you would go straight to Hell. And in small town religious circles, there were lots of things lurking around that had Hell-like consequences.

It took a while, but most of the time I can let go of my "permanent record" thinking and feeling, my having to please others all the time, and my strong worries about what people will think of me when I have the courage to be more authentic. It is a conscious effort. For me, I learned about cognitive restructuring and learned how my thoughts patterns of "having to please" made it imperative that I please everyone. Not pleasing, in my mind, led to catastrophic consequences. I had to learn to change my thinking patterns and get to the point where I could not only survive without pleasing all people, but I could also thrive. Yes, the demons still raise their ugly heads, but helping other people face their demons has always been affirming for me. Fortunately, I have affirmed as healthy behavior my sensitivity to how others feel, my empathy, my relationship skills, and my passion for a better world. And with this learning came the broader and more obvious learning that no one can please everybody, no one is perfect, and that we all have some life-long learning patterns that keep us from living life more fully at home and work. These are our armors, as noted earlier, that we learned early in life to protect ourselves from hurt, pain, and shame.

My hit songwriter, recording artist, and music producer friend, Steve Azar, wrote and recorded one of his many top-selling hits, "I Don't Have to be Me (Til' Monday)," in 2001. In this song, he describes the secret dream we all have of not having to armor up for three whole days. Google the lyrics to this fun song and hear the themes: Long weekends, not having to face the reality of a time clock, no boss to answer to, leaving stress all behind, and being authentic.

Who doesn't need more three-day weekends where you can choose to be the real you? We all need timeouts from the daily grind with no pressure, no problems. That surely is the original definition of vacation. In addition, Azar's song captures what millions of American workers did during Covid when they quit their uninspiring jobs. They decided they wanted jobs where they could "be me" more, 24-7. People wanted to be valued at work as well as at home, during the week as well as on the weekend. They quit jobs with traditional bureaucratic bosses and toxic bosses who didn't value them being themselves, didn't see them as the most important asset.

But taking off armor 24-7 is hard. Behavior change is hard. Old habits are old habits. They have been around a long time. When we want to change, as I did with wanting to be more me, less "pleasing others," it does take time and commitment. It seems overwhelming at times. When you have protected yourself for so long, it is scary every time you speak up at a time when you would normally be silent. It takes practice, it takes acting differently more often, and it is freeing. We will talk about learning how to be more assertive, which is a great communication tool for breaking out of passive, silent, and non-assertive behavior patterns. Responsible assertive behaviors are behaviors that help us express ourselves in ways that respect the other person and ourselves. Our goal becomes valuing ourselves without having to be aggressive, increasing our chance of being heard.

Obviously, workplaces that openly invite people to be themselves and share their ideas freely will be the ones that will thrive in the future. Think how freeing it is to be invited to be courageous.

I was surprised, for example, with how hard it was for me to accept that the early hearing loss I inherited from my mother meant hearing aids at an early age for me. I remember hearing the squeal of hearing aids in older people when I was growing up. I kept thinking, unfairly, that people would judge me as "old" and irrelevant based on the fact that I was wearing hearing aids, plus they would squeal with that high pitched tone, and I would be embarrassed. So, I found myself resisting and delaying. "I will just have to listen harder, learn to read lips better," I thought. Finally, my young daughters, less patient than my wife with my ill-advised delay in getting help, brought me to reality with a blinding flash of the obvious. Elizabeth and Steph were sitting in the back seat of our car, and I was driving on a family trip. After I had said "what?' or "could you repeat that" for the hundredth time and was obviously lost during the telling of a funny story, Elizabeth said, "Dad, you're not hearing us and haven't been hearing us for too long. Get some hearing aids! Don't you want to hear us?" The obvious. I was missing a lot, letting my fear of what others would think drown out the voices of our two delightful daughters. Why did that take so long? For me, it took the courage of my daughter to state the obvious in a direct and caring way. She named it. I heard it. It inspired me to act. She modeled assertive communication with me.

The story of my wrestling with the hearing aid decision was based on a hidden fear of inadequacy and imperfection, both associated with potential shame. Would I think any other person to be "less than" because of early hearing loss? Of course not. It was another remind-er of how powerful feeling vulnerable and "found out" we all are. For me, it was another freeing moment. I had been missing so much of conversations that I truly valued. I would treasure what I learned. But it was still hard. I often think of E. E. Cummings writing, "To be nobody-but-yourself in a world which is doing its best, night and day, to make you everybody but yourself—means to fight the hardest bat-tle which any human being can fight—and never stop fighting." Being me, being you, takes practice and courage.

I would suggest a little adventure if you wanted to speed the process of becoming more authentic as a person or leader: seek out a mentor, counselor, or coach.

Dr. James Downing, CEO at St. Jude and a model leader for think-ing and acting like a leader for Better Normal, talks with enthusi-asm about choosing a coach to help him become a stronger leader. Downing, a researcher by training, thought he needed a coach to be more effective as a leader. He wanted to learn about his strengths and weaknesses. He wanted feedback. He wanted to avoid the trap of mistakes so many people live out when they move into leadership positions. Now, he recommends coaches for all his leaders.

Obviously, great teams play and work for Win-Win outcomes within their team. When writing Real Dream Teams, we talked to leaders of mountain climbing teams, a Medal of Honor military helicopter rescue team pilot, Nobel Prize recipients, national basketball and football national championship coaches like John Wooden, and successful business leaders. Great organizations and teams work for Win-Win-Win outcomes within the organization and with all stakeholders, internal or external. But Win-Win is not an intuitive or knee jerk response as noted. Even with the Covid-19 pandemic, individual states had to compete for basic supplies and equipment, a classic Win-Lose scenario where some won at the expense of others. Even face masks became political, many refusing to wear masks, a classic lose-lose scenario with everyone at greater risk and everyone losing. Whether conscious or unconscious, intentional or unintentional, we see win-lose and lose-lose play out every day with less than optimal, even devastating, and cruel results. To disengage from our knee-jerk competitive culture, leaders must change their mindset intentionally and consciously.

We can't build our team, our home, or our organization when some are winning at the expense of others. As parents with two children, we thought a lot about fairness and house rules that applied to all of us in the family. We worked hard to discern the impact of our behaviors on each other. Simple things like if we wanted our children to pick up their shoes or clothes in the den prior to bedtime, we as parents did the same. Anything left in the living room was placed in a box and could not be worn the next day. I got down to my last pair of shoes quickly! If we expected our children to call if they were running late getting home, we owed them the same respect if we were going to be later than we thought. Why? The worry impact is the same for parents and children.

As I indicated in the last chapter, we had the chance to work with both Nucor Steel and several Kimberly Clark facilities as they were sustaining their "good to great" stock performance during their 15-year period of becoming good to great companies. It was evident to us at the time that the senior teams at Kimberly Clark plants, as well as the Nucor facility with whom we consulted, wanted to fine tune their team and collaborative practices. All their teams wanted to be even more efficient, effective, and focused on their core mission. They clearly wanted to distinguish their brand from the competition and working better collaboratively was one way to do it. Obviously both companies were doing well at the time. The caveat was they wanted to consistently improve the process, be better. So, we particularly worked on identifying any roadblocks or hurdles that kept them from working together even better. Normal was not good.

One of the first Kimberly-Clark senior teams with whom we worked wanted to work together better as a senior team. I wrote about this briefly in a previous chapter. They had never been off-site as a team for training, but off-site would work best for the mission-driven team building process we designed after interviewing each of the team members. They needed to be intentional, and in a place where they could really focus on their team. We were in a lodge and cabins living arrangement for 3 days and 2 nights. It was a great opportunity to get to know each other better. As usual, we interviewed each senior team member individually a couple of weeks prior to the retreat to assess where they saw themselves as a team, strengths and weaknesses. Then, we developed the framework of the retreat to address what they needed most. A greater sense of their interdependence and how each one connected their individual team to the company mission emerged as top items of concern, so we developed a process to accommodate these needs.

Some of the team members were coming in for the retreat from corporate headquarters on the first evening. We decided to have these guys bring their best Wisconsin bratwursts for dinner. Some would do the prep work, some would cook, and some would clean up. It was a team project, and everyone had a role to play. It was a cool opening night activity and quite different for them. Working together on a fun, shared, interdependent common mission set the tone nicely for the following two days. In the next days, they clarified their common work mission and what it meant to each of them, built a deeper trust level, were able to talk about what strengths they appreciated about each person on the team, and identified what they needed from each other to be even more successful. They used the role-clarification exercise in the bibliography to be specific about the requests each had of the other. The helpful and revealing questions were, "What can I do to help you be more successful in your role?" and "What specifically do you need more of or less of from me, and what am I doing that you want me to continue doing?" Before the retreat ended, they dug into the win-win concept and committed to the specifics of how they would be accountable with new win-win agreements going forward. They had defined what winning or success would be for them. They were already savvy young pros. They wanted to keep winning team championships.

> **People who have power and control and win at the expense of others rarely change their behavior without significant new information and a desire to change.**

People who lose at the expense of others are always the ones who feel the pain, hurt and disappointment. It is difficult for winners to want to change the system when they are winning. If you don't see the negative impact winning has on those not winning, behavior doesn't change. So, if there are even unintended win-lose situations existing, they are roadblocks. Identify them and help those who feel they are losing express the negative impact it has on their performance. Help those who are winning listen and understand. Most who listen closely to the stories of those who lose will be shocked at what they hear and be willing to alter their behavior.

Even with new information, the financial, political, or psychological payoff is so huge for those who win that the counter-productive behavior often continues. The key to getting past the destructive impact of Win-Lose behavior is this:

1. The person who is winning at the expense of others must be willing to seek feedback on the behavior pattern and learn from those negatively affected,

2. Those who are losing and negatively impacted must be willing to help the winner understand the negative impact, and

3. After sharing information with each other, the former winners and losers must be willing to seek a solution that is acceptable to both parties. In organizations, teams, and family with a common mission, often the person who is winning at the expense of others is unaware of the negative impact of the behavior. The ideal scenario, with mutual desire to reach the same mission or goal, is that both parties see the opportunity to remove a roadblock in the relationship or system and believe that both can win with a new behavioral agreement. In other words, both learn how changing can be beneficial and both want to change.

Worst case scenario. What to do with people in leadership positions that don't change their toxic behavior?

People who have a toxic impact on others must be confronted. Do it with respect and be honest about the specific counterproductive behaviors. Often toxic people stay toxic or obnoxious because no one wants to confront them. No one wants the wrath and anger of a toxic person. They are not pleasant people to confront. So, confront with respect. They must see the consequences of their actions and given a reasonable amount of time to change. The people negatively impacted by the behavior must see change. That is part of the confrontation with the toxic person. The toxic person must own the toxic behaviors and understand that developing new relationships with those colleagues who have suffered is part of the deal. Ideally, a mentor or coach would be assigned to work with the leader struggling to change on a weekly basis. Very bright and talented people often lack emotional intelligence and simply are not aware how their behavior affects other people. Most people can learn to be more emotionally intelligent and more aware. The key is this: does the person want to change and learn? If not, this person may not be right for this position or this place of work. Regardless of the individual talent, toxic people cannot continue to be toxic. Only two people I have worked with in the past were unwilling to change when confronted. One person self-selected out, as most people do, who are not a good fit. The other person was fired. Yes, these are difficult and hard conversations. A mini-malignant normality is created when toxicity is permitted or perceived to be ignored. The goal is to make a "work divorce" a healthy separation where all learn. Remember the initial invitation that leaders for a better normal offer to those that are colleagues? "You are invited into a culture where we want you and those around you to be engaged, inspired, and successful." Most people love an inspiring and collaborative work environment.

COMMUNICATION: BEING SEEN AND HEARD

When I worked as a psychologist with couples to repair or heal a crumbling relationship, the most common issue was lack of understanding and poor communication. "He doesn't understand me," "she doesn't listen to me," or "we're angry with each other all the time." In organizational settings I would hear "you guys don't have a clue what we're thinking" and "why don't you check with the people who actually use the computers every day before buying a new computer system?" "How can I feel a part of the team and do my best when no one ever asks me what I think?"

Developing a collaborative mindset and thinking and acting within the win-win framework is all about learning to communicate differently. Communication issues have long been at the top of the "biggest problem" list for couples and organizations. We all want to be heard, respected, and understood.

The two most critical people skills that lead to Win-Win thinking and acting are active listening and responsible assertiveness. Both yield new information. When leaders listen, they discover information they could not get otherwise. When leaders or team members responsibly assert their thoughts and ideas, new information is gained. Leaders will inspire others when they listen because they show they care about what others think and they need the unique perspective of everyone. Leaders inspire others when they are open and honest about their expectations.

The Johari Window of Awareness is a helpful way to conceptualize the basic issue of shared information. The Johari Window has been around a long time and is still hard to beat as a straight-forward way to visualize the communication process. It is easy for people to discuss and understand how they can improve the communication with specific people on their team. When I first used this model years ago, I thought "Johari" must have some mysterious symbolism associated with the term. Then I discovered the two men who produced the model were named Joe and Harry. Pretty disappointing, but the model no less helpful. Below, you see four arenas or windows:

1. **Open** arena where people are feely sharing information. This is transparency. This is the home of psychological safety, where it is safe to be vulnerable.

2. **Façade** arena where you have information you have not shared with others, so others are unaware of the information you have. Home of vulnerabilities. You can make choices about what to share with others.

3. **Blind Spot** arena where others know and see things you don't know or see. You are unaware of their information (much like your blind spot when you are unaware of a car right beside you and you cannot see it in your sideview mirror or rear-view mirror). Others can make choices about what to share with you.

4. **Unknown** arena. The home of discretionary energy and unrealized human potential that no one knows about. This is available information in a psychologically safe environment. Any person, organization or family that wants to be healthy and authentic is working to expand the open arena and reduce the underutilized potential arena. Leaders will want to learn how to get good feedback from others and give good feedback to others. With innovation, entrepreneurial thinking, self-actualization, and best thinking so critical to authentic living and eloquent solutions, inspiring leaders will always want to tap into the underutilized human potential window and expand the open arena. The leadership goal: Expand your Open and Public arena, reduce your Façade arena by sharing more information with others (Responsible Assertiveness), reduce your Blind Spot arena by seeking more information from others (Active Listening), and reduce the Unused Human Potential arena by learning more about leadership, vulnerability, psychological safety, and inspiring others. Then, you want the same for the people you lead, creating an environment that maximizes the sharing of information, and fostering a culture of inspiration.

	Known to self	Not known to self
Known to Others	Open area or Arena	Blind spot
Not known to Others	Hidden area or façade	Unknown

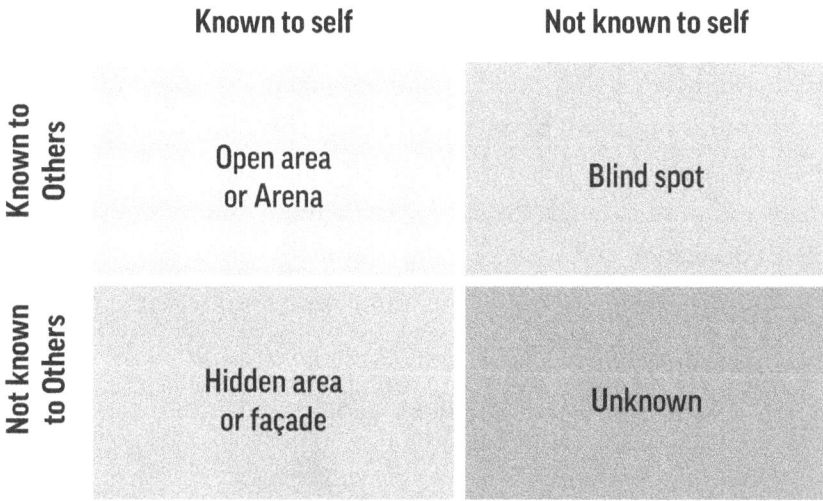

THE JOHARI WINDOW MODEL

Expanding the open arena in a personal relationship or a business environment does not happen accidentally. You know how difficult it is to talk about situations or issues that you and your partner have avoided, sometimes for years. At the same time, inappropriate, hurtful behavior is often a blind spot for people. It is not uncommon for one partner in a relationship to be totally surprised to discover how painful a behavior has been to their partner. I have often seen tears flow from marriage partners and business partners when learning about how they were perceived. "I had no idea. I never knew you felt that way. I am so sorry."

I am always shocked when touring movie or television studio sets to discover the difference between the "set" and what I perceived when I watched the movie or television show. The "set" is a believable façade that looks so real when viewed on the TV or movie screen. We know people use façades to protect themselves psychologically. It is like an armor we have learned to use to protect when we feel threatened, frightened, or anxious. A façade is protective, but it is also stressful and can be very counterproductive in personal and business relationships. Bottom line. If most people see only our façade, they come to believe only what they see. Perception is reality! We want to maximize courage to move beyond the facade. Therefore, a huge piece of your role as leader is helping create psychological safety for people to share and push through the self-imposed and culture-imposed armor of self-protection and sense of vulnerability.

ACTIVE LISTENING

Active listening is the most potent people skill to build trust and inspire others to want to be and do their best. Listening is an engaging process, inviting the person you are listening to, to tell you more. Listening is the ability to fully focus on another person and convey accurately back to the person what they are feeling and thinking, to the other person's satisfaction. Notice that it is not agreeing or disagreeing from your own frame of reference. You are focusing totally on the other person's feelings and the content behind the feelings. I found active listening to be the toughest communication skill to teach to graduate students working to become counselors or psychologists, believe it or not. And listening is the essential core communication skill for relationships, for developing emotional intelligence, and conveying to another person that you understand how they are thinking and feeling. For example, I never recall an angry person feeling better or less angry with someone by telling the angry person all the reasons they should not feel angry. Conflicts are reduced or resolved when we understand the depth of the feeling and why we are feeling the way we do. Listening calms and deescalates the situation. Perceived understanding must be there. Remember the learning sequence discussed earlier: increased awareness leads to increased understanding and increased understanding leads to new actions and behaviors. Active listening and empathy encourage a person to hear themselves, become more aware, and understand themselves. Once the new insights emerge, meaningful action can occur.

In a 2016 article I wrote for the Nashville Tennessean, *"Big Dreams, Bold Leadership, and Collaboration."* I suggested that Nashville became a magic place to live, work, and play primarily because of a coalition of community leaders committed to long-term vision, urgency about solutions, and willingness to collaborate. The CEOs of the Nashville Chamber of Commerce, Ralph Schulz, and Convention Visitors Bureau, Butch Spyridon, the mayors, Phil Bredesen, Bill Purcell, and Karl Dean, and one of the top city leadership programs in the country, Leadership Nashville, worked hand in hand for over 15 years, building a strong coalition of community leaders supporting Partnership 2020 in Nashville. At the community level, it was as close as it gets to regional Win-Win thinking and acting; seeking solutions to complex infrastructure, educational, housing, safety, and transportation opportunities. Over 250 top leaders from every sector of the region were and are engaged in an on-going process of collaboration. During this time span, I mentioned earlier that Belmont hosted the first-ever Presidential Debate. The 2008 Town Hall Presidential Debate became a model for university, city, and state leaders working together on a major undertaking that was mutually beneficial.

Carl Rogers, a psychologist and writer, had a profound impact on my thinking about relationships and human behavior. His contribution was the strong belief that all of us humans need to experience unconditional acceptance from at least one person in order to grow and thrive. The unconditional acceptance vehicle came through Active Listening and being "empathic with another person. Empathy is the ability to convey to the other person that you have heard them. You hear their feeling. You are not agreeing. You are not judging. You are showing you listened. Are they angry, sad, happy, confused, scared, or conflicted? How intense is their anger, sadness, or conflict? The closer you get to the intensity of their feeling, the more you "get it." Feelings are nuanced and complex. How a person feels and being able to convey back to the person accurately their feeling is the heart of empathy.

Helen Riess, M.D., writes about the power of empathy in her recent book, *The Empathy Effect.* She discusses the neural or "hardwired" substance of Empathic Leadership and says that "neurobiology seems to predispose us to a preference for leaders who above all else express empathy and compassion. These have a clearly positive effect on neurological functioning, psychological well-being, physical health, and personal relationships. Richard Boyatzis, professor at Case Western Reserve's Weatherhead School of Management, emphasizes that 'lack of empathic concern in organizations results in multiple disasters, including losing touch with the hearts and minds of your staff, your customers, your suppliers, and community. It goes hand and hand with lack of moral concern.'" Riess significantly notes that "true leadership----whether you command a country, an army, or an organization---hinges entirely on the success and well-being of the entire group." Imagine what would happen if every leader at every level of the organization were taught this learnable gift of empathy. Can you imagine the impact on your leadership as a long-time leader or as someone on the journey to become a leader?

Let's listen in on a conversation shared by someone I was coaching at the time. Melvin was one of the top performers in his organization and the leader of a small team working on an important, time-sensitive project. Susan, the leader of Melvin's division, became concerned when Melvin missed some key deadlines and a couple of Melvin's team members expressed concern about his distracted behavior. "He's just not himself." Susan asked to talk with Melvin. Instead of giving him grief about the blown deadlines, she led with wanting to understand what was happening from Melvin's perspective. Listen in on the conversation.

Susan. "Hey Melvin. I have been concerned about the project timeline. Seems there have been some delays. And a couple of your colleagues have said that you seem distracted lately. I just wanted to check in with you to see if something were going on that I could help with."

Melvin. Tears welling up, "I'm sorry. I thought I could handle this without bothering anyone. My wife, Jessica, you met at our Christmas party, was diagnosed 4 weeks ago with stage four breast cancer and it, well, has just turned our world upside down."

Susan. "Oh my gosh, Melvin. I can imagine how scared you must be feeling."

Melvin. "I am. That's all I can think about. This was just so unexpected. She had had regular checkups. We were shocked and scared. I feel bad that I'm behind at work, but it has been hard to think about anything else. I know I'm letting you and the team down."

Susan. "You're worried that you are going to disappoint us?"

Melvin. "Of course. This isn't like me. Jessica and I are doing all the right things and our options are hopeful. It has just been tough."

Susan. "Tell me more about what you all are facing. I know it has been overwhelming. I want to know."

This was the start of the conversation between two leaders in the same company. I can tell you that Melvin was greatly relieved. "It's like a weight being lifted off my shoulders." I can also tell you that when Melvin's immediate project team heard his story, which he shared with them after talking with Susan, the team immediately pitched in to get the project back on track. They also asked about Jessica on a regular basis and made the leap from colleagues to fellow human beings.

When we look in on this conversation through the lens of the Johari Window, we see the power of good communication. 1) Susan opening the conversation with an invitation rather than judgement, 2) Melvin dropping his façade that had been up for 4 weeks and sharing hidden information, 3) Empathy from Susan as she gets new information and which encourages more information from Melvin, 4) Melvin's relief and willingness to be vulnerable and assert himself by sharing with his teammates, 5) Greater openness with more transparency resulting in positive human interactions and sensitivity to Melvin from his teammates, 6) With more information, willing teammates picked up the slack on the delayed project. Win-win outcomes. Call this a short-term win in team communication. It is self-reinforcing and increases the likelihood of occurring again.

In fact, one of the discoveries that came from Google's multi-year research into high performing teams is illustrated in the example above. Susan created a "psychologically safe" environment for Melvin to talk about something very personal. Melvin in turn shared his story with his team, demonstrating to his team that he can have these personally relevant, hard conversations. The atmosphere shifted with Melvin's team. The impact was a new understanding, a new humanness, appropriate sharing of personal information, and a new desire to help each other. The team's performance improved. It was okay to ask for help. As one team member said, "We can't do this with a lot of talented individuals working independently. We need each other."

Rogers believed experiencing unconditional acceptance freed an individual to make good choices and live more fully. In daily relationships as leaders, this translates into active, non-judgmental listening, walking a mile in the shoes of a colleague, teammate, or partner. We all need to "be felt," as Mark Goulston writes in his excellent book on listening, *"Just Listen"*. How powerful is empathy and listening? As Goulston has discovered, when someone gets "you," perhaps for the first time, and conveys understanding of your feeling and why you feel as you do, the relationship can change instantly. Recall, this is the environment that Gore and Company deliberately designed years ago, a culture where scary personal matters didn't have to be left at the door when you came to work. People care about people with whom they work. When people "have your back" and convey they care, relationships can indeed shift immediately.

ACTIVE LISTENING BENEFITS

Medal of Honor Dust-Off rescue helicopter-pilot and commander of a medical evacuation unit during two tours of duty in Vietnam, Major General Patrick Henry Brady shared this stark comment during our interview with him. "The leader better be listening or he's dead." "People have to be able to give you feedback at any moment. If somebody sees something on the instrument panel that I'd overlooked or if I had been blinded by a flare or something, or don't see an obstacle of some kind, it is understood that they say, 'Stop!'" This is the kind of urgency about process, relationships, teamwork, and how we work together that makes sense for any leader and any team anywhere.

ACTIVE LISTENING IS A PROCESS FOR:

- Getting new information
- Correcting old misinformation
- Removing blind spots
- Creating deeper understanding and learning
- Avoiding mistakes
- Showing respect
- Making better decisions
- Building trust
- Developing positive expectations for future listening
- Getting others to want to listen to you
- Creating a more positive connection with an individual or team
- Demonstrating **empathy**: showing you care, just being with someone at a difficult time, unconditional acceptance.

A second people skill and relationship builder is responsible assertiveness, the courage to express one's own thoughts, feelings, and opinions and sharing new information with others in a responsible manner.

RESPONSIBLE ASSERTIVENESS BENEFITS

Five F-16 jets are in tight formation as they begin one of their many difficult aerial maneuvers at speeds approaching 500 m.p.h. Excellence and survival depend on listening and assertive sharing of information. The wingtips are as close as 18" at times. No room for error. The arena of open communication is wide open, and no maneuver begun until every piece of information is checked off and verified. Open organizations thrive on "top guns" who specialize in shared information: listening and asserting, listening and asserting. Leaders invite feedback and speaking up. "Yes people," silence, and compliance do not add value.

Responsible Assertiveness is a communication process for:

- Talking directly and honestly.
- Being courageous in spite of feeling vulnerable.
- Being clear about expectations: what you think, want, believe, and feel.
- Sharing important information with others.
- Increasing understanding and getting results.
- Communication without being abrasive or demeaning.
- Building trust.
- Showing respect.
- Making better decisions.
- Assuring that organizational, divisional, and individual goals are communicated accurately.

Responsible Assertive communication should be distinguished from Non-Assertive communication, which is more passive, indirect, and unclear. It should also be distinguished from Aggressive communication, which is disrespectful, hurtful, and offensive. Intentionally sharing misinformation, for example, is toxic and dangerous.

CONFLICT RESOLUTION IS A PROCESS FOR:

- Using the information gained from active listening and responsible assertiveness in a helpful manner.
- Committing to act on the blind spots and hidden information that has been discovered.
- Removing identified roadblocks and obstacles.
- Building a healthier relationship.
- Making decisions based on good information.
- Getting to win-win outcomes.

Think of any good relationship and the Johari Window of Awareness. The open arena is the psychological safe place where at our best we are listening to others and asserting ourselves. With another person, there are two big containers of information and the only way to tap both of these data and information sources is to listen and assert. When we live together or work together toward a shared vision or common mission, there is just no way to get a best outcome without this amazing process of sharing information. It I need you. You need me. We both have much to offer. It may be a procedure for a shift change in any plant, removing barriers to implement a strategic plan, or listening to real customers share their experience with your product or process. When differences, conflicts, or need for more information result from what we discover, as they predictably will, we keep sharing information till we reach a mutually agreed upon solution. If you have a coach or mutually trusted colleague available, ask for their input. The key: *don't settle*. Unresolved conflict becomes a roadblock and a waste of energy.

LEADERS FOR A BETTER NORMAL ARE THE "HOPE GIVERS" IN THE CULTURE WARS ERA

As we seek to change the leadership narrative and see the need for people to collaborate, our hope rests with other leaders for a better normal. Better normal leaders will create a culture of inspiration where it is psychologically safe to actively listen, express thoughts and ideas honestly, be vulnerable, learn from each other, have hard conversations, and work toward win-win outcomes. Corporate leaders, ministers, priests, rabbis, "common good" political leaders, and business leaders of all stripes everywhere are called to be the compassionate ones, the listeners, the gatherers of good information, and the ones who create a process for solving conflicts and reaching solutions that help people in the arena where they lead and have influence. The benefits of leaders being the hope givers and seekers of win-win solutions are multiple and life-changing.

THE BENEFITS OF CONFLICT RESOLUTION

Conflict resolution and eloquent solutions come from listening to others, learning, and sharing information. Better normal organizations currently and in the future are and will be learning organizations. People in open organizations, like firemen and firewomen, run toward the problem, not away from it. The sooner conflicts and hard conversations occur, the sooner energy can be spent on resolution and solutions. The longer there are unresolved conflicts and unacknowledged issues the more people will live below their potential. Unresolved and unacknowledged issues are a huge energy drain and take time away from the mission and strategic priorities. Other benefits of conflict resolution and solution seeking:

- People build trust and gain confidence in themselves and others.
- People learn from new information and become more innovative and creative.
- The psychological safety that comes with open communication creates more short-term wins and momentum. The flywheel turns faster.
- Active listening and responsible assertiveness build emotional intelligence and compassion for others.
- People feel a stronger bond with each other, are more hopeful.
- Win-win outcomes increase significantly.

One of the most helpful tools for increasing awareness and understanding and agreements to new actions in the relationship is a simple exercise called "role clarification" which I mentioned earlier. I used this exercise with couples in counseling and role clarification was an integral part of every vision-oriented team-building process. It could easily be called a "what we would like from each other" discussion or a "process clarification" conversation related to any conflict, roadblock, misunderstanding, or new opportunity to work together differently. The worksheet with specific instructions on how to use the worksheet is provided in the bibliography as Exhibits A and B. We have used this exercise successfully with thousands of workshop participants to enhance working relationships with co-workers. It is the most stress-free and psychologically safe tool we have found to improve working and living relationships. It gives permission to be vulnerable and share with another person 3 things they could specifically do that would help you work more productively with them. The activity calls for each person to be assertive, actively listen, and then negotiate an agreement to resolve a conflict and/or act differently in the relationship going forward. This is a Johari Window moment, moving information from the unknown into the open arena!

A similar process is emerging that already has a great track record of reducing the raging public acrimony and mutual contempt after

2020, called "authentic dialogue." According to Pew Research Center, the divisiveness in this country is so great that people in both political parties abhor people in the other party, so much so that people often feel they have lost their existing relationship with family, friends, and co-workers. Authentic dialogue joins role clarification as one of the few communication tools available to stop the bleeding. And the future of our organizations, families, and friendships depends on how we deal with the bitter political, religious, cultural, and racial divides. Having a louder voice, more power, more control, and winning at the expense of others will only make matters worse.

My wife and I are wired differently. Our differences and the various roles we like to play make us stronger as a team. After we married in Memphis, we came back to live in the little house I had been living in for a few months with my new job in Chattanooga. The first time Rubye Lynn went to the mailbox, she discovered my bank statement. Not good news. She learned I had written two checks with insufficient funds. From that moment on, we made one of our first wise decisions. Rubye Lynn would oversee our finances. She clearly was our detail person. Play to your strengths, right? Incidentally, my financial skills or lack of I blame on my mother. After her death a few years ago, I found her last checkbook. The last note she entered in the "Total" column were these two words, "Not enough."

Another discovery about my relationship with Rubye Lynn would not come as quickly. It took a while for us to learn, but we finally had an epiphany about what energized each of us. It was a big awakening. The trigger for talking about this came after a large party we attended. When we got home after mid-night, I was ready to fix breakfast and talk about what a fun party it was. I was pumped. Rubye Lynn shared that the party was ok, and she was exhausted. And besides that, "After you got me a glass of wine when we first got there, I never saw you again till it was time to come home. You disappeared! What's that about?" We came back the next day to talk about our different views about large parties or gatherings. A tipping point for a broader conversation had occurred because Rubye Lynn had the courage to be honest with me about the impact of being with a lot of people and how my behavior impacted her.

I am energized by people and Rubye Lynn is exhausted by too many people. She is great with people, but it requires more emotional energy. She prefers small social events with 2-4 couples. She has more friends. I have more acquaintances. Finally talking about the impact of our social styles and preferences, triggered by one event, was a huge awakening in our relationship. It clearly was a Win-Win for us. And, neither of us was right nor wrong. We are just different, wired differently. And the more we understood those differences, the better we were.

Think of the people you work with. Isn't it tremendous they are all not like you? If all were like you, a lot of great work would not get done. Our work teams require a lot of conversations about how we like to work, how we are different. The first-ever person I hired to do a lot of detailed work in my office had a personality style similar to mine. I learned quickly that I did not want someone like me to do the details as error-ridden letters and brochures emerged as a result. From a leadership standpoint, the quicker you can learn your strengths the better. The quicker you can learn the strengths of those around you the better. And there are lots of options for learning about your preferences and strengths: Myers-Briggs, Social Styles, Strength Finder, Enneagrams, and other self-assessments as well as 360-degree assessments from your colleagues. The highly effective "Dream Teams" we wrote about always maximized the talents and strengths of each person on the team. Each role was important. We will talk more about connecting each person's role to the compelling vision in the next chapter.

I also want to reinforce how much stronger relationships become when there is a common goal that requires you and your team to work together to successfully accomplish it. For marriage partners, there are lots of common goals that emerge through the years. For Rubye Lynn and me, one of the most fun and bonding adventures that we enjoyed for years was playing mixed doubles together. We kicked into high gear in the beginning of this partnership by going to a tennis weekend for couples at Vic Braden's Tennis College in southern California. We went with another couple; our good friends Charlotte and Charles Nabholz and it was especially fun because of the shared experience and because "the" Vic Braden made it fun. The instructors built the learning around positive reinforcement, encouraging progress, improvement, and having fun. Rewarding progress toward goals and key initiatives is a great tool for any leader or parent or friend. A whole chapter is coming up on "seeing" and recognizing your colleagues when they make a difference.

This fit perfectly with the deal Rubye Lynn and I had made earlier. She had made me promise, when she agreed to try tennis, that the only way this would work would be on one condition. She made me promise that I would never criticize her, only encourage her. She said, "You know I will always do my best and that criticism or being frustrated with me will never help me. Positive feedback will, but no criticism, or putdowns." I knew already that most married couples had big trouble playing together, primarily because the men dominated the court and criticized their partner. Sound familiar? At any rate, I made the promise and kept it, and we turned out to be a pretty darn good mixed doubles team. My only feedback early on was this. "It would be helpful if you don't hold your breath till the point is over. Breathe, okay?" She had never played tennis before and was really working hard to get it right! We did laugh often about breathing and relaxing in the beginning of this new tennis relationship. Most of all, we had fun and for years had a consistently positive "together" time playing tennis. So, whether its doubles tennis with your partner or common work goals and missions with colleagues, collaborating on common tasks can be great fun and highly rewarding. It spills over into the total relationship. Collaboration is also the only way to be successful with a mutually shared objective.

Active listening and responsible assertiveness, when communicating with those we live and work with, is essential for Win-Win collaboration, simply because leaders have to understand how to work differently with different people. You cannot get to Win-Win and a collaborative mindset without active listening and the courage to be assertive, as Rubye Lynn was assertive with me in the tennis promise. The open window of the Johari window enlarges with the information gained from both these people skills. Then, and only then, is it possible to more easily work out and negotiate any roadblocks that exist. The role clarification process I invite you to use at the end of this chapter is the most useful tool I have found to allow productive active listening, responsible assertiveness, conflict resolution, and creation of new agreements with people who live or work together. It is a part of your invitation when you hire people to work with you. You are sharing your commitment to create a culture of inspiration where each person will be heard and valued, and each person will make a difference.

Earlier, in the first part of the book, I described our work with the US Department of Transportation when the Coast Guard was still a part of DOT. We were into our 4th year of working with the Department to help create Secretary of Transportation Rodney Slater's vision of ONE DOT, a broad-based initiative for collaborative thinking and acting designed for the different modes of transportation to be strategic and intentional about multi-modal solutions.

Admiral James Loy was Commandant of the United States Coast Guard when the JFK, Jr. plane tragedy occurred on July 19, 1999. We asked Admiral Loy soon afterwards for his description of the process leading up to that fateful evening and how so many agencies worked successfully together throughout the ordeal. Here is his story.

WORKING BETTER TOGETHER

"The motto for our change initiative was "Working Better Together." It was designed to unite all agencies of the United States Department of Transportation to work together more effectively. Prior efforts to unite the Department had failed or had dwindled out when newly elected government officials took office. However, we felt that this time around, things would be different because we had a united, committed group behind it. We had a Secretary of Transportation who was passionate about the vision and a strategy that was judged "Best in Government" by Congress. We had a strong communication program to keep people informed of our progress."

Admiral Loy continues, "We were making some progress. We in the U.S. Coast Guard had redefined our rescue strategies. Instead of working independently and calling on other agencies when needed to aide us in a rescue mission, we created a systematic approach that included the necessary people, resources, and skills across various Department of Transportation agencies as well as military branches. For instance, we planned on working with the National Oceanographic and Atmospheric Administration for their expertise in sonar to track fallen planes and sunken ships at the bottom of the ocean, the Federal Aviation Administration for their expertise in radar to track missing aircrafts, and Navy and Air Force for helicopters, planes, and ships for search and rescue missions. Instead of just depending on team play from within the Coast Guard, we were now going to depend on inter-agency team play to make rescue missions as successful as possible. We made progress on this, and were pleased, but there were still plenty of disbelievers and resistors. The 2000 election was just around the corner, and I could tell that people were expecting the new administration to come in with their own agendas and priorities, and there goes "Working Better Together." People were less enthusiastic and energetic about continuing the change initiative because they thought the new administration would wipe away the effort.

Then on July 20 I got a call from the district commander at 2:30 in the morning. I lifted the phone to hear, "JFK Jr.'s plane is missing. We think it might have gone down off the coast of Long Island. His wife and sister-in-law were in the plane with him. Let's get a move on."

The rescue effort was launched immediately. Over 300 people from various agencies and military branches were immediately involved in the search mission. We instantly gained assistance from the Federal Aviation Administration (FAA), the National Transportation Safety Board, the Navy, The National Oceanographic and Atmospheric Administration (NOAA), the Air Force, the Air National Guard and various other agencies. We worked with the FAA and NOAA to locate the exact point of entry where the aircraft hit the water, and we did so in a matter of hours. We worked with the Air National Guard, the Air Force and the Navy to get equipment, helicopters, and search boats to the area quickly and efficiently. We worked with the White House to keep the families intimately informed and to deal with the persistent media frenzy. Instead of fighting about who was in charge, we exchanged information so people could do their jobs. We had multiple meetings every day to keep all parties informed and made consensus judgments, so everybody knew their role to contribute to the whole. I had a systematic set of teleconference briefings, four times a day, throughout the entire length of the ordeal with members of other agencies. We all had never worked so closely together, but with our collaborative efforts, the meetings went as smooth as glass. It was collective cooperation at its best.

After two days of intensive searching and no sign of survivors, we had to transition the search and rescue mission into a search and salvage mission. Again, we worked closely with the various agencies to deal with the situation quickly, effectively, and extreme sensitivity to the families involved. We were able to cut through all the red tape that existed in the past and quickly get equipment to the scene without arguing about from whose budget this will come.

The media was everywhere. The entire nation was glued to their seats in anticipation of what was going to happen next.

When the plane was found at the bottom, the White House made it very clear that this information was NOT to get out until the families had been advised. With such a huge operation encompassing so many different agencies, and with an aggressive media hounding us for breaking news, someone could have unknowingly slipped the information to the media. However, with the new collaborative change initiative and the structural nature of our teamwork, we all knew about and complied with the order.

At the end of the mission, in a press conference, Senator Kennedy emotionally acknowledged the effort, "We also thank in a very special way the men and women who have worked so well and long and hard in these past days to find John, Carolyn and Lauren. We will never forget the dedication, the professionalism and the sensitivity they have shown." That touched all of us deeply. Our success in handling this tragedy gave our whole effort to operate in a new way a gigantic boost. This was not talk; it was action, and action that was visible to everyone. We could do it. It was not just another 'good' idea, but something that could make a difference to real people, and to our nation."

The JFK, Jr. story and the massive effort to save the three people involved, reminds us of the massive efforts of healthcare workers during Covid-19 to save lives and reduce the pain of the disease for thousands of families across the country. When the mission and vision are calling our best, it is inspiring. It becomes a driving force for heroic efforts even when the outcomes are sometimes immensely sad.

THE MORAL IMPERATIVE, URGENCY, AND COLLABORATION

These first three inspiring leadership practices form the moral imperative of "how" we will work together to inspire the best in others.

- The Ethical Heart with its three chambers of character, courage, and compassion.
- A Sense of Urgency about strategic direction and your people.
- The Collaborative Mindset: Win-Win thinking and acting.

With these three "how" leadership practices in place, the other four practices gain new strength. You have built relationships and trust.

As you move toward becoming an inspiring leader, the first measuring stick is how equipped you believe you are and have been with these foundational practices of "how we will work together." Do the people you lead appreciate and understand the kind of environment you want to create to help make them successful?

A word about why these first three foundational leadership practices are the "hard" ones. These are the people skills, the heart of leadership. As I have said before and as others who write about leadership have said, if we don't get this right, we fail. These practices have become even more important now that we have connected the dots to find that only people who are inspired sustain best individual and collective efforts. They have become more important since we have discovered that psychological safety is the number one dynamic for the highest performing teams, allowing team members to be more vulnerable, open, and willing to tap into their discretionary energy and full potential.

On top of this, the powerful revealing forces of 2020 slammed us with a new awareness of our shared humanity and the need for all leaders to inspire the best in others with a new sensitivity to systemic inequities. More is required of leaders going forward. We can't engineer emotion, compassion, and vulnerability out of our people systems. We don't want to. In fact, we can capitalize and leverage what we know about emotion, compassion, and vulnerability and tap into the discretionary energy available in us all. Think about this. Did you learn how to do this in undergrad or grad school? No. But it is learnable as are all the non-negotiable leadership practices that inspire.

SUMMARY

Win-lose and lose-lose patterns of behaving at work, home, education, and politics are unsustainable. This is why the leadership practice of The Collaborative Mindset is non-negotiable for better normal leadership and a better normal world. This is a practice for the common good, a better democracy, better home, and better work environment. Most all of us don't like being on the losing end of policies that discriminate. We don't like being marginalized. When we dig into the systemic inequities, we can understand why "we've come a long way" seems hollow. Leaders can address the systems and practices driven by inequity now. They can call inequities and unfair practices by their names. They can challenge the normal, just as W. L. Gore & Associates, Kimberly-Clark, Nucor, Belmont, St. Jude, WD 40, and others have done over the past few years. Being intentional about a win-win, collaborative mind set is motivating and inspiring, and we know how to create and live this practice. Active listening, courageous assertiveness, and resolving conflicts for the common good help create the collaborative magic in relationships.

BEING INTENTIONAL ABOUT THE NON-NEGOTIABLE LEADERSHIP PRACTICE OF THE COLLABORATIVE MINDSET

1. I refer you to the bibliography and the Role Clarification Worksheet with instructions (Exhibit A and B). I invite you to use this with a colleague in the next day or two. As I mentioned earlier, we have used this exercise with hundreds of couples and team partners. We saw this simple intentional exercise reap huge dividends in hundreds of organizations small and large. I experienced couples and families learning to listen to each other more and learn healthier communication. After you use the worksheet a few times and write your requests of your partner, teammate, direct report, or leader, the process will become natural and comfortable for you. You can easily initiate the conversation with a simple, "let's talk about our frustration in switching from a stockholder-based organization to a stakeholder-based organization and see what we need from each other to get this right." Or "Our Meyers-Briggs profiles are really different.

Let's talk about what we need from each other based on our style preferences and see what we learn that helps us work better together?" This simple communication tool, used as suggested or tweaked in any form that works for you, will save you and your colleagues or you and your family lots of heartache. When this happens in real time, it is mutually inspiring and hope-giving. "We can actually talk about the hard topics," is a powerful thing to discover.

2. I recommend for any couple the CliftonStrength Finder assessment which can be found in the book *Living Your Strengths*. You will discover your top five talent themes. In addition, this is a valuable tool for any group of people whose work is interdependent, which is true for most organizational teams. For teams that work together every day, I suggest posting your Meyers-Briggs results or your Enneagram number outside your office or prominently inside to invite conversation with teammates. Of course, if you do this, make sure each person is trained on how to best use the results to initiate productive conversations with others.

3. I also suggest reading Michelle Obama's personal story of "*Becoming.*" It is a beautiful account of one woman's journey to be authentic, strong, and make a difference with her life. We are all in the process of becoming.

A Compelling
Shared Vision
Is The Powerful
Magnet
That Draws People
To The Future

CHAPTER SEVEN

SHARED VISION: CREATE YOUR OWN FUTURE OR SOMEONE ELSE WILL

"All human beings should try to learn before they die what they are running from, and to, and why."

— JAMES THURBER

I f you have a strategic plan and it is collecting one particle of dust on any leader's bookshelf, you should be worried, very worried. If you have a strategic plan that was created before 2020, you should be worried. This was a chaotic, fast moving, rapidly changing world prior to 2020. Now, there is greater urgency for our new world and rethinking leadership and what it means to be a leader. Organizations must also rethink their strategic plan. We have considered the first three non-negotiable practices of leaders that inspire and create a culture of inspiration. Now we move to four additional inspiring practices that answer the why, what, when, and where of leadership, starting with the powerful and compelling "why" we do what we do.

SENSE OF DIRECTION: THE POWER OF EVERYONE INSPIRED BY SHARED ASPIRATIONS

Envision Charlie Brown and Lucy together. Lucy has her "Psychiatrist is in" sign proudly displayed and is giving advice to Charlie Brown. "Charlie Brown, on a cruise ship, some people have their deck chairs facing toward the front of the ship so they can see where they are going. Others have their deck chair faced to the back of the ship so they can see where they have been. Charlie Brown, on the great cruise ship of life, which way is your deck chair facing?" Charlie Brown's puzzled response, "Heck, I can't even get my deck chair unfolded." Ah, don't we feel like Charlie Brown at times. Knowing where we are going and being able to see where we are going is non-negotiable for people and organizations.

Sense of direction is inspiring and a powerful motivator. Leaders who have children can appreciate constant questions about "where are we going?" and "are we there yet?" Can you imagine working hard to get the right people on your organizational bus and then not knowing where to drive the bus? This chapter, and the next one, discuss the essence of what comes from strategic thinking and acting. Good strategic plans start with "where we want to go." It is called vision and it becomes "true north" or the north star for an organization. Most organizations spend some time thinking and walking through the process of planning for the future. However, only a few align their daily actions and priorities with the plan. Here's the problem, particularly in the new world with new information and a new sense of urgency.

Whatever your current vision, mission, and strategic priorities are, if they are pre-2020, you are missing critical information about the reality of the post-pandemic world. If you ignore the reality of 2020 and beyond, spend your energy only on "getting back to normal", it will be catastrophic.

You will appear to your colleagues as out of touch, naïve, or uncaring. Their perception would be right. The new world is calling you and your peers to be better. Leaders must help people dream bigger. If you do choose to ignore 2020, you are missing thinking deeply about your moral compass. You are missing struggling together with a new perspective on the process for how you and those you work with, teach with, and live with can inspire the best of each other and your larger community. You are also missing creating a powerful new vision that goes beyond returning to normal. You simply are missing out on the greatest opportunity of a lifetime to make a difference and do something that will impact your world in a most positive way.

Think about this.

> **The ultimate test of your success as an inspiring leader will be asking those who work with you to be able to articulate their role in helping move toward the new future vision you have mutually created. Yep. Every person. Leaders want everyone working every day to think about the vision and how they and the organization can move closer to the vision.**

In addition, each person should be able to articulate the conditions necessary for them to be inspired to do their best work. How do you know what inspires them personally? Ask them. Then ask them what inspires them about the organizational vision. You can't live it if you can't see it. The companies, the religious institutions, the organizations that will influence the future for good will be those where all stakeholders know the vision and why the organization exists. All the stakeholders. If someone asked you, right now, to share your organization's vision and how you contribute to it, could you do it?

I know you have heard the term "elevator speech." This is the speech you would give if you got on an elevator on the ground level of some building where you work and the other person in the elevator is your CEO. Your CEO asks you, "Tell me, what excites you about working here and what is your role?" You have roughly 90 seconds before you reach the top floor of the building. What would you say? Think about what needs to happen prior to the hypothetical elevator speech for a person to be able to respond thoughtfully and with some degree of enthusiasm to the CEO question. For this to happen, everyone, regardless of their role, would have to know why. Why do we do what we do? Why are we here? How does our little non-profit, big corporation, religious community, or company make a difference in this world?

THE NEW BOSS IS THE VISION, MISSION, STRATEGIC PLAN, AND TOP STRATEGIC INITIATIVES

Bureaucracy means a boss. Traditional management style means a few leaders at the top know the vision, mission, and key strategies and most of the people in the organization do not. In open, better normal organizations, most people are expected to lead, know strategic direction, and know how they can advance the strategies. The strategic direction is the new boss. The strategic plan tells you what your priorities are and what is most important. You are not sitting around waiting for someone else to tell you what you need to do. Your motivation comes from within. You don't need an external boss to reward you or incentivize you.

I vividly remember going to Washington years ago as a recent high school graduate and working a month for my local Tennessee Congressman, Joe L. Evins. He gave hundreds of rural young people an opportunity to discover a bigger world and learn valuable history lessons about how democracy works. I also learned to dream bigger that summer. I made a point to cram as much as possible into my time there. One fascinating place to visit for me was the National Cathedral. I was "all ears" as our tour guide told the story about the original construction. It seems that a group touring the construction site asked a lot of repeat questions about what different construction workers did on the job. The standard answer was something like you would expect. Most of us answer questions about our jobs by telling people what we do, what our specific role requires. "I'm an electrical engineer working on the outside lighting" and then a little more about how outside lights would be used around the cathedral, or "I'm working on the logistics of the seating areas in the cathedral" and here's what we do. In other words, lots of descriptions of the specific work they were doing. The real surprise came from a stone mason who got a rousing applause with his atypical response and big smile, "I'm helping build a magnificent cathedral."

Leaders want to inspire people to build cathedrals, to feel they are a part of something bigger than themselves. From a personal standpoint, the Mary Oliver question, "Tell me, what is it you plan to do with your one wild and precious life?" is not a "what" question as much as it is a deeper "why" question. Recall Tony Deitfell and the Harvard Business School Portrait Project. Remember the Mary Oliver question used with MBA graduates since 2002. Recall also that Tony is now founder and Chief Evangelist of WDYEDWYD, Why Do You Do What You Do? A shared collective vision is the vision an organization creates basically by asking Why Do We Do What We Do? Like, why do we exist? How will we make a difference in this world? Vision is about inspiring others to imagine a possible, "make-a-difference" future, and then acting to move toward that imagined future. In short, a compelling and challenging vision will inspire use of discretionary energy. Inspiring leaders help others make the leap from "just a job" to "building a cathedral."

As a leader or potential leader, I would ask you to consider challenging your current vision as a test of its relevancy for this new world we live in after 2020. Does it still inspire you, your colleagues, and your customers? Inspiring visions are possible futures that are significantly better than where you are now, a future that is compelling, challenging and reachable with the best collective efforts. This is a leader's invitation to colleagues to create a vision of what the desired future might be, whether 3 years or 5 years out.

> A meaningful and compelling future vision creates a gap between where the organization is now (current reality) and where the organization wants to be in the future (vision).

A meaningful and compelling future vision creates a gap between where the organization is now (current reality) and where the organization wants to be in the future (vision). Many people have participated in a SWOT analysis where your team or organization has worked to determine your **S**trengths and **W**eaknesses, **O**pportunities and **T**hreats. Done well, this tells you a lot about where you are now and creates a picture of current reality. Future vision is the picture of the desired future and always creates a gap that can only be closed with strategic thinking and acting.

Future Vision

(Gap) Tension

Current Reality

A Gap Analysis begs the question, "How do we close the gap?" The beauty of experiencing the gap as a team or group or organization is the gap creates tension. Visualize holding a rubber band between your two thumbs. Even better, if you have a rubber band handy, grab it right now and place in over your thumbs. Now, raise your right thumb higher than the left thumb and pull your thumbs apart till you feel the tension. Your higher right thumb represents the vision of the future, and your left thumb represents current reality. The tension is a healthy tension. As a leader, you want to create tension between where you are now and where you want to be in the future.

You want people to feel the discomfort of healthy tension. The pull of the future can be like a magnet pulling on current reality, encouraging people to grapple with what they need to do to move toward the future vision.

The formal process for grappling with how to get to that compelling future becomes strategic direction and strategic initiatives.

Peter Senge and *Learning Organization* theory made a major and meaningful contribution to framing how we need to think about strategic planning when he suggested that we see Current Reality and Future Vision as the bookends of a strategic planning process. Bookends, personally, mean a lot to me as a former college professor in the pre-digital era. Between my many bookends were my beloved psychology, counseling, and higher education books along with books that reflected my early interest in organizational psychology. We could now call "bookends" the "alpha and omega," "current reality" and "future vision," or "base camp" and "mountain top." Every process has a beginning point and desired outcome. Multiple steps must be taken in a thousand-mile journey and a journey begins with the first step. The bookends frame the process if you will. Senge proposed that we think of organizations as "learning organizations" much as you would think of yourself as a life-long learner. Robust people and robust organizations are continually learning. Individuals, families, and organizations get old and dated when they stop learning. In learning organizations, people are committed to learning and seeking solutions. They are constantly innovative, creative, and entrepreneurial. According to Senge, organizations need to be transparent and honest and intentional about learning.

I recall the "why" questions that just kept coming from the mouth of our babes when they were small. Every one of our parent explanations was followed with another "why?" I know this is the reason parents quickly default to "Because I said so." In learning organizations and more open organizations, child-like curiosity is rewarded.

People start discovering when they ask more "why is that?" questions. Remember the "gloves on the Boardroom table" story? Leaders (managers, supervisors, team members) are responsible for learning and helping others learn. And learning is rewarded.

According to Senge, organizations particularly have to be intentional about two things. One, they must be brutally honest about current reality, "where are we right now?" Current reality is not a place leaders of learning organizations want to stay. Current reality is the truth about "now." As Scott Peck says in *The Road Less Traveled,* "The more clearly we see the reality of the world, the better equipped we are to deal with the world." Brutal honesty reveals so much about the organization or team, or group. Where are we most vulnerable in all our systems, including the human systems? Where are the minefields? Are there elephants in the room? Are there sacred cows and undiscussed issues with system-wide inequities that may have existed for generations? The magic is being honest without blaming or critiquing people and focusing on the truth, the facts, the fallacies, the roadblocks and structures not working well, at least not good enough to get to the vision. The enemies are the broken systems, systemic roadblocks. Leaders must call the brokenness by its name, even if they don't know exactly where to start to deal with the brokenness. We know how to speak the truth, even when it hurts. And yes, I can tell you, as a leader you have to risk being vulnerable. The inequities have been in our systems for years. Despite that fact, as a leader you will get pushback. Therefore, eliminate the blaming and finger pointing. Blaming is a common waste of time and energy. Blaming others is an inspiration killer. Solutions are inspirational.

THE POWER OF VISION

It is not uncommon for me, in any city at any time of the day, on any street or highway, to be clueless as to which direction is north. "Go north" has no meaning for me, left to my own devices. Fortunately, most of us carry a compass around with us on our iPhone along with maps, camera, weather, Podcasts and a zillion other finger-tip apps. With a compelling shared vision, any team or company has a true north calling them in that direction every moment of every day. The vision is the North Star if you will. It is a powerful source of inspiration and provides the "why" for working where you work, why you do what you do. Vision inspires any organization or team that wants to raise their thinking and acting from "good to great" or great to greater.

The litmus test for the power of vision is the degree to which every person in the organization can align their role with the vision and mission. Each team, each person contributes in some way to supporting the vision and helping move the organization toward the vision. Whatever true north is for an organization, project, or community, the greater the alignment of people with that overall dream, the greater the success. We will look at several examples of powerful visions in the next few pages. Visions of great opportunities inspire us to want to be a part of reaching the vision. We will see the power of vision vividly at St. Jude, for example, as true north for St. Jude is "no child dying in the dawn of life" from childhood cancer. We will learn how the thought of "no child" inspired them to move from a great vision to an even greater vision. Then in the WayFinding chapter, we learn how they align every role on the St. Jude team with their powerful vision. Everyone knows the vision and aligns what they do to contribute to the vision.

> Whatever true north is for an organization, project, or community, the greater the alignment of people with that overall dream, the greater the success.

In a previous chapter that included leadership gifts that led to my vision of a new model for leadership, I talked about my capstone leadership experience of leading at Belmont University, implementing leadership practices that inspire others and make others successful. Current reality in 2003, in the early days of new leadership, Belmont was a good small private University with regional influence and a faith-based background. It was one of many institutions of higher education in Nashville, once known as the Athens of the South. The board, faculty, and staff were fairly content with little change. No one had seriously asked the question, "What will happen in five years if there is little or no change?" There was no driving or compelling future vision. There was no "tension" and no gap between what existed in 2003 and the vision of what Belmont might become in the future. That changed dramatically.

New President Bob Fisher used the phrase "You ain't seen nothing yet" in his welcome reception in 2000 as the next President of Belmont University. The phrase came from the 1974 music Billboard # 1 hit by the same name, and Bob showed his passion for music, for big Dreams and big Ideas, in one celebratory moment. It was the beginning of a transformative period rarely matched in institutions of higher education. "You ain't seen nothing yet" was prophetic.

"Good to Great" thinking permeated the strategic planning process at Belmont. The seeds of a new vision emerged that would become "seeds of greatness," to borrow from Dennis Waitley's book entitled *Seeds of Greatness*. The seeds that emerged were:

- Become Nashville's university
- Become a nationally recognized brand
- Grow enrollment
- Invest in new facilities to accommodate growth
- Capitalize on Nashville's music and healthcare industries creating new programs and strengthening existing ones
- Attract more diverse students, faculty, staff, Board members, and friends to match the new vision
- Create a new economic engine to support the dream

All the above "seeds" were planted in the 2005, 2010, 2015, and 2020 strategic plans and nurtured with urgency. The vision created an exciting and healthy tension to close the gap between where we were in 2003 and what we envisioned for the near future. The envisioned future was compelling, exciting and filled with short-term wins. The future was so compelling. I liked talking about the vision as "the pull of the future." It felt like it. Our external stakeholders were engaged to the point of asking at Rotary meetings or other Nashville events, "What's the next big thing for Belmont?" The next big thing or next big artist is a Nashville "thing" anyway. Doing great things and doing good things became expected of Belmont. These positive expectations and on-going accolades were highly reinforcing, giving frequent opportunity for all Belmont stakeholders to experience the power of the vision and why we did what we did.

I find the following illustration helpful in visualizing the power of shared aspirations.

Vision-Driven Organization

Organization

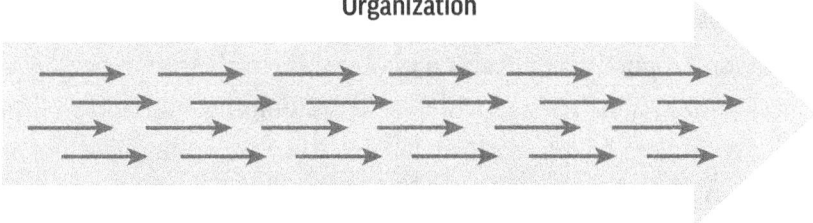

Traditional, Highly Bureaucratic Organization

Organization

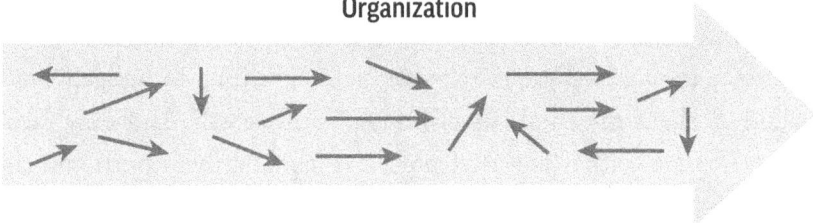

With a mutually shared future vision, everyone is seeing the desired outcomes. The first big arrow represents the vision-driven organization. All the smaller arrows represent the people and the roles they play within the organization. They are aligned with the vision and core values. The focus is on True North, the future vision. All systems and policies are aligned with the vision and values. When this happens, the human resources create great energy, and that energy is directed toward the vision and values. People know how they can devote their time and energy to make a difference. Can you see the powerful energy source when all roles are aligned with true north (the vision)? This represents win-win collaborative thinking and acting at its best. Alignment with the vision is inspiring. Alignment encourages teammates to notice people contributing to the vision and allows leaders opportunity to reward individual and team efforts that are vision-driven.

Now, imagine traditional bureaucratic organization without clear vision. Most people don't know the vision or the core values. When this happens, well-meaning people go in different directions. People want to succeed, but everybody needs a sense of direction. Think about the energy drain when the roles of individuals or groups of people are not aligned. People and teams are left to their own devices as to a clear direction. They are vulnerable to stomping out the fire of the day or waiting to be told what to do next. They are pulling in different directions, negating the impact of others. The energy drain and damaging impact are enormous.

One of the Dr. Seuss books that is relevant for today and a beautiful example of what happens when there is no common direction is the story of the North-Going Zax and the South-Going Zax. They meet face to face and toe to toe with neither willing to budge. "Never budge, that's my rule. Never budge in the least!" And they tacitly agreed that neither will budge even if it made them both and the whole world stand still, for 59 years no less! As a result, of course, they both lost. But the whole world did not stand still. The world grows up around the stubborn Zaxs. The Zaxs are acting like two ego-driven, lose-lose toxic leaders. "I may not win, but you sure as hell won't."

So, when teams in the same organization compete against each other, when people on the same team compete against each other, it can be deadly. The vision needs to be strong enough and the leadership strong enough to eliminate Zax behavior.

Vision and Mission-Driven enterprises strive for excellence and are driven by a passion for distinguishing themselves from others who do similar work. At Belmont, we thought we were positioned better than any small university to do something uniquely different in the academic world. No time to waste. All the people playing a multitude of roles had to be focused on the same direction for us to succeed. When this happens, the flywheel of momentum does spin faster and faster. People begin to expect success. It becomes a part of your DNA, a culture of inspiration. There are many "wins" and people know why they won.

> Vision and Mission-Driven enterprises strive for excellence and are driven by a passion for distinguishing themselves from others who do similar work.

Tom Peters, one of the first writers to examine what excellent and great companies do that distinguishes them from others, often told the story of challenging the strategic planning team of a major company working to craft their future vision, mission, and core values. A few hours into the process, with Tom pushing them to think more creatively about what separates them from the competition, one frustrated senior leader blurted out, "Come on, Tom. We're no worse than anybody else." Tom's retort, "What? Is that what you want for your mission statement?" It's like Tom caught a real thought, a secret thought, and it just tumbled out. So, Tom says, "Here's your new mission statement." Then he writes the following on the flip chart for all to see. *"We're no worse than anybody else."* Pausing a moment to let this sink in, Tom continues. "Imagine what that looks like in your ads and on your letterheads as what you want to strive for every day? . . . Want to think about this a little more?" Another lesson for raising the bar for leadership. Leaders must be intentional. No worse than the next guy is not good enough.

A compelling future vision is one of the strongest opportunities that leaders have for inspiring others. Great visions are so much bigger that any one person or any organizational team. People have to work together to accomplish a big dream. Most of us are familiar with the President John Kennedy challenge to be the first to put a man on the moon. The various teams working toward this vision had to reset many times. As one person on the teams told me, "It was almost like starting over." At a reset moment, the best thing a team can do is learn from what happened and go on, and that's what they did. They could not waste time or let conflicts, frustrations, or miscommunication become roadblocks to reaching the moon vision. With big urgent visions, there is no time for winning at the expense of others or wasting time. All the people in the big boat working on this project had to row together and pull together to get there. All in the same direction. As we know, Kennedy did not live to see the completion of his dream, but he will always be remembered as a visionary and the originator of the first "moon-shot." In addition, his moon-shot team did not quit when he was tragically assassinated. The dream was bigger than John F. Kennedy and so inspiring it became reality. Great leaders create and inspire visions that outlast them.

The second iconic vision that is embedded in almost everyone's memory bank is the Martin Luther King, Jr. "I Have a Dream" speech made on the capitol mall in Washington on August 28, 1963. The speech lasted 17 minutes and immediately created a vivid, robust picture of human equality and a beloved community.

The impact of the visions of the first man on the moon and "I Have a Dream" are the ultimate standards for future visions: bold, compelling, attractive, challenging, and inspiring our best. You can see it, taste it, feel it, and appreciate the fulfillment of significant steps that move you toward the vision. We want our visions to inspire the process of choosing to struggle through all the roadblocks that could prevent us from closing the gap between where we are now and where we want to be in the future. The challenge for this beautiful dream of a "beloved community" is to match more actions and supportive policies with the celebration of the dream. We need the dream to inspire more actions and policies and more leaders to do what's right in the organizations they lead. What would success look like if we lived the dream in our organizations and communities more urgently? The events of 2020 challenge leaders everywhere to lead for more just and equitable workplaces and communities. A Better Normal leader now has this new role responsibility.

"TELL SOMEONE I AM HERE"

I first wrote about the miracle of St. Jude Children's Research Hospital in the Ethical Heart chapter as we discussed the core values and Guiding Principles of St. Jude. Since they are vision-driven by "no child should die in the dawn of life," a recent two-year strategic planning process led St. Jude leaders to finalize something they had wrestled with for some time. They concluded that "no child" meant no child, period. No child anywhere. Why would the vision be limited to children from the United States? Realizing their hearts and souls were with children around the world, St. Jude Global was launched on May 24, 2018. The new vision will ensure that every child with cancer and other catastrophic diseases in the world will have access to quality care and treatment. Carlos Rodriguez-Galindo, M.D., traces the seeds of the St. Jude Global initiative to war-torn Nicaragua on Christmas Eve, 1986.

"Every night, Dr. Fernando Silva, director of the children's hospital (in Nicaragua), would visit the children, looking at all of them to try to figure out how he could distribute the resources. And when he saw a child with cancer, he put a cross beside his name, so that the nurses and the rest of the doctors would know this child couldn't be cured—that they should let the child die in peace. They didn't have the money and didn't have the resources. Every day he put a cross beside the children that had to die.

One Christmas Eve, Dr. Fernando Silva was making his final rounds before going home. A young boy, orphaned in the war, dying of cancer, and left alone to die because of lack of resources, tugged on Dr. Silva's coat as he was passing and said, "Decile a alguien que estoy aqui'." *Tell someone that I am here.* This powerful story became the tipping point for thinking "no child 'anywhere' should die in the dawn of life."

St. Jude leaders began to see without a global vision and a Way-finding strategic process to reach the vision, all they would be able to do over the years would be to make incremental progress with limited success for childhood cancer-cures globally. Their experience in the past 20 years told them that continuing to do what they had been doing would simply not be enough. There would be too many "Tell someone that I am here" stories. They thought "we're making progress" or "we have come a long way" was not enough. Leaders dug deep. Normal would never be enough. Let's set this big, hairy, audacious dream goal and do it. This will be our new moonshot. But the dream goal alone was far from enough. They had to define what success would look like, what big strategies were necessary to find the way forward, then the actions needed to move each Wayfinding strategy along. They also needed leader-champions at St. Jude and around the globe to bring the necessary collaboration and urgency to the process. St. Jude chose the man who traced the seed of the new global vision back to that event in 1986, Dr. Carlos Rodriguez-Galindo, Chair of the Department of Global Pediatric Medicine, to be the Director and Champion of St. Jude Global.

The new journey for St. Jude, taking all they have learned to the world, has begun. This is St. Jude's moonshot. Already a great and inspiring organization, the leap to the global vision is a leap from great to greater. They will share all cancer protocols, research findings, and their best resources with doctors and health care professionals in facilities across the globe, particularly to those who live in lower- and middle-income countries where treatment abandonment is the biggest threat to their lives. Imagine the sharing of healthcare intellectual capital with the world. Imagine the perspective change that comes when every child, every human is valued.

St Jude folks know why they come to work every day. They are helping find cures for childhood cancers around the world. They are playing a part in making lives better for families with sick children from around the world. Whether you are a doctor, nurse, housekeeper, or receptionist, each role is connected to "finding the cure." This is cathedral building!

NEW ROLE FOR LEADERS IN THE PANDEMIC WORLD

The St. Jude and astronaut perspective of a fragile world is revolutionary. As we discovered during the pandemic, we are all in this together. As Dr. King noted years ago, "We may have come here in different boats, but we are now all in the same boat." In America, we are witnessing with shock the exposure of glaring healthcare disparities between the poor and the rich, between people of color and others, between those with health insurance and those without. We are seeing first-hand the impact of mass incarceration and the disparity in the justice system between the rich and powerful vs. the poor and vulnerable. We are seeing the many broken systems that perpetuate inequity and the vulnerability of millions of Americans.

The current reality of where we are vs. where we are fully capable of being in the future creates a gap that is stunning. These are solvable human problems, and we have the resources to solve them.

The great organizations of the future will be intentional about their moral compass and willingness to seek solutions for man-made and systemic brokenness. Inspiring leaders must stay informed about these huge social issues that impact the wild and precious lives of millions of people. Leader awareness and sensitivity to these big issues become a part of leadership. These issues become a part of the vision, mission, and strategic plan. The final chapter will deal with the new role of leaders to activate their social consciousness and make a difference in their local communities. St. Jude leaders, for example, saw the need in the world, and decided to lead in confronting childhood cancer around the globe. Every leader can look more closely and see the needs of people in the larger community. The challenge is to broaden the scope of leadership and ask two questions. 1. Why not identify the inequities that exist right now in this organization and make a commitment to make it right? 2. Why not make a bigger difference in the broader community with an existing inequity that affects the people and the families of the people who work here?" Then leaders, make the new commitments a part of your strategic plan.

In our interviews for our book, *Real Dream Teams,* we had the opportunity to interview, Gertrude Elion, a woman who broke barriers in the male-dominated field of medical science. She and two of her colleagues received the Nobel Prize in Medicine in 1988. Her research had led to significant treatments for childhood leukemia and the first drug for treating patients with HIV. She had partnered particularly with Dr. George Hitchings, a co-recipient of the Nobel Prize, for many years and was known for her determination and tenacity. We discovered that she was driven by the memory of her grandfather's dying of stomach cancer when she was 15. "I decided that nobody should suffer that much."

Although her research saved countless lives and brought hope to millions, she never found a cure for stomach cancer. But saving lives became her passion and vision. As leaders ourselves, we asked her to tell us about her motivation and how she inspired others to work so hard. She responded, "I don't motivate them. All I do is help them to see what is possible and to remind them of their responsibility to achieve and help people have a longer and better-quality life." She continues by sharing with us a lesson about creating internal motivation and the difference between external motivation and internal motivation. "When someone new comes to work here, I sit down with them and talk about how important our work is. When we were focused on the leukemia research, I would tell them that there is a child out there who will die of leukemia today. There are others who will die tomorrow. There are some who will die next week, and who will die next month until we find a cure. We've asked you to join our team because you and all the rest of us have the ability to solve this problem if we work long enough and hard enough." The internal motivation she created was inspiration.

Even though I am clueless about medical research, listening to Dr. Elion at this moment, I said to myself, "I would love working with this woman." Elion continues, "Once the team members catch a sense of that vision, I don't have any trouble getting people to work hard---in fact, I have more trouble getting them to take time off for themselves and their families! . . . We faced many medical problems, and each was exciting and challenging."

Obviously, there are so many of us who work with team visions that are less dramatic than immediately saving lives, so we asked Elion about how we could equally inspire a similar commitment for people we lead. Her response and our first "too casual response" were breath-taking. She asked us, "Is what your team doing important?" One of us meekly replied to her unexpected question, "I guess so." We then saw her fierce determination, intensity, and caring emerge as she said, "You guess so?" she asked incredulously. Here was her challenge to us and any leader, "I think I see the problem with the group you lead---your group has a leadership problem! You need to go away from here and think deeply about what you're doing with your life and decide if it's important. If you don't believe that what you are doing is important, then you need to get out of the way and let someone who believes lead." She jumped all over our sloppy, "I guess so," and we could do nothing but thank her.

This pioneering, barrier-breaking, life-giving woman provided us with another leadership gift. Gertrude Elion knew we were writing about teamwork and told us we could make a difference. Her message came through. It was like, Ok guys, you need to be more intentional here if your writing is really important. Team leaders must lead by inviting others into important work. You are inviting them to be a part of something exciting, challenging, and worthwhile. You want them to tap into their discretionary energy and give their best. Got it? Lesson learned.

Lesson learned, again? Yes. The theme of "intentional" will run throughout this book. Great things happen because of strong belief in doing what is right, sticking to your knitting, being persistent, and making a difference. We don't have control over many things that happen to us in life, but we do have control over how we respond to what happens. These challenging moments create choice. They become tipping points that can send us over the edge to giving up or getting up.

> We don't have control over many things that happen to us in life, but we do have control over how we respond to what happens.

Having control over how one responds to heartbreak, loss, and challenge has always fascinated me in my career-long work with individuals and organizations.

So, I was particularly drawn to the story of Du Nord Craft Spirits, a Black-owned distillery in Minneapolis, after the murder of George Floyd in 2020. They had no control over the situation itself, but I was inspired with how they dealt with deliberately set fires to their business and home following Floyd's death and the ensuing protests in their neighborhood and hometown. They chose to use their sadness and anger as fuel to get up and make a difference. In the words of founders Chris and Shanelle Montana, "From all this we had a choice: Go back to business as usual or build something better in the ashes of what was."

Du Nord was a 7-year-old business in 2020, unique in the sense that it is one of the few, Black-owned distilleries in the country and unique in its location. They didn't start with a grand plan, but the circumstances came to them and became the tipping point for an inspiring response that was good for their community, good for business, and good for humanity as another model for making a difference. They are another example of win-win for all the stakeholders. Out of the ashes from their burned business and home came the Du Nord Foundation which provides economic opportunity for the historically excluded. Here is their unique version of an exciting, "getting up," worthy mission statement:

Social in Manner & Mission

RAISE UP YOUR WORLD

We want to change the rooms, open the doors and help people who have not traditionally held power see how we can make it in this business, this town, this life, this world. We can make it better and in our own way.

The Montanas talk about roadblocks and obstacles and encourage a refreshing new way of thinking about the roadblocks built into the system. Their advice on making life better in your world is to quit celebrating those who have overcome so many obstacles and start removing the obstacles. Start removing the inequities where you are. Open the doors and help where you are as leaders. There really is a better way of doing things. It starts with "how" you choose to respond, and then make it a part of your purpose, the "why" you do what you do.

Patagonia is a manufacturer of upscale outdoor clothing. Their imagined "make a difference" vision for the future:

"We're in business to save our home planet. We aim to use the resources we have—our voice, our business and our community—to do something about our climate crisis."

As a leader, imagine what you might do if you frame your future vision around something that makes a difference for people or the planet? As a result of Patagonia's vision, they attract committed talent who want to be a part of the vision and customers who take pride in using their products. These are Patagonia people who know they are contributing to the environment and making a difference with their lives. Think about the power of vision as the creation of "want to" in yourself and others. "Want to" is so drastically different than "have to," "must," "afraid not to," or "not my idea." I "want to" is an affirmation. Kouses and Posner in *The Leadership Challenge* define leadership in a way that has been helpful to me and thousands of others. "Leadership is the art of mobilizing others to want to struggle for shared aspirations." The "want to struggle for shared aspirations" calls for a commitment to the shared aspirations of vision, mission, and values, a commitment strong enough that people are willing to struggle through conflicts, disagreement, and other roadblocks to discover new solutions.

On the biggest world stage of all, we are seeing millions of vulnerable Ukrainians forced to flee their homes while millions, who are able, stay to fight. They care so much they are willing to separate their families and fight for what is right. This is what it means to struggle for shared aspirations. Many people reading this book have sacrificed fighting for democracy. You know what it feels like.

BEING INTENTIONAL ABOUT THE NON-NEGOTIABLE LEADERSHIP PRACTICE OF CREATING SHARED VISION

1. As a leader or aspiring leader, if your vision is already compelling, engaging, and most of all inspiring, you are one of the fortunate few. Otherwise, find a way to help make your organizational vision attractive and inspiring. If this is not possible, why does the team you lead exist, and what would not get done if you guys disappeared? Create a team vision statement.

2. Ask the Tony Deitfell question to yourself and those you lead. Why Do You Do What You Do? Plan a listening session around this question and learn. Your enterprise can equally learn in strategic planning by asking, "Does our vision reflect in a compelling and inspiring way Why We Do What We Do?"

3. The real litmus test is this: You will be successful with this leadership practice when everyone on your team can talk about the shared vision or shared vision in their own words and talk about how they personally contribute to the vision and/or mission. This is the 90 second elevator speech. This was an annual event for my Belmont team. It became clear how important each person on the team was. Each person knew how they made a difference and could talk about it. When this happens, people "want to" struggle for those shared aspirations with much greater willingness to improve communication and reduce roadblocks. St. Jude is willing to struggle together to save lives and find the cure. Nobel Prize recipient Gertude Elion recruited people to work on her team with the vision in mind. Remember her question to us? "Is what you are doing important?" If it is, clarify the vision and make it compelling enough that people will want to pull together to move toward it. As with Du Nord, if you have a social mission built into your business model that connects with systemic issues, it is very potent.

4. If you want to dig deeper into the power of vision, read Simon Sinek's excellent book, *Start with Why: How Great Leaders Inspire Everyone to Take Action*. I say start with How, but I define "How" differently. Both my "how" and Sinek's "why" fit under the big umbrella of inspiration. We both are passionate about getting people inspired.

Successful Moon Shots Inspire the Best

- Bold Strategies
- Persistence
- Short-Term Wins
- Sustained Collective Effort

CHAPTER EIGHT

WAYFINDING: STRATEGIC DIRECTION AND SHORT-TERM WINS

An organization's shared future vision is their moonshot. It is true north on the organizational compass. Done well, a carefully crafted vision is strategic, informative, motivational, and inspirational. There is, however, always a gap that exists between the present and the future. That gap creates a healthy tension and sense of urgency, always asking the question, "How do we close the gap between here and there?" Good information and direction are required to achieve a vision and organizations must determine what strategic steps it will create to move forward on the pathway from current reality to future vision. From a personal perspective, the same thought process is true. If you have a dream, you ask "how do I turn that dream into a reality"? I call the process that transforms visionary dreams into reality "Wayfinding." It is a strategic thinking and reinforcement process that helps people find the way to that moonshot vision, creating short-term win opportunities along the way.

Many people have shared with me the intensity and good intentions of their strategic planning process only to see it hit the shelves and never mentioned again. <u>It is better not to plan than plan and not implement.</u> Imagine sitting down with your family and planning a family vacation. Then, you don't go. And you do this every year with the promise that this time we are going to take it seriously. You never do. When this happens in an organization, there is little wonder why so many people dread strategic planning, don't trust the process, and roll their eyes at the mention of the process. Therefore, I have included two chapters related to the strategic planning process: Shared Vision and Wayfinding. Although both should be a part of the overall strategic planning process, I separated the two concepts to highlight the powerful inspirational qualities of both. People are motivated and inspired to be a part of creating something bigger than themselves, bigger than senior leaders, and bigger that any CEO. It is the "why you do what you do" and it can inspire people to invest their one wild and precious life in a higher calling. And great organizations and great leaders help each person see how they contribute to that something bigger than themselves. Then, every practice and policy should live out the mission and move you toward the future vision. This is the value of Wayfinding. It is the role of all leaders to demonstrate how individual work and teamwork connect to the strategic plan. When we say we want the strategic plan to be a living, breathing document, this is what we mean. The life, breath, and inspiration pieces of the plan comes from leadership. Leaders make it come alive and make it robust. You know what happens when leaders consistently demonstrate and call out how individual and team efforts lead to success? Others learn to see the connections as well, and the momentum builds. Here's the deal. Everyone in the organization has to know the vision, mission, strategic initiatives, and their role in making it happen. At the end of the day, each person should be able to articulate how her/his role makes a difference.

> It is the role of all leaders to demonstrate how individual work and teamwork connect to the strategic plan.

Making progress, short-term wins, successful Wayfinding is not accidental. When it happens, notice it. Make connections. Reinforce it. Celebrate it. This is inspiring stuff, and we will get to this in the Difference-Making chapter.

I first heard the term "Wayfinding" from my friend Lance Utterback who, at the time, was CEO of a large signage company. I loved the term as it so accurately described the process; how do we find the way from point A to point B and beyond to reach our ultimate destination?

Wayfinding has multiple purposes from a signage standpoint. We need signage or markers that inform, guide, direct, and reinforce us as to the way to go. The same is true with establishing a strategic direction and active plan to accomplish an organization's vision.

"I-40 West Exit." This sign message informs of a pending major decision to set the correct course. We also need signage to confirm that we are on the right path and making the correct turns throughout the journey as we progress toward the ultimate destination. "Are we there yet?" "No, but we're making progress." This is a short-term win, vital to success. Finally, signage offers more information that is helpful on a journey, like "Road Work Ahead, Expect Delays." Signage at airports tell us how far away we are from our gate of departure or if our flight is on-time, delayed, or canceled. Wayfinding informs us and helps point the way when our GPS has done all it can do! Wayfinding signage is there for all to see as we travel or enter a strange facility. Good strategic plans, progress toward the vision, and identification of what short-term success looks like should be common knowledge for all in the organization to see. Leaders help people see success and then help individuals and teams celebrate short-term wins.

For our purposes, leaders are responsible for telling the truth about current reality (transparency) and communicating that message as a powerful element within the overall wayfinding strategy. Wayfinding creates the messages that point the way to the vision.

> **Wayfinding becomes the strategic steps or series of initiatives that help steer the team or organization toward accomplishing the vision, closing the gap between the present and the future.**

Wayfinding is therefore inspiring. We know we are correctly moving in the direction of true north, and we're excited about the progress. We can see the big steps we need to make to move toward accomplishing the ultimate vision, we can identify short-term goals and objectives associated with every big initiative, and we can identify and celebrate short-term wins with team members along the way. We can also monitor and adjust as we learn. People are inspired by progress! Wayfinding serves as the roadmap that sets the stage for recognition and appreciation of groups, teams, and individuals which we discuss in detail in the next chapter.

As leaders, we want to identify a limited number of Strategic Big Steps or Initiatives that will be the signs that point the way from the present to the future vision. When we identify with and implement strategic Big Steps with urgency, we close the Gap that always emerges when we are honest about current reality and imagine a much better and inspiring future vision. For example, commitments to enhanced technological quality, a culture of inspiration, increased market share, new facilities, customer service, or an innovative culture are all Strategic Big Steps.

What leaders want to communicate to everyone is that the Vision and the few Wayfinding strategic steps lead the way to the future and should guide everything they do. Each person's role contributes in some way to helping move the organization forward, toward the vision. People should never have to guess what the most important work is. In short, each person is either serving the customer or serving and supporting those who do serve the customer. Since moving toward the vision is so important, the Wayfinding process is urgent, becoming a critical accountability tool. I suggest a written executive summary, shared and discussed by all, for each key wayfinding strategic step that includes the following:

WAYFINDING PROCESS: USING THE TENSION OF CHANGE TO POWER LEADING CHANGE

The Inspiring Vision Statement
The Guiding Principles
The Strategic Initiatives
Goals and objectives for each Strategic Initiative
Short-Term Wins
Elevator Speech

MY FIRST PERSONAL JOURNEY WITH WAYFINDING

I want to share this personal experience with finding my way because it was the first time in my life that I had been intentionally purposeful for a long period of time. For others, the personal Wayfinding experience might have been a time in the military, a time-out after high school, service corps, trade school or college, a year learning in another country, peace corps, or a parent's delayed dream of education or career. It could be anytime you were intentional with a purposeful vision or mission. My personal wayfinding journey just happened to be the pursuit of a graduate degree. I had to commit to some major strategic steps for the first time in my life. There is nothing more special about my journey than that so many of you have made. It's just my way of sharing what Wayfinding looks like and felt like to me.

My wife, Rubye Lynn, and I were in our late twenties. We were in our third year of marriage and working with young people at a large Methodist church in Chattanooga, Tennessee. We loved what we were doing and found real joy through the young people who were willing to include us in their lives as well as the young couples that volunteered to work with us. Even though I didn't play a guitar, a must requirement for youth work, Rubye Lynn made up for my shortcomings. Through this three-year journey, we bought millions of Krispy Kreme donuts and thousands of McDonald's hamburgers. I loved teaching and I taught part-time in the Psychology Department at the University of Chattanooga (now UT Chattanooga). It was the good life for a young married couple. We felt loved and appreciated. We believed we were making a difference, which for most of us is one of the research-proven, strongest internal motivators. Deep down, we all want to make a difference and know our life counts for good. We were inspired.

I was settling into our work and Chattanooga. Other teaching opportunities were emerging. Rubye Lynn sees and experiences the "settling in" process building in me and one afternoon she asks, "What are you planning to do with your dreams of a PhD and a career in higher education?" This fledgling dream had gotten buried in all the neat things we were doing. Her question jolted me. After a few days, I discovered that well of excitement that goes with big unrealized dreams. And then another question, "If you really want to do this, now is the time." Now? Yes. It was the time.

The decision to pursue another graduate degree helped me realize why I had buried the dream. A PhD meant two years of statistics, computer science, plus a proficiency in one and a language proficiency; scary as hell for me as I was a pitiful, uninspired undergraduate student in statistics and French. I was so bad in conversational French with my east Tennessee accent that I repeated the first year! Two years of French for one-year credit. It would pay off later. All I knew was that I wanted to work with people, and a psychology major was a late undergraduate junior- year choice. So, I hung around after graduation, worked with young people in a church youth program, got a master's degree in counseling, and was selected for some major leadership positions on campus. What I learned during this 2-year period was striking. Other people believed in me more than I believed in myself! This was a big insight. I later saw what a key part of leadership this is, believing in others more than they believe in themselves. Inspiring leaders see potential in others and nurture that unrealized potential.

At any rate, I had found a path with youth work, teaching, and a life partner who was powerfully supportive. Rubye Lynn's gentle questions stirred the dream, and I was inspired in a new way. The potential prize of a bigger degree outweighed the fear that went with it. Three months after the fateful questions from Rubye Lynn, we left for Ohio University with everything we owned in our Chevrolet Impala. Things had moved so quickly that assistantships and housing were uncertain, both critical. We had little money. This was a leap of faith and a potential "what were we thinking" moment. But our new friends at OU said, "no problem," and we drove on. There was no Plan B. At the time, some of my friends and family were openly questioning our intelligence. They thought the leap of faith might be over a cliff.

We were rewarded quickly for the faith to act on the inspiration. I want to say it was a courageous decision. It was more likely a mixture of naivety, courage, and believing more in my underutilized potential. I quickly got an internship, a student loan, and we were able to find housing. My very first purchase in Athens, Ohio, was the statistics book for the first semester of the course I feared most. I knew I had to be more intentional about learning. I had to adopt new study habits and be more focused. This was serious and it was not just me anymore. It was us. I had to reset the way I learned. Failure was not an option. Statistics is a program of study that punishes and rewards immediately. If you miss the basics and get behind, you get punished quickly. In the first semester, I felt I was jumping into the frying pan of learning. Make or break. Here's the power of choice. We always have choices. Always. I chose to do this. I raised my hand. We chose this adventure into the academic wilderness. There were statistic wolves howling and one thing I knew I had to do right away was prepare and stay vigilant.

This was the first Wayfinding challenge and strategy: be prepared. Non-negotiable. By the opening day of the first semester's statistics class, I had read ahead and understood the basics. I also decided that I would ask questions in class about anything I did not understand from the lecture or stay after class till I understood. I knew I could not let one day pass without understanding everything presented. I could not fall behind. I know this sounds elementary, but I had never done this before. It was important and urgent.

I also had to be honest about how easily distracted I am by competing cues and stimuli in the classroom. I am not ADD but my attention wanders easily. I am somewhat like a racehorse and need blinders, so I don't get distracted. Wayfinding challenge number two. To meet this challenge, my strategy was to sit front row center, right in front of Professor Sligo, statistics maestro. Had this been a Broadway play, I would have had the most expensive seat in the house. Every day he called roll and never failed to call me Mr. Bethel instead of Mr. Thomas. For an entire semester! He never got my name right, but he knew he could count on me being right in his face every day. I also had a second strategy for extra focus on examinations and tests. Get this. I literally pulled my desk into a corner with my back to the room and two walls on each side. It was a self-imposed "time out," but it worked for me.

Validating my learning with peers was important. Learning in isolation made it too easy for me to think I was doing better or worse than reality. Wayfinding challenge number three. My strategy was a learning group and I found 3 buddies right away who were eager to do the same. Almost like with exercising. In fact, 2 of these guys became handball competitors and partners as well. Easier for me to stay motivated with others. Plus, this fit with my extroverted tendencies and needs for interaction.

With all this academic focus, where's the balance, where's the fun? Fun is a rich part of my life. The academic world and too much emersion in constant critical thinking can be very boring. Wayfinding challenge number 4. This strategy became a unique combination of exercise and fun, both energizing and mentally renewing. The twice a week handball game filled the bill for exercise and fun. Here's how that worked. The winner of the cutthroat handball match earned a half-gallon of A&P's Coast to Coast fine table wine! The wine added to the fun weekend party at someone's apartment, enjoyed by all the couples. We celebrated our short-term academic wins along with fun family stories from diverse backgrounds.

It is one thing to have a dream, another to reach it. My wayfinding journey meant a complete learning reset. It was intentional and strategic. There were four basic strategic initiatives that moved me closer to my dream of this terminal degree. Each one was significant in closing the gap between the current reality of no degree, no internship, no housing, no student loan and the future vision of the PhD. I was fortunate to have a marriage partner who believed in me and committed to the three-year process. This is a big deal. We all need support systems. This initial support system grew with the comradery of many friends on the same journey and supportive professors who wanted me to be successful. Here is a summary of my Wayfinding and big strategic steps I had to take to successfully reach my vision of a PhD and that I never altered. The best support system in the world could not take these steps for me.

Let me quickly add there is nothing especially sacred about earning a PhD, as such. It is an indication that one has been persistent and has somewhat mastered a field of study at some moment in time. I am immensely proud of the accomplishment but knew and still know if I don't continue to grow and learn, the value of the degree diminishes along with me. Persistence does pay off. Big dreams, whatever they are, mean sticking to them, never giving up. I also know how many brave men and women have accomplished so much by being more persistent than I have ever been. As I write now, I am thinking particularly of the women that Chelsea Clinton recognized in her recent book for children entitled *She Persisted, 13 American Women Who Changed the World.* These are, Clinton writes, "women who have spoken out for what's right, even when they had to fight to be heard." These strong women have persisted in following their moral compass to do what is right and includes inspiring women like Harriet Tubman, Helen Keller, Ruby Bridges, Sallie Ride, Margaret Chase Smith, and Oprah Winfrey. Observing Chelsea grow up in Arkansas where we both lived at the time, it was easy to see and appreciate her talent and persistency as a child. She now celebrates that quality in the lives of other women who have persisted to make the world and this country better places. These women serve as role models for all leaders for a Better Normal. I should note also that in addition to writing and family, Clinton is a global health advocate.

There are opportunities everywhere and leading examples of leaders in every walk of life who never gave up on equity, fairness, diversity, or inclusion. For example, we are familiar with the persistent struggle of the U.S. women's soccer team who have fought for years to gain pay equity with the men's soccer team. On Feb. 22, 2022, the dream became reality with a discrimination settlement and a commitment to equalize pay and bonuses to match the men's team going forward. Megan Rapinoe, the star midfielder and leading advocate along with Alex Morgan for equity, reflected on this huge win. "I think we're going to look back on this moment and just think, 'Wow, what an incredible turning point in the history of U.S. Soccer that changed the game and changed the world, really, forever.'" These are women who persisted for years and model a quality for all leaders who want what is right and fair.

The key for me, then, was not the degree itself. It was a dream of something bigger. The degree would open doors and this degree was a necessity for college teaching, which I wanted to do. The vision for me was that this degree would help me make the world a better place. I would be in a helping profession. I would have a lot of opportunity to influence others in positive ways.

> This graduate school journey was the first step in a life-long journey that would lead to this book and a new dream that we humans could all work together and lead to create a better than normal world after 2020.

Below is the account of my "wayfinding" path from the scary reality of dropping everything to chase a dream and finally catching the dream three years later. I had been inspired before in my life for short periods of time. This would be the longest period of intentional sustained inspiration that I could document as a "wayfinding" process with multiple short-term wins along the way.

MY WAYFINDING JOURNEY AND LEARNING CREDO

- **Preparation and understanding.** I will always be prepared before every class. I will never fail to ask a question about anything I don't understand. If I still have questions about the material presented in class, I will stay afterwards with the professor until I do understand.
- **Focus.** I will sit front and center in class to avoid distractions. In examinations, I will self-explore additional steps if needed to stay focused.
- **Study group and collective learning.** I will form a study group of 2-4 people and we will meet weekly.
- **Exercise and fun.** I will exercise two to three times a week and plan fun time with my wife and friends.

Implementing my Wayfinding process was non-negotiable if I were to be successful. This was my first experience with explicitly calling a process non-negotiable. "I will try to," "I will do my best," or "hopefully" were not going to cut it. I knew I had called out my points of vulnerability and named them. This was explicit, "I will." After five or six weeks, I had great confidence in the process and was affirmed by it. It was inspiring for me. I earned an A in Statistics (celebration) and my other classes that first semester. I learned that being inspired and committed required me to identify in advance the conditions necessary for me to succeed. My graduate school learning was so powerful that it became the foundation and inspiration for the leadership model I taught, coached, personally adopted, and now write about.

WayFinding, then, is a process for digging deep to identify the few top strategic steps you need to take to move you toward your personal future vision or the shared vision of your team or organization. The process answers the question: How will people or leaders know they are making progress toward the desired dream? For me it was identifying a few success indicators or signs that would tell me I was being successful. They were signs of progress and signs of success. They were short-term wins. They were powerful. They were inspiring.

By the way, our first child, Elizabeth, was born in Ohio. No degree could top that joy!

Belmont University, my last hands-on leadership experience, was driven by an overall growth strategy for its traditional liberal arts undergraduate program and its professional programs, particularly in health sciences, law, and pharmacy. As a result, the economic engine became the institutional reserve funds created by the annual enrollment growth and a sound budgeting process based on enrollment numbers from the last academic year. We were able to invest more quickly in new facilities, faculty and staff salaries, and spectacular new residential housing, much of which looked over the city from the highest elevation in Nashville. The vision was to become a leader among teaching universities by bringing together the best of liberal arts and professional education. The strategic investments, therefore, aligned perfectly with the vision. It has taken a long time for colleges and universities to treat students and their families like customers, the most important stakeholders. They are customers and they have many choices. We "got it" and were student-centered and became more intentional about diversity and inclusiveness. Our top-rated music business, entertainment, and film programs put Belmont on a national stage and attracted students from across the country and around the world. Belmont is physically located at the top of Music Row and just blocks from the heart of Nashville. Nashville grew as Belmont doubled and tripled in size and it was logical to partner with the Mayor, the city council, the Chamber of Commerce, and the Nashville Convention Visitors Bureau, the music industry, and the healthcare industry. It was obvious that Nashville was on the cusp of becoming a go-to destination city and we wanted to leverage the attraction of Nashville and our relationship with the city as another reason to choose Belmont.

I have already made the case that Belmont University made the leap from good to great for higher education in the 15 years from 2004-2019. Jim Collins selected 11 companies to write about in his book *Good to Great* for their stock market performance over a 15-year period. Obviously, stock market performance was a great indicator to choose to explore in depth the common characteristics shared by the 11 companies who performed so well. What did these 11 do that other didn't do? At Belmont, we studied and learned from the discoveries and insights found in the *Good to Great* research and applied them to higher education. Hedgehog and Flywheel concepts were just as valid for higher education as other organizations. President Fisher was the former Dean of a Business School, had advance degrees in Economics and Management, and led with the traits of what Collins called Level 5 leaders. "Level 5 leaders are fanatically driven, infected with an incurable need to produce sustained results. They are resolved to do whatever it takes to make the company great, no matter how big or hard the decisions." At this writing in 2021, Belmont has sustained great results over an 18-year period, most recently announcing a new Medical School in partnership with healthcare giant, Hospital Corporation of America (HCA).

To reach the on-going vision of Belmont noted earlier, I want to describe a few of the Wayfinding big strategic steps that led Belmont from a good, sleepy little liberal arts regional university to a robust national university in the heart of Nashville. During these same years, Nashville was exploding into a good to great city, making Belmont University even more attractive.

Wayfinding Strategic Initiatives during this magic time were many, but I will describe just a few. Obviously, many strategic big steps overlap as they do with any Wayfinding process. Wayfinding is a synergistic process that energizes and feeds momentum. The strategic steps create over time an organizational "fly-wheel" that turns faster and faster. The fly-wheel concept was beautifully described in the Collins book. It is a gradual process that is inherently inspiring. Each big step creates a short-term win, and more people begin to believe. It is hard to say which step led to a breakthrough since great organizations are led by senior teams that keep pushing and pulling in the same direction for some time before others outside the organization begin to notice. As Bob and I discovered when visiting with John Wooden, the legendary UCLA coach who won 10 national basketball championships in 12 years, John had coached the Bruins for 15 quiet years before he won the first title! We were astonished. We also discovered something else significant about the man, John Wooden, that speaks volumes about him. He wrote a note, a love note, to his wife every day. Every day for years! He was a model coach, but he was a model husband prior to his coaching fame. My wife is encouraging me to think more about the husband John Wooden!

Strategic Big Wayfinding Steps at Belmont University

- Creation of a growth strategy and economic engine. We decided early on to implement a growth strategy that would create enrollment growth. In an increasingly competitive higher education market, enrollment increases continued each of the

> Wayfinding is a synergistic process that energizes and feeds momentum. The strategic steps create over time an organizational "fly-wheel" that turns faster and faster.

following 15 years. Enrollment more than doubled. The budget process was based on the previous year's enrollment figures. As a result, each year new institutional reserves accrued, providing attractive opportunities to reinvest in Belmont to move more quickly toward the future vision. Institutional reserves became the economic engine.

- Selection of the right people to the right senior leadership positions. This intentional process led to two new senior positions. One, a new VP of Spiritual Development was added to affirm our commitment to our ethical and moral compass. Two, a new VP of Institutional Effectiveness was added to assure we lived into our vision of becoming student-focused and a leader in liberal arts and profession education as a teaching institution.

- Investment in new facilities. We quickly invested in new facilities to accommodate the growing number of students, including new academic space and student housing. The new facilities made Belmont even more attractive.

- Underground parking. In 2003, Belmont had roughly 3,000 students and sat on the estate property of the old Belmont mansion. It was a charming old little campus, and most students were commuting students. Strategically, the big step was to become more student-centric, provide a better student experience, while maintaining the charm and feel of a small campus. How do you double in size, double the number of students living on campus, add all the needed parking spaces and keep the small campus atmosphere? Here was the big strategic step that kept the small campus "feel." Parking lots, even above ground parking garages, make any campus larger and puts more focus on cars than people. Tons of asphalt parking lots are not attractive or environmentally friendly. We chose to build every new building on top of an underground parking garage to accommodate both students, faculty, and staff parking. The massive concrete and asphalt lots seen on most campuses don't show up at Belmont. You see green instead. No one had to walk blocks on a rainy day to get to class. It was safer for all. Belmont is still a charming, lovely campus, one of the most attractive in the country. The additional cost per parking space as opposed to surface parking was significant as you can imagine. But this big step-strategy of safety, convenience, and campus beauty moved us toward the vision of becoming more student-centered and a national brand.

- Sustainability initiatives. Another commitment to doing the right thing related to the environment. Belmont's commitment to sustainable initiatives is expressed proactively in its Conservation Covenant. As with most things, we did not want to just give lip service to conservation and protecting the environment. Let's put what we want to do in writing and do it. As a result, Belmont achieved the first Platinum LEED certification for a New Construction project in Nashville for the Janet Ayers Academic Center and Gold LEED certification for the Milton and Denice Johnson and Randall and Sadie Baskin center facilities. Unique composting and geothermal heating and cooling systems have emerged because of the Covenant as well as a partnership with the Nashville Metro Transit Authority that allows all students, faculty, and staff to use public transportation to and from Belmont free. There are 13 other sustainable initiatives in the Covenant.
- Quality-of-life salaries. The Big Step Strategy of investing in merit increases of salaries for faculty and staff for over 15 years has led to nationally competitive salaries and made Belmont an attractive first-choice place to be for the best and brightest teachers and leaders from across the country.
- Intentionally spiritual environment. Belmont underscored its commitment to create an atmosphere of service, learning, and spiritual growth by adding a Vice-President of Spiritual Development to its small senior leadership team. The university

was deliberate in inviting students to grow their faith, discover their God-given talents, and find ways to serve and transform the world. As a result, it became the fastest growing ecumenical university in the country.

- National branding. "From Here to Anywhere" became a new marketing tag line in 2003, fitting beautifully with the Belmont mission to prepare students to use their God-given talents to transform the world. Shortly afterwards, we had an opportunity to partner with National Public Television on a major project. Belmont has a world-class Entertainment and Music Business program as well as an outstanding traditional music program and musical theater major. Therefore, it is a country to classic, pop to Christian, rock to rap to dance, multi-music-genre powerhouse. Christmas at Belmont was already an established tradition when I arrived at Belmont in 2003. The major project that would create a national stage for Belmont was a partnership with Nashville Public Television and National Public Television to share Christmas at Belmont with a national audience, delighting millions of new fans across the country. In addition, as I mentioned earlier, we discovered an international stage by successfully hosting the 2008 Town Hall Presidential Debate, the first-ever Presidential Debate in Tennessee. By intentionally partnering with the Governor, the Mayor, the city, and the state, hosting bi-partisan events and the Debate itself, the event showcased Nashville and Belmont internationally. The "building brand" Wayfinding step also supported the vision of becoming Nashville's University, willing to partner in every opportunity.

As you can see, Wayfinding is an intentional strategic process that creates synergy, builds on each success, creates short-term wins, and spins the flywheel of momentum faster and faster toward the desired vision.

At Belmont, we think we had big dreams and big ideas that inspired the big strategic steps and the best work of most everyone. As a witness to and leader in this sustained effort over my 12 years at Belmont, I saw it happen. More importantly I "felt it" as it happened. I originally committed to 5 years of my one wild and precious life, and that of my life partner, when I accepted the challenge from my old consulting partner to come to Belmont and help create something special in higher education. I planned to go back to consulting after 5 years. I ended up staying 12 years. Why? The simplest way I know to explain why I stayed longer than originally intended is that this leadership experience confirmed for me the enormous power of inspiration and investment in relationships. Gertrude Elion's simple question from years past still echoed in my head, "Is what you are doing important?" I could affirm that, and I knew our work was making a difference in multiple ways. The success indicators were there.

The miracle story of St. Jude Research Hospital in Memphis is the epitome of inspiration and the model for an inspiring vision, mission, and wayfinding process. As discussed in the Visioning chapter earlier, St. Jude made the leap from great to greater when it committed to expand their vision of "no child should die in the dawn of life" from America to the world. In America, since St. Jude was founded 65 years ago, cures for childhood cancer have increased from 20% to over 80%. The new global vision was announced on September 27, 2018. "St. Jude Children's Research Hospital today announced a five-year collaboration with the World Health Organization aimed at transforming cancer care worldwide to cure at least 60 percent of children with six of the most common types of cancer by 2030." Dr. Downing talked about the founding idea of "no child" and said this new vision for what can be in the world "will provide the tools and resources to shape how childhood cancer is addressed globally, encouraging national health systems to make childhood cancer a priority and dramatically improve cure rates for children with cancer."

The first big Wayfinding strategy or step for St. Jude is no surprise but is a tribute to how they think about leading. It's not about St. Jude, it's about finding cures for children with cancer. So, it is not shocking at all that a headline strategy is "Collaborating to Cure." To them, the global vision was bigger than St. Jude, bigger than the World Health Organization, and bigger than the healthcare partners in other countries. It would take the best of all of them. All of them had to collaborate, share, discover what they could do to help each other in curing childhood cancer. St. Jude would share their successful protocols, countries would make childhood cancer a priority, and all would be inspired by the collaborative effort.

The second strategic Wayfinding step was another process commitment: Urgency. If this collaborative initiative and dream were to be realized, 60% cure rate for 6 of the most common childhood cancers by 2030, the collaborators had to commit to a sense of urgency. Dr. Downing agreed to put the weight of St. Jude behind this and help hold all the partners accountable. Urgency is a continuous process and on July 13, 2022, St. Jude pledged an additional $1.4 billion to expand the hospital's campus, hire additional staff, invest more in patient care and research capabilities, making it the largest strategic expansion in the hospital's six-decade history. ($12.9 billion by 2027) "This expansion was the work of hundreds of individuals across the institution," said Dr. Downing. They asked, "How can we further accelerate progress? How can we do things that other institutions can't do? How can we make lasting impacts that will affect children?" Urgency is about asking questions that push beyond normal, pushing people to think beyond anything done before. Better normal.

> Urgency is about asking questions that push beyond normal, pushing people to think beyond anything done before. Better normal.

The third Wayfinding Big Step was Increasing Access to Care. The key to success in low and middle-income countries was earlier diagnoses and increased availability to effective treatment. Therefore, the strategic actions and goal objectives for this Wayfinding initiative would include 1) Supporting clinical care for the most vulnerable children, 2) Ensuring all children with cancer can access high-quality medicines and technologies, and 3) Strengthening training programs by developing centers of excellence. Downing revealed early on that the partners indicated high-quality medicines would be no problem, but when pressed on this issue, the quality medications, and the logistics of getting them to the right centers was much more difficult than expected. Urgency demands of leaders that they push themselves and others to follow-through, not just assume it's no problem.

**Big dreams have unexpected hurdles and roadblocks,
so all the energy needs to focus on solutions,
not blaming others, and figuring it out.**

Which they did.

A fourth Wayfinding strategy was Developing National Centers of Excellence. Strategic actions include development of regional, national, and hospital-specific efforts in education, capacity-building, and research. To make this happen, expert technical support would come from St. Jude faculty and other healthcare leaders from around the world, St. Jude would make a programmatic investment of 15 million, and they would engage and collaborate with the "all important" government leaders and healthcare leaders and work together with WHO support. Imagine this happening without the support of key government and political leaders? Government support was absolutely necessary since another key Wayfinding big step in low- and middle-resourced countries was influencing the national policies enough to make childhood cancer a healthcare priority.

In summary, leaders seek to get the best thinking and acting from themselves and their colleagues through a strategic planning process.

It is an inspiring process to be heard, to see your ideas become productive actions, result in new policies that value all the stakeholders. The impact of vision and mission-driven strategic planning, implementation, and connecting of individual work and teamwork to the plan is inspiring. As a leader, this is what you can expect from a shared future vision and a shared Wayfinding process.

- A clear sense of direction. True North.
- Big step signs or strategies that point toward true north.
- Action steps that are specific and measurable.
- Synergistic impact. The impact is more than the sum of its parts.
- Momentum. The flywheel is spinning faster.
- Short-term wins.
- Opportunity to recognize and celebrate individual and teamwork successes.
- Deeper trust and belief in the strategic process.
- Greater confidence.
- Increased productivity.
- Enhanced innovation and entrepreneurship.
- Inspired and motivated team members.
- And, in cases like St. Jude, a great vision and dream could inspire an even greater dream.

BEING INTENTIONAL ABOUT THE NON-NEGOTIABLE LEADERSHIP PRACTICE OF WAYFINDING: ACTION STEPS

1. Train all people on the vision, mission, core values/guiding principles, and strategic initiatives of the organization. It is absolutely critical for all to know the strategic direction and the role they play in helping move the organization in the desired direction.

2. Consider attractive vision-mission-wayfinding-strategy displays for every place there are team meetings. Train leaders on how to connect individual and team actions and successes to vision-mission, Wayfinding Big strategies, and short-term wins.

3. As new team members are added, review the "connecting process" of their roles to vision and mission. Leaders want to continuously help people see how they make a difference. Wayfinding connects directly to the inspiring leadership practice of "Difference-Making: Recognizing and Celebrating Individual and Team Successes."

4. Consider how you might influence a better normal by creating a Wayfinding path to equity for women and Black and Brown colleagues in your organization. Remember, any organization can inspire their people by adding "just" causes to their vision, like Patagonia with the environment.

If I could give you
just one gift, it
would be this one

Love Your Awesome
Imperfect Self

Then, Add Recognition
and Appreciation
of Others To Your
Inspiring Leadership
Practices.

CHAPTER NINE

DIFFERENCE-MAKING: RECOGNIZING AND CELEBRATING INDIVIDUAL AND TEAM CONTRIBUTIONS

What if you knew that 70% of the people that work in your company or organization told me that they were not engaged with their job, were unmotivated to do better, and were uninspired? What if you knew that these same disengaged and uninspired people were 87% more likely to quit than those who were engaged and motivated? Would you believe this data from the Gallup research, University of California research, and others? Would this information be strong enough for you to act? Apparently not. This information has been around for years, as long as we have had truckloads of information about the importance of exercise and diet for good health. Neither of these scientifically based information pools have had a great impact on healthier people or healthier organizations.

If the Gallup studies haven't fully gotten our attention, let's add more encouragement to answer the wake-up call to lead for a Better Normal. The O. C. Tanner Company combined their years of observing the power of recognition around the globe with a ten-year in-depth research of workplace productivity by HealthStream Research. Over 200,000 interviews were conducted by many research analysts from HealthStream with managers and their employees. The collaborative effort allowed the researchers to quantify the critical connections between recognition, employee satisfaction, and business outcomes. So, this is bottom-line, attention-grabbing information. Check out these headlines:

- 79% of employees who quit their jobs cite a lack of appreciation as a key reason for leaving.
- 65% of North American employees report that they weren't recognized even once last year. Not once in 365 days. Can you imagine not hearing any recognition from someone who cared about you for 8,760 hours?

> 79% of employees who quit their jobs cite a lack of appreciation as a key reason for leaving. 65% of North American employees report that they weren't recognized even once last year.

From the O. C. Tanner article. "The simple act of a leader recognizing a person in a meaningful and memorable way is the missing accelerator that can transform the speed and quality of performance. (Here's the key) But it must be purpose-based recognition. And it tops the list of things employees say they want most from their employers. When employees know their strengths and potential will be praised and recognized, they are significantly more apt to produce value."

I would be a wealthy person if someone paid me for every time I have heard this comment from a manager or leader, "Why should we reward anyone for doing the job they are paid to do? It's their job!" Here's why, leaders.

The news about purpose-based recognition is another gold mine for inspiring others and getting bottom-line results.

The Tanner article reports that companies that effectively recognize excellence have significantly increased retention and lowered turnover rates. They tell us that some estimate it costs as high as 250% of a person's salary to replace them. In addition to increased retention, acceleration of business results with excellent recognition is stunning. According to the data, companies that effectively recognize excellence:

- Enjoy more than three times Return on Equity (ROE) than those that don't.
- Enjoy more than three times Return on Assets (ROA) than those that don't.
- Companies in the highest quartile on recognition of excellence report an operation margin of 6.6% while those in the lowest quartile report 1%.

Want one more reason for adopting this non-negotiable and inspiring leadership practice? Recognition outweighs tuition reimbursement, higher pay, and competitive vacation and holiday benefits for employees. No question, these are huge additions for any company. Investment in additional education and time off to do that is significant. Higher pay is critical to quality of life. Vacation and holiday benefits are important to people. But they are not as powerful as recognition when seen through the eyes of employees. Leaders for a Better Normal will strive to lead with

> Recognition outweighs tuition reimbursement, higher pay, and competitive vacation and holiday benefits for employees.

the whole package. Interestingly, the only cost of purpose-based recognition is the cost of training and education of leaders on this additional "hard skill." Of course, included in the education process would be helping all people learn the business strategy of the organization along with the directional forces noted below in my definition of purpose-based recognition.

One big clue for why recognition isn't as important as other incentives is this: 1) Most organizations don't' train new leaders (managers or supervisors) on any management or leadership skills, and 2) Most senior leaders still have a total disconnect with their employee/associate base on what is most important. Note that most senior leaders still think other incentives are more important than recognition and being valued as a human being.

HUMANIZING LEADERSHIP

Purpose-based recognition? Good to be clear about this since it is far more than the traditional "good job" or thumbs up. It is what it sounds like. Recognition that purposefully makes a difference. Recall from the Wayfinding chapter the chart that focused on Vision, Mission, Guiding Principles or Values, Strategic Initiatives, Goals and Objectives, and each person's Elevator Speech? These are the directional forces that drive the company forward.

> When leaders connect recognition to the above directional
> forces, we call the recognition "purpose-based." We
> reward people for being purposeful and intentional.

We help people feel valued. We help people see they are making a difference. Similar terms that I have used in my consulting work have been "vision-driven," "mission-driven," or "purpose-driven" recognitions. Our team-building sessions, for example, were called

Vision-Driven Team Building. Great teams have a shared vision and common purpose. The work together is driven by a higher calling.

Whatever your tile is, you are a leader. You are a "difference maker." What you do influences others and has an impact on others. As these proven, non-negotiable leadership practices become more comfortable to you, you will have more influence and positive impact. Your colleagues and associates are eager for you to encourage, give hope, believe in them, and help them be successful. One of your major roles, in fact, is helping those you lead be successful. When they succeed, you succeed. So, whether you are a supervisor, rabbi, manager, priest, coordinator, minister, CEO, or designated leader of any kind, you are a leader and difference-maker. You will help those around you be successful by empowering individuals and teams, by finding ways to recognize contributions to the vision, mission, and key strategic objectives.

All of us want to make a difference, individually and collectively. We live in an interdependent world. We are wired for connecting and interacting with others. We strive to belong, be accepted, and grow toward our best selves. As a psychologist working with individuals and organizations, I was always moved by this basic human need that we all have. In our inner-most self, we want to count for something. We want to leave a positive mark.

> In our inner-most self, we want to count for something, we want to leave a positive mark.

You now understand more clearly how you can create a culture of inspiration for those you lead, even if you work in a normal, bureaucratic company. You may be the only one who is choosing to lead for a better normal. If so, you must work within the parameters of the organization. But within those parameters, you can lead change and improve the individual and team performances within your team. You can also influence other leaders to lead differently. You can make a difference and help others make a difference.

Recall the founders of W. L. Gore and Associates, Bill and Vieve Gore? The genius for their company was the belief that they could inspire innovation, creativity, and spark the best in others by maximizing the work environment for personal and collective growth. Where the heck did this unique, one-of-a-kind business model come from? When we dig deeper into the genius driving the Gore enterprise, we learn that Bill had been highly influenced in his past work experiences at Dupont by Maslow's Hierarchy of Needs as well as the positive impact of small, task-force teams. You will recall Maslow's widely respected identification of basic human needs from an earlier chapter. As lower-level needs are successfully met, people grow, become more confident, self-assured, and gradually more creative and curious. So, here are two concepts that Bill experienced as powerful. One was a model for how people grow, become more creative, innovative, and thrive when basic needs are met. The other was a model for collaborative thinking and acting in task-force teams that led to more ideas, better ideas as well as greater productivity. I am not sure exactly how this played out in the minds of the Gores, but these two concepts led to a gigantic "Aha" moment. I can only imagine, but it must have been something like, "Why not create a unique enterprise built on a Maslow culture that rewards personal and collective growth and inspires the best of everyone?" And, they had the guts and courage to do it.

The Gore brand promise remains the driving force for their success over sixty years after their dream was implemented in the basement of their home in 1958: *"Together, improving life for all Gore Associates, customers and the communities we serve."* Yep. That's it. Guess what? *"Together, improving life"* has led to 3,400 unique inventions worldwide in a wide range of fields and recognition as one of the best places and most imaginative places in the world to work. W. L. Gore and Associates is the model for the ultimate case study in the power of a culture of inspiration and improving life. Here is the way Terri Kelly, CEO at Gore from 2005-2018, summed it up, "Our beliefs and principles are not just about creating a great place to work. They foster creativity and shared ownership for success and help us continue to innovate and deliver products that improve lives and industries." The Gore message is powerful. They are saying to all of us who aspire to be leaders or who are already leaders, "People really are our most important assets and if we invest in an environment that believes in people and supports and recognizes the amazing talents in people to grow toward their best, creative and amazing things will happen."

By the way, Gore is intentional about something else. They decided early on against "going public." They believed they could remain true to their core mission, values, and unique culture only by remaining a private enterprise. While most large companies during the same time frame prioritized return to shareholders, Gore and Company did not. They were and are focused on prioritizing Associates, customers, and the communities where Associates live and work around the globe. All with a culture of creating uninhibited minds and collaboration. By the way, they are very, very profitable.

The intent of this book, right from the beginning was to create a pathway to inspiring leadership for every person who leads whether a parent, supervisor, pastor, manager, CEO, Board member, or for-profit or non-profit leader. We have made the case that the traditional "soft skills" are now "hard skills" because they are rarely taught in graduate or MBA programs. We have made the case that a new normal is not good enough for the new world after 2020. And, we have made the case that you can learn the new "hard skills" of leadership along with the traditional leadership skills that have always inspired others. Bill and Vieve Gore got it right in 1958, creating a culture unlike anything seen before and rarely seen afterward. This has been the real "hard skills" Gold Mine in our own leadership backyard for decades. "Why not mine this leadership gold for a better normal?" I ask. Why not build a leadership model for a Better Normal that includes the "Aha" of Bill and Vieve Gore? Why not think of improving the lives of our associates, customers, and people in our community with a focus on the most powerful motivating forces known to man as the Gores did? Why not be intentional about helping people learn how to work more collaboratively?

In the earlier chapter, The Collaborative Mindset, we made the striking contrast between win-win, win-lose, and lose-lose thinking and acting. In this current chapter on the leadership practice of Difference-Maker: Empowering Individual and Team Contributions, I want to show the empowering qualities that the Gore's found in Maslow's Hierarchy of Human Needs.

The Gores believed if we intentionally designed the culture to meet basic human needs and if people learned to collaborate, were recognized for individual and collective excellent work, people would be inspired to be their creative best selves.

Throughout this book, we are connecting the dots of leadership gifts from the past to build an even better leadership model for a better normal. The Gores left a huge legacy that few leaders have adopted. Gary Hammel, London Business School and Director of the Management Lab has written beautifully about W. L. Gore and Associates and their unique management model. The Gore enterprise has also had the attention of other management writers for years and received numerous awards consistently for Best Places to Work, not only in this country but in every country hosting their global enterprise. Yet, the fact that so few leaders of major corporations have adopted the management model that makes Gore and Associates successful is astounding. My lifetime of leadership experience and leading personal and organizational change resonates with the big idea of humanizing the enterprise. They believed, as do I, that people soar and exceed expectations when given the freedom to do so. These thoughts have led to this moment in time and have influenced my need to make a difference by authoring this book. Therefore, I want particularly in this chapter to dig deeper into Maslow's Hierarchy of Needs to help you understand why believing in yourself and your colleagues is so empowering, tapping into the most powerful motivators of human behavior and the source of our discretionary energy.

Maslow's basic human needs structure moves from Basic Needs to Psychological Needs to Self-Fulfillment Needs. Maslow believed that people could reach their full potential if all the Basic Needs and Psychological Needs were met first. With lower-level needs met, we would be free to be more creative and innovative or what Maslow called Self-Actualized. The basic physiological and safety needs are at the first level of the hierarchy. Most of us take food, water, rest, a safe environment, and personal security for granted. However, many people we work with do not. The second level are the psychological needs, the need for belongingness, fitting in, and knowing people care about you, and then prestige, a sense of accomplishment and making a difference. The third level of the hierarchy at the top of the pyramid is the magic place where people can do their best work and meet their needs to live into their full potential, becoming self-fulfilled. In short, the Gores intentionally sought to create a working environment that assured basic, psychological, and self-fulfillment needs were met. In the process, they empowered the best of individual and team performances. In the next few pages, I will discuss in detail how Maslow's hierarchy of needs influenced the culture, policies, and practices of W. L. Gore and Associates. They provide the ultimate model for a culture of inspiration and empowered associates. In this model of "growth" not only can leaders recognize and appreciate the growth and contribution of others, but the individuals also recognize it in themselves. It is self-reinforcing. The insights for what leaders do in a culture of inspiration and empowerment is radically different from bureaucratic, command and control leadership and back-to-normal leadership.

> My lifetime of leadership experience and leading personal and organizational change resonates with the big idea of humanizing the enterprise.

I know that some of you are ahead of the leadership curve and hoping to find a few good ideas for your leadership toolbox. You may already be in a work environment that is inspiring and empowering. Others of you are working in a more traditional and less inspiring work environment. Regardless, every person who leads can engage colleagues to want to do their best. All of us, deep down, want to contribute and make a difference. Therefore, as with the other non-negotiable leadership practices, I trust you will find a way to implement some version of the powerful concepts in this chapter that tap into discretionary human potential and empower the "difference-maker" in the people you lead.

After the events of 2020 and early 2021 created a leadership crisis, I have suggested we bring brutal honesty to the crisis. I have suggested we seize the moment, if you will, and view the crisis as the greatest leadership opportunity of our lifetime. To do so, we must radically shift our thinking about normal, traditional, and bureaucratic leadership. In addition, since "malignant normal" leadership emerged in force during the years from 2016-2021, there is even more urgency to create a new leadership paradigm that empowers our best selves. We must change how we think about leadership and the role of leaders. Leaders for a "Better Normal" must be intentional about leading with bold, courageous, and human-honoring actions. Leaders must act on the premise that people are our most valuable assets, making the enterprise as amazing as the people within the enterprise.

A "paradigm" is a way of looking at something. It is a perspective or a standard way of seeing something. Think how long the paradigm of a flat world was commonly accepted. For example, with leadership, an old paradigm related to leadership was that people were born with leadership qualities and leadership belonged to a privileged few. Some were leaders, most were not. It was that simple.

*We now know that we all have leadership potential and all of
us can lead, whether it is leading in our personal and family life
or leading others in an organization to make a difference.*

All can learn to lead. Leadership is teachable and learnable. This is a new way of looking at leadership and it is significantly different than the old paradigm, the old way of looking at and thinking about leadership.

Another false and widely accepted paradigm about leadership was that people could not be trusted to make good decisions, people needed a lot of supervision and management, and that people needed to constantly be incentivized to work better or harder. Inherent in this line of thinking was that many people were not very motivated, and someone had to "motivate" them, either through fear, threat, or external rewards. We discussed much of this earlier, but this was and still is a powerful way of thinking about leadership. This thinking permeates bureaucratic leadership and supports the belief that immensely powerful, brilliant, charismatic leaders are the only ones capable of being CEO's or senior leaders of large enterprises, deserving to be paid millions of dollars to make the really big decisions. Certainly, there are some very smart, even brilliant CEOs and senior leaders, but this old paradigm fails to honor the multiple people talents throughout the organization, the power of inspiration, unused human potential, and over-rewards the people at the top. Then, common in leadership circles has been the belief that good organizations need top-down leadership and decision-making. Or that young people needed to sit at the "kid's table" while the grownups made the big decisions. Or that Human Resource departments need to find ways to "manage" performance or that money is the most powerful incentive. These paradigms, traditional ways of thinking about managing and leading, are simply inadequate for the new world and better normal leadership. Now we have evidence that there are much better ways to lead and motivate. The practices and policies in a bureaucratic environment in no way reflect that "People are our most important assets."

And, by the way, over half of American workers are 27 years of age or younger. That half of the worker population is particularly annoyed by the old paradigms.

Thinking of paradigms shifts think about Ferdinand and shifting the paradigm about bulls in chapter one. In reality, still living the old leadership paradigms has much the same impact as a bull in a china shop.

W. L. Gore and Associates started with a major paradigm shift that led to other positive paradigm shifts about leaders and leadership. The major shift was a radically new leadership model based on "how." How do people become the best they can be? How can people live up to their potential? They went directly to a human growth model that had been around for years. Not a management model, but a human growth model. Surprisingly, no one had done this before, and few have capitalized on it since. The paradigm shifts about leadership inherent in W. L. Gore and Associates reinforce every basic concept in my new model of leadership for a better normal. They answer the questions I pose above. The paradigm shifts will help transform the way we think and act as leaders. The focus is on people and how leaders can be difference-makers, empowering individual and team contributions to excellence. Hear and see the different narratives about the leadership for the future. You will find empath, vulnerability, courage, awareness of how the leader's behavior impacts others, and new definitions of winning throughout the following narratives and mindset shifts.

Leadership Paradigm Shift 1: Everyone Can Lead.

The first shift in thinking is that each person can be a leader and a difference-maker. In 1958, this was radical, but it is now the foundation of what we call "open organizations" that all build on parts of the Gore and Associates growth model for leadership. The heart of the matter is that you, the reader, can lead and be a difference-maker. All of us can make a difference and we have leadership choices available to us every day where we work and where we live. All of us can inspire others by how we chose to act and lead.

Most leaders would say YES to the question, "Do you hope to make a difference with your leadership?" Just think how the scale of people saying YES to this question would exponentially change if everyone with whom we worked believed they were leaders and could make a difference by seizing opportunities to lead. This is why this paradigm shift is so super important. It is the leadership game changer. This means that whatever kind of organization you are in now, open or more traditional, you can be a difference-maker. Whether you lead with a title of supervisor, manager, or another title or you are in an organization with few titles and no bosses, it is critical that you believe you can make a difference. Believing what I do makes a difference is extremely important to me personally. It has always been. Equally important to me and what we know to be true about human potential is that this "making a difference" belief is empowering to most all of us as human beings. Open organizations thrive on practices built on top of this paradigm shift. Every inspiring non-negotiable leadership practice in this book draws energy from this basic shift in thinking.

"I believe I can make a difference." Where does that come from? For people with a faith background, whether you are Christian, Muslim, Jewish, or another faith practice, many would answer that we are created in the image of God. Others might say we are created with a spark of the Divine. The belief about making a difference is inherent, therefore, within the broader context of being part of the creation. We are "on purpose" if you will. We are intentional. Without sounding too syrupy, we are

> We are "on purpose" if you will. We are intentional.

special in the sense that we are one-of-a-kind. Ok, I will not use the snowflake example. The point is, deep down, most people could own the belief of being created for a purpose. We might also own that we are living with a fair share of potential that we haven't lived into yet.

My oldest daughter Elizabeth grew up with Mr. Rogers in the early 70's. Based on the bright, confident woman she is today, I think two early lessons she learned from Mr. Rogers before she was six years of age were 1) "I am okay just the way I am," and "The Mr. Rogers neighborhood of Make-Believe unleashed her life-long curiosity and passion for learning." Millions of children and many of their parents share the lasting positive impact of having a kind and caring, sweater-wearing adult tell them, "I like you just the way you are." In any language the translations are "you never need to be anyone else but you," "you are good enough just the way you are," "you are special," "we are all special" and fill in your own thought if you grew up with Mr. Rogers.

Call it whatever fits for you in your belief that you can and do make a difference: Divine spark, ok just the way you are, one wild and precious life. Belief in self and belief in others leads to passion. Passionate people can do most anything. Purpose-driven recognition allows leaders to "catch the passion" of colleagues.

Leadership Paradigm Shift 2: People Are the Most Important Assets.

Many CEO's and senior leaders proudly tout their people as their most important assets. This popular declaration is hard to miss. It is part of what I call "CEO speak." Don't ask the follow-up questions to determine what policies and practices are in place that support their believe in people as the most important of all stakeholders. I can't tell you how many times publicly traded companies in the past have included increasing shareholder value as the real basis of their strategic planning process. If you are a "low-cost provider," like a Wal-Mart, check out the history of the benefit-plan for part-time employees. Check out the number of lawsuits filed against large companies in the past because of multiple inequities that are considered by many top leaders as just the cost of doing business. Somebody pays for the lower costs. Often it is thousands of employees who struggle to make ends meet. Examples are abundant. It's hard to drive on any interstate without catching up to an 18-wheeler with these words emblazoned on the rear doors, "Our most valuable asset is sitting 52 feet ahead."

In short, bureaucratic leaders and old normal leaders have not led in acting as if they believed that people were their most valuable and important asset.

W. L. Gore and Associates designed the company on the concept that their people indeed were their most important asset. They believed first and foremost in creating a work environment that intentionally fostered individual and team learning and growth. They believed in the Maslow growth model which we highlighted earlier, and they went about building their work environment as a place where every facet of the enterprise supported becoming your best self. You didn't have to wait till the weekend or vacation or go somewhere else to grow and learn. You could come to work with Gore and Associates and live your passion all day every day! Isn't that amazing? We already know from the extensive Gallup research that people thrive when they have an opportunity to do what they do best every day. The same research shows that people thrive on frequent recognition for good work.

So, the powerful second paradigm shift we see lived out at Gore and other "open organizations" create new narratives about leadership. This allows leaders to talk with people about the creation of a new work environment that means they won't need to worry about basic needs being met. For the new associate, the message is you aren't wasting precious time concerned about your physical and psychological safety, belonging, feeling "a part of" something special, or self-esteem. You are free to let your best thinking and best ideas fly. We want you to soar. We want you to exceed your own expectations. You will grow and you will get better in this strange, new, and wonderful environment. Yes, you will feel uncomfortable for a time, maybe months, but that's okay. This is what being out of your normal comfort zone feels like. We foster the courage it takes to make mistakes, be challenged, and work things out with your fellow associates. We know, because of this growth environment, you will be more innovative, creative, and entrepreneurial. You will have better ideas and we will create better products. It is a win-win-win-win deal. You will be more inspired and productive, which makes our enterprise more successful, our shareholder value enhanced, and we create more value for our community stakeholders around the world. We will be better citizens of this world.

Do you see the paradigm shift from the models of toxic leadership and normal bureaucratic command and control leadership to inspiring, better normal leadership? The narrative is radically different. The mindset totally different. Imagine coming to work every day and getting to live your passion. You can grow and live fully at work, home, and play. Your "one life" can be honored, respected, and enhanced everywhere you are.

The takeaway for leaders. You can share your passion about being in a place where people are intentionally valued as the most important stakeholder. Leaders recognize and appreciate innovation and creativity specifically when it happens.

Leadership Paradigm Shift 3: Power with Purpose.

Terri Kelly, former CEO at Gore from 2005-2018, believes the fundamental key to success is how leaders think about their role. She says the leader's job is to not get in the way. And hear this: Kelly also says it takes courage to change the paradigm we have held for years as traditional, normal, and bureaucratic leaders. Courage. Courage to shift out of that comfort zone of control and learn to use power in a different, more purposeful way. Her insight from what worked so well at Gore since 1958: "Leaders have to give up control to get results." And,

I might add, the results at Gore have been spectacular. Kelly says the role of the leader is to make everyone else successful. Isn't that a new definition of leadership? Make others successful. Gore and Associates spend a lot of time with associates helping them discover or clarify their passion. Then they position them in the best way and on the best teams to fit their passion, a new formula for success. At Belmont University, we believed a big part of our mission was to help students discover their God-given talents (their passion) to transform the world by serving others in whatever career that might be.

Terri Kelly's CEO story is quite interesting. She worked at Gore for 22 years before becoming CEO. Notice that they did not go outside to pull in some master leader from outside. They chose someone from within who people already trusted. In fact, she appeared surprised when chosen, but over the years there was a pattern of followership, if you will. She just kept being a person who helped others be successful. The teams she chose to be on just kept doing great work and creating great products. People wanted to follow her. So, she became CEO because she basically had made so many people successful and had helped more than anyone make the enterprise successful.

The takeaway for leaders. You can be transparent about not having all the answers and that you value the unique strengths others bring to the enterprise.

You learn the unique strengths of each person and recognize how the strengths of many led to success.

Leadership Paradigm Shift 4: Passion.

All the paradigm shifts are synergistic with each other. Passion particularly depends on Believing You Can Make a Difference. Then, you are more open to finding your passion. Since you have a reservoir of underutilized potential, where your passion lies, believing in yourself is like having those "seeds of greatness" within you. You just have to find the environment that nurtures those seeds, allowing you to grow into your best self.

What is your passion? Haven't you heard someone sometime somewhere utter these words, "I am just so lucky to get paid to do every day what I love doing." Or "I feel so blessed to do something every day that I love to do and believe I am making a difference." Well, if you have a similar feeling about what you do at work you are one of the fortunate few. At Gore and Associates, helping create this feeling for every associate is built into the system. They intentionally hire passionate people or work immediately to help talented new associates identify their passion.

Recall our earlier discussion in the Creating a Culture of Inspiration chapter of untapped human potential or under used personal potential? Working below potential is common for most people with either toxic leaders or bureaucratic leaders. Remember that we only volunteer our best work when we are inspired and fully engaged. Inspiration is passion is engagement is fully invested is best effort! At Gore, they go directly to the "P" word: passion. The narrative is we want your passion. We want you to be doing every day what you do best and what you love doing. Our growth model for our work environment is designed for you to grow into your best creative, innovative, entrepreneurial, and self-actualized self. Jason Field, who became President and CEO of Gore on April 1, 2018, mentioned his passion on assuming his new role following Terri Kelly. "We have strong organizational momentum, and I look forward to creating value for all our stakeholders by applying my passion for exceptional customer experiences, innovation, and Associate engagement to improve life for our customers, communities and Associates."

Recall a time when you were in your zone, really clicking, running on all cylinders. Athletes describe peak performance as being in a zone where they are mentally, emotionally, and physically focused. No distractions. They describe being able to tap into their full potential and perform at the top of their game. When I am writing at my best, I think of what I am writing as "flowing." Years of teaching, learning, practicing, consulting on "what leaders do at their best" can be enhanced for this new leadership opportunity with a new sense of urgency for the lessons of 2020. I do have this reservoir to draw energy and new insights from, this deep wellspring of experience and practice flowing from my years of passion for making a difference and helping others make a difference. I know when I tap into that wellspring, I am sharing the best of what I have learned with you. My goal is to help make you more successful in your leadership and help you discover your passion for helping your colleagues and associates find their passion. We all have it. It's there. And we are powerful when we have the courage to live it and be it.

Takeaway for leaders.

> *Passion, one of the most powerful emotions, is our friend. We want to leverage passion to help make us more curious, more questioning, and more willing to fight for what we believe in.*

As a leader, learn and share stories of how individual and collective passion have helped create better results and better products.

Leadership Paradigm Shift 5: Collaboration.

I devoted an earlier chapter to this non-negotiable leadership practice, so I will be brief here. In addition to the Maslow hierarchy of needs growth model adopted by the Gores in 1958, collaborative teamwork was the second piece inherent in the Gore magic. Bill Gore had seen and experienced the exceptional outcomes and stronger results that came from teams at his earlier workplace. In short, collaborative work, from his experience, was more powerful in generating more ideas, stimulating better ideas, challenging others to think differently, and brought out the best in creative thinking and acting. Coupled with the supportive ideas that anyone could and might generate the best idea or concept, success was success regardless of where it came from, and courage to be uncomfortable was rewarded, collaboration thrives in the Gore environment. The key here, as I have stressed throughout the book, is the synergistic effect and impact of valuing, respecting, and believing in people. It is like a subliminal message of "yes, yes, yes, yes . . . ," encouraging associates to trust themselves and trust each other to create and produce things that have never been done before.

I have mentioned before about Friday night and movie night at our home with our grandson. This past Friday night, we were quickly engrossed in *Raya and the Last Dragon*, a beautiful piece of storytelling from Walt Disney Animation Studios. We found ourselves in the fantasy world of Kumandra where humans and dragons lived in harmony together long ago. But when an evil force threatened the land, the dragons sacrificed themselves to save humanity. We pick up the story 500 years later when the same evil has returned. Humanity had been saved, but now there are 5 warring tribes. Could the harmonious land of Kumandra ever be restored? Could this one humanity live and act together as one humanity again and find joy with other living things, like dragons? It is up to a lone warrior, Raya, to track down the legendary last dragon and begin the perilous journey. Along the way, she will discover that even a dragon cannot save the world alone, it's going to take trust and collaboration as well. Raya is willing to risk her life to earn the trust of others.

Takeaway for leaders. Leaders for a Better Normal are on a journey to find Kumandra. Like Raya, they refuse to be complacent and do nothing. They have the courage to trust their fellow human beings and collaborate for better work, better products, better stakeholder value, a stronger democracy, and a better community. So, be proactive in celebrating examples of "courage to trust". Trust building always touches our willingness to be vulnerable. We grow in the process.

> Trust building always touches our willingness to be vulnerable. We grow in the process.

Leadership Paradigm Shift 6: Core Values.

At St. Jude Children's Research Hospital, they tap into the passion potential in all their employees through a focus on their vision, mission, and core values. They know that some of their 5,000 plus employees are passionate about medical discoveries, some are focused on healing, and some are in support roles to discovery and healing. But all are motivated every day by the mission of finding cures and saving lives, and they are driven by a set of core values. Everything relates to the mission and core values. Everything. I mentioned earlier how they have found a way to capture people living out those values in a very concrete way. I am looking at a 98-page booklet entitled *Living Our Values*. It contains 39 stories about St. Jude employees who have been seen by their colleagues living out one of the 7 core values that undergird the mission of "finding cures-saving lives". This is an annual celebration of St. Jude people: researchers, housekeepers, bookkeepers, medical doctors and nurses, those who work with the parents of sick kids, and others.

Diane McGarry, for example, has worked for 2 years to develop an app called Our St. Jude. She had countless meetings with families, consultations with staff, discussions about technical details, and revision after revision to get it right. She saw the need for another resource to improve the patient and family experience 24/7. When patient families arrive at St. Jude they are filled with hope and terror and have hundreds of questions. What will my child's schedule look like? Who will make reservations for housing and provide the meal cards? Remember that families pay not one cent out of their own pocket for any cost associated with their child's illness. Danny Thomas thought families should be able to spend all their energy on their sick child and never have to worry about how to pay for anything. Still, hospital staff spend hundreds of hours compassionately responding to the fears of families, offering comfort, and explaining unfamiliar policies. No one can magically remove all those fears, but people like

Diane make sure families have detailed and personalized information at their fingertips through Our St. Jude. Why? The number one core value is "Always recognize that ADVANCING treatment for children with catastrophic diseases is at the center of everything we do." Families are part of the treatment process and need the best information to remain calm, helpful, and reassuring to their sick child.

Another St. Jude core value is expressed in these terms, "Work with PURPOSE and URGENCY—your efforts matter." This core value helps everyone know that every role contributes to finding cures and saving lives and working with urgency means more children will live. Another employee snapshot of what is typical in this distinctive children's research hospital is researcher Barthelemy Diouf, PharmD, PhD. Born in Senegal, educated in France and Germany, and now a United States citizen, Diouf brings a global perspective along with new ideas and new strategies. How valuable it is to St. Jude's new global initiative to have a number of people like Diouf, who happens to be fluent in French, English, and German. Because he is so inspired by what he does, he volunteers from his reservoir of potential extra time to help his colleagues in the lab and collaborate with multiple departments across the St. Jude campus. He is known for giving his best through his research and willingness to help others, "a shining example of the success of St. Jude—taking unexpected findings and pursuing them to their limits."

Clinical Operations is necessarily a team sport—and the head coach for that team is Colette Hendricks. Colette was featured as exemplifying the value of "Do what is right; take Ownership of what you do." She works assertively to enhance collaboration among the many groups who keep St. Jude's multiple clinics working smoothly. She is known for insisting gracefully that everyone needs to do the right thing. "She reminds people of the mission, and wasted time slows the process. Initiatives need to proceed quickly and efficiently, and she encourages others to think about solutions in a new way."

Then, there are people like Summer Freeman, Director of Executive Communications, who helps leaders communicate better and more often, in part because she knows how to inspire employees as well as enlighten scientists on the other side of the world. Her leader, CEO James Downing, was able to communicate so well, so often, and in multiple formats during 2020 that over 97% of St. Jude employees rated his communication of the St. Jude mission and strategies during the Covid crisis as inspiring.

Employees at St. Jude and associates at Gore and Associates share a common thread. The only way they can do what others have never done before in their respective fields is this: they help make others around them successful and stay razor focused on their vision, mission, core values, and strategic objectives.

Takeaway for leaders. Find ways to communicate in every format available the vision, mission, core values, and strategic objectives. Relate every individual and team success to these 4 strategic driving forces by purposeful recognition. As a result, people will never have to guess whether they are making a difference or not. This concept has great synergy with the Wayfinding practice. Wayfinding has already defined the pathway to success and then, great difference-maker leaders recognize the short-term wins when they happen.

Leadership Paradigm Shift 7: Making Others Successful.

Another "big idea" and shift away from toxic or bureaucratic leadership that will help new leaders approach their leadership differently are finding ways to build on the power of making others successful. The "big idea" at Gore turned into the action step that became part of the Gore culture.

Every new associate would have a sponsor within the company who was charged with the responsibility of helping make the new associate successful.

The sponsor was the new associate's part-time coach, mentor, encourager, listener, connector, teacher, and hope giver. These are my descriptive words, but this is what a sponsor does. It makes so much sense that, when you read it, it's like "duh," why doesn't every company do this? Ok, you might say, "Isn't that what a good supervisor or manager should be doing as part of their job?" Yes and no. It's just that most supervisors and managers don't see this as part of their role. In addition, most supervisors and managers are charged with evaluating the people they supervise and manage. Plus, we know that many, many people don't have a good enough relationship with their boss, unfortunately, to have the kind of discussions that sponsors have with a new associate. With a sponsor, there is none of the traditional baggage. By definition, the sponsor is there to help the new associate be successful! The sponsor has been through the uncertainty and newness of an enterprise with no traditional hierarchy, few titles and no bosses, and experienced the freedom of being able to go directly to talk with whomever you think can be helpful. That's at Gore.

If you are in a more traditional company, think about how to use the "sponsor" concept and how to implement strategies designed to help the people you lead be successful. There are so many successful people in most enterprises who have a hidden sponsor or teacher within. It is amazing what happens when successful people are asked to identify and talk about the strategies they used to become more successful. They learn so much from the process of telling and articulating. Often, the process of mentoring and sponsoring will be a first-time experience for many seasoned colleagues. The sponsor/new associate relationship is a two-way deal. Both learn. I have also discovered that most successful people relish in the opportunity to help someone else navigate the first few months in a new enterprise. Bottom line: Any leader will benefit from this overall concept. It is one way of creating psychological safety for a new employee or colleague. It only enhances your role as a leader for sponsors to build relationships with new associates, discover their passion, and do all they can to help make others successful. The sponsor is just another powerful resource which is available to you as leader.

Takeaway for leaders: Since every new associate or new person on your team can have a sponsor, make time for the new members of your team to share one example of how their sponsor has helped them become more successful.

> I have also discovered that most successful people relish in the opportunity to help someone else navigate the first few months in a new enterprise.

Leadership Paradigm Shift 8: Best Case Wins.

In the Gore enterprise, the best case for a new strategy or product wins, regardless of where it comes from or who it comes from. Gore is an example of a growing number of what we call "open organizations." Yes, finally more organizations are catching on to what the Gores started in 1958. Open organizations, writes Jim Whitehurst, now former CEO of Red Hat, are intentionally designed for the world of speed, connectivity, and greater competitiveness. In his book entitled *Open Organization,* Whitehurst defines an open organization as "an organization that engages participative communities both inside and out--responds to opportunities more quickly, has access to resources and talent outside the organization, and inspires, motivates, and empowers people at all levels to act with accountability." Red Hat itself is one of the most revolutionary companies in the new era. With greater transparency, engagement, collaboration, and inspiration, Red Hat and Patagonia, are two great examples of big companies that have created the workplaces where people want to be and believe they can make a difference. Unlike all toxic environments and most bureaucratic cultures that are hierarchical in nature and dictate who gets heard, Whitehurst writes that "the most influential voices at Red Hat aren't necessarily tied to someone's title or even his or her longevity within the company. Instead, the respected individual tends to be those who have a track record of being consistent and selfless. You can't assume that your job title gives you credibility, any more than it does in a real community. . . . There really is an objective beauty to this principle because titles, experience, and politics begin to matter far less than insight and sound reasoning." The term for all of this is "meritocracy." Based on merit, the best reasoning and the best case win the day. Meritocracy was part of the driving force for Nucor in their "good to great" years.

As we discussed earlier regarding Gore CEO Terri Kelly, she became CEO because she had the most people who wanted to follow her lead. She had the greatest influence. Most importantly, it flies in the face of the old myth that the CEO is always the smartest person in the room, therefore getting to make the final decision. Leaders for a better normal will look more like the leaders in open organizations, always seeking the best thinking of all and the better solutions that result.

Takeaway for leaders. Document some examples of winning ideas that led to new policies or products or led to greater value for a stakeholder. Share those and recognize your colleagues. You cannot over-communicate and over praise examples of good thinking and acting and how people make a difference. I have never, ever heard one person say she was over recognized or over appreciated!

Leadership Paradigm Shift 9: Leaders Everywhere.

Another big paradigm leadership shift that comes from Gore and Associates plus a new group of open organizations is the belief that organizations need many more leaders. In fact, in open organizations, everyone is expected to lead with their unique expertise and thought leaders emerge over time. Many of you work in traditional hierarchical organizations and you can still tap into the core concept here. All your colleagues have leadership potential. They just need to know that you believe that. If your organization itself is traditional, you can still benefit from how you work with your colleagues and your team. You will need to be more proactive since the organizational culture does not support you conceptually and practically. That said, you want to tap into that underutilized potential in each of the people you lead. By being proactive, I mean you work on listening, actively seeking feedback and ideas from each person. They will need to learn that they can trust you and that you sincerely want to hear all their ideas, however crazy they might think they are.

Takeaway for leaders. Catch others leading. Catch people making a difference. Then recognize them in the form of feedback they prefer. Some would prefer private personal feedback. Others like to be recognized publicly. So, find out what people prefer.

> This is the "platinum rule." Treat others as they
> want to be treated is the principle that people are
> different and we should treat people differently.

I like a surprise. My wife absolutely, unconditionally hates surprises. We are beautifully different and that is the human magic.

Leadership Paradigm Shift 10: Courage for the Community.

Leaders for a better normal lead change. They go beyond just "managing" the rapidly changing dynamics that impact daily organizational life, although they are often forced into a reactive mode. The reactive mode certainly kicks in when leaders are blindsided, must put out fires. But, far and away, leading change is a characteristic of great leaders. Leading change is a proactive mindset. Now, after 2020, leading change calls leaders to be proactive in speaking up on community and national issues that have a direct impact on their stakeholders, especially the ones who are their most important assets.

There is a significant paradigm shift emerging for leaders after the 2020 **leadership** crisis and opportunity. Many would call this new emergence a moral imperative for leaders. I do. This is a "the trumpet call cannot be unclear" moment. There has never been a time in recent history where business leaders have been called so strongly to lead in their own organization and the broader community related to structural inequities and the environment.

The impact of systemic inequities negatively impacts millions of people directly and all of us indirectly, the impact of environmental change negatively impacts all people around the globe, and the new challenges to democracy itself create a common threat to us all. Remaining silent and being complicit is not an option.

Courage to lead in the community is a leadership opportunity of grand proportion and deserves a larger discussion in the next two chapters.

SUMMARY

This chapter has been devoted to the power of recognition in touching the core humanness in people. People yearn to be valued for who they are and the difference they make. The beauty in the leadership shifts that emerge from these models for Better Normal leadership is the applicability for leaders in any organization or enterprise. They come from a human and personal growth model, and they are all about relationship-building. As you learn them and apply them, your relationship with others will improve at work and home. Obviously, it is easier if the leaders within an organization are on the same page with you, but regardless, you can implement with the colleagues you lead. The takeaways share common threads:

- Since the concepts are rare to most bureaucratic, traditional, or normal organizations, the leader must do what great leaders must do: build trust, build relationships, spend more time on the front end of leading change by making your case for working differently than normal. Recall that normal is the enemy of better normal. Get to know your people. Listen to your people.

- Use some form of the St. Jude model of capturing what inspired people do when they are living out core values and guiding principles. In great organizations, core values and actions consistent with those values are easily documented. St. Jude inspires and lives out its values. You can find a way to do that even though your mission may not be finding cures and saving lives. All leaders anywhere can lead for a just cause within their enterprise. Find a way for people to discover their passion and make a difference. Then, recognize the people and teams as they make a difference.

Make "story catching" a part of the culture. Document the stories. Show your colleagues how their actions make a difference. They need to see what "making a difference" looks like. A story that became famous in our Advancement team at Belmont was the story of a lifelong piano teacher in her early 80s. Her husband had died earlier and left her with a small fortune. Vicky Tarleton, our planned gift leader and the person on our team who had the best relationship with this sweet woman, asked this woman if she might consider a proposal that would allow her the opportunity to have a lasting impact on the music program at Belmont. She agreed and in a few days Vicky and team leader Jason Chandler returned with a proposal for her to create an endowed scholarship at Belmont that would generate enough interest each year for perpetuity to fund scholarships for piano majors who might not otherwise be able to go to college. In addition, she could also complete the funding that would allow Belmont to become an All-Steinway University, meaning that all future music majors would be learning, practicing, and performing on Steinway pianos when they came to Belmont. As the explanation of what her money could do for future piano and music students for generations to come was ending and this dear woman realized the scope of what she could do, tears flowed down her face and she said, "I now know the purpose of my life. This is exactly what I was intended to do." She then got up and played the piano to celebrate and express her joy. This beautiful story connecting passion and purpose was told often as an example of the joy of giving, helping others find their passion and seeing how they can make a difference in the lives of others.

BEING INTENTIONAL WITH THE NON-NEGOTIABLE LEADERSHIP PRACTICE OF MAKING A DIFFERENCE: RECOGNIZING INDIVIDUAL AND TEAM CONTRIBUTIONS

By this time, in your journey to being an inspiring Better Normal leader, you have listened more intentionally to the people around you, discovered what they plan to do with their one wild and precious life, why they do what they do, how they contribute to the vision, mission, and core values, and what their goals are for their role. You have a lot of new information about the people around you and several new leadership practices to apply to help make them successful. Recognizing others is connecting and it trumps every other perk that people want. It is about relationships. It is another non-negotiable leadership practice that humanizes the workplace and builds a culture of inspiration.

1. Good recognition is frequent, purposeful, specific, and timely. Make the time this week to talk with the people you lead and recognize either a contribution they have made personally or collectively. This can be something you saw that was progress toward a goal, a collaborative effort taken, or something else you appreciated. At the close of a meeting, for example, a simple comment like the following will be a breath of fresh air. "I appreciate the way you guys received the feedback from our customers on Monday. The feedback was harsh, critical, and informative. You listened and asked for more information. You worked to understand the issues from the perspective of the customers. And you are acting quickly to demonstrate to them

that you heard them. This will only strengthen our relationship with them. Well done."

- Say "thank you" often for specific work-related behavior through verbal interaction in the hallway, office, or over coffee. Write thank you notes and leave sticky notes of thanks in people's workspace.
- People love hearing their name. Be the "Cheers Bar" leader who knows everybody's name.

2. Leaders, find individual and collaborative success stories that live out core values, mission, and strategic initiatives. They are all around you and they are powerful ways to demonstrate what "good work" looks like. Multiple people are part of the story, the good work. I suggest finding a way in every meeting with your team, group, or division, to recognize individuals or teams that made the story possible.

3. Although some people prefer praise in private, the reason I suggest public recognition is that leaders can use each public recognition as a teaching moment for others in the organization. The behaviors and actions you take to recognize others are the ones that you want to become intentional, conscious, automatic, and comfortable for all. These are new habits that you can quickly learn.

4. Of the 9 paradigm shifts that have occurred, changing the narrative for leadership, which one resonates most with you, and which one will be hardest for you? Share your ideas with a friend or mentor who you trust.

- Note: Should you be in New York and love music, you will be inspired by third and fourth generation piano creators when you visit the Steinway & Sons factory in Astoria, N.Y., a real Steinway Village in Queens.

See the World through
the Eyes of the
People You Lead

Feel and Understand
Their Pain and Passion

Be Compassionate
and Act

Use Your Power and
Influence To Help
Make Lives Better

CHAPTER TEN

EMPATHY INTO ACTION: THE NEW LEADERSHIP ROLE TO LEAD CHANGE FOR THE COMMON GOOD

"The only thing necessary for the triumph
of evil is for good 'people' to do nothing."

— EDMUND BURKE, 18TH-CENTURY IRISH PHILOSOPHER

Turning Empathy into Action is the last of the 7 non-negotiable inspiring practices of leaders for a Better Normal. This practice is inspirational because it makes life better for the people leaders work with every day. From the opening sentences of this book, we have shined a light on a new perspective of leadership that humanizes the workplace and creates a culture of inspiration. Diversity, equity, and inclusion (DEI) are "musts" for MBA programs and "musts" for the new leadership narrative. St. Jude has been a model for making the lives of children with pediatric cancer better along with their families and friends. They have gone from great to greater with their global initiative moonshot. Patagonia has been a model for responding to the environmental crisis with their strategic commitment to the environment. Leaders everywhere and anywhere can inspire the same kind of hope within their organization, their community, and the world with new strategic commitments to make life better for their people and the environment. New strategic commitments to people for diversity, equity, inclusion, and justice in a culture of inspiration will make other strategic commitments to customers, stockholders, and stakeholders even stronger.

> **Deep down, people want to do what is right, do good, and make a difference. This motivator and inspiring phenomena "runs deep" in us humans.**

As I write the chapter that I hope will be the "turning point" for your decision to strive for "Better Normal" leadership, I feel compelled to share something personal with you. I know first-hand about significant events that change lives forever and want you to know why I feel so strongly about this new role for leaders. I have written that things can never go back to the old normal and that we all must lead from a new perspective with new urgency. I have spoken of our one humanness and vulnerability. No one has supported this notion that leaders must enter the culture wars and be a voice for marginalized people more than the three most important women in my life: my wife and two adult daughters. The "fragile and vulnerable" nature of life hit our immediate family of four in the most personal way possible in 2020. One of us died. Steph's "one wild and precious life" ended in 2020 from a freak fall and fatal head injury. Our lives will never be the same again. There are no words.

Steph and I talked often about this book, and she felt most strongly about the message of this chapter. She talked passionately about the need for good people to find their moral compass and stand for the common good. Thus, my compulsion to share these thoughts and this pain with you now.

Steph had great empathy and compassion for those with less opportunity simply because of the way they were created or the conditions they were born into: gender, race, sexual orientation and identity, poverty, or geography location. In her opinion, good people should use their influence, their compassion and empathy, to reduce the pain and hurt in this world and make a difference. Her most common expression echoes in my head as I write.

"What is the end game for people who have the power and resources to make a difference in the lives of hurting people and don't? What do they want?"

THE END GAME??

The end game must start with being human and seeing the people around us as fellow human beings. In Ian Morgan Cron and Suzanne Stabile's book on Enneagrams, *The Road Back to You,* the last chapter begins with the story of Rebecca, a nurse who works with children with profound visual impairment. She also works with the parents of the children who have just been diagnosed. These are mostly young mothers who are shocked

> The end game must start with being human and seeing the people around us as fellow human beings.

by what they have learned. They are also hurt, uncertain what to do, and sometimes angry at this unexpected life challenge. Rebecca leads support groups to help parents understand, in part, how their child literally sees the world. "Apart from the practical advice, the most invaluable part of the workshops come when Rebecca hands the parents' eyeglasses that correlate to each child's specific disability. Almost always, the parents burst into tears. 'I had no idea that this is the way my child sees the world,' they tell her. Once they have the experience of observing through their children's eyes, they never experience the world in quite the same way again. They may still be angry about the diagnosis, but they're not frustrated with their child, because even a brief exposure to the reality of how hard life is for these kids inspires in their parents only compassion."

Leaders and aspiring leaders, here is your invitation: put on the glasses and look through the lens of the people with whom you work.

Look through the lens that correlate to the stories of women, single mothers, people of color, and others who have had less opportunity, those most affected by inequity. Feel, experience the reality of how hard life is for most of these people and be inspired by compassion. Care enough to act. Use your influence to make a difference. These are your associates and colleagues. These are the people that you work and live with every day. These are your teammates. These are the people that can make any leader and any organization successful. These are our fellow human beings. They are us. When some are marginalized, all of us are diminished. And, the environmental crisis directly affects us all, poor people and people of color even more.

You recall Maslow's hierarchy of needs from an earlier chapter. You recall also that the wildly successful and innovative company, Gore and Associates, was founded on the premise that people would be inspired to bring their best to work in a culture that intentionally fostered personal growth and self-actualization as well as collaborative teamwork. People at Gore thrived by building a unique culture around Maslow's hierarchy and win-win collaborative thinking and acting. At the core of the hierarchy is the gateway to innovation, creativity, and exceeding expectations: love and belonging. Yes, love and belonging are non-negotiable and part of the new leadership language and narrative. These sound like God-like qualities, don't they? And they are. Love and belonging are at the heart of humanity, and they are "thriving qualities" at home, at work, and in community. We are hardwired for wanting to be a part, to be valued, to belong, to be connected to others. But fitting in is different than belonging, as Brené Brown has illustrated beautifully. From her research on vulnerability and connection, came another book, *Braving the Wilderness.* In this work she dived into what participants meant when they reported often about feeling "spiritually disconnected" and a "diminished sense of shared humanity. Over and over, participants talked about their concern that the only thing that binds us together now is shared fear and disdain, not common humanity, shared trust, respect, or love." Brown admits that it was counterintuitive for her, so I am guessing it is the same for most leaders and would-be leaders. Maybe even shocking to discover that "connection to a larger humanity gives people more freedom to express their individuality without fear of jeopardizing belonging." She goes on to declare something we all wish we had heard and appreciated long ago. Belonging means "I can be myself when I know that I'm with people who recognize the inextricable, unnamable, spiritual connection that is shared humanity, because belonging is not in jeopardy. True belonging doesn't require us to change who we are; it requires us to be who we are."

A culture of inspiration is a culture that intentionally offers people a chance to grow and be who they are. And get this. "Our sense of belonging can never be greater than our level of self-acceptance."

> A culture of inspiration is a culture that intentionally offers people a chance to grow and be who they are.

Therefore, in this critical new role for business, community, religious, and political leaders, all must listen to understand the people they lead. They must acknowledge the shared humanity, help people feel listened to, and help them secure a place to belong. Leaders must stand for, speak up for, and inspire compassionate practices and policies. I am inspired by my daughter's spirit as I write. My hope is that her sensitive awareness and empathy for people will impact my writing in a way that will help you see the world through the eyes of the people you lead. She would want you to be open to and see the hurt, pain, dreams, and potential of the people with whom you live and work. She would want you to be open to the environmental crisis and how you and your organization can lead in making a difference. The worst possible scenario for her dream, our shared dream, would be that "good people do nothing."

The culture wars are raging and create a time when real leaders are needed most. We need leaders who seek good and truthful information, demonstrate concern for all, and take actions to reduce inequities at work, in communities, and in the world. We must look to "Better Normal" leaders to lead us out of the wilderness. We cannot always depend on some political leaders to do the right thing. In fact, political leaders may make it more difficult for other leaders to lead for the common good. "Malignant Normal" political leaders are incapable of leading for a "Better Normal." "Bureaucratic Normal" business leaders so far have been largely complicit or silent with the growing destructive behaviors of the "Malignant Normal" political leaders and the media that support them. Thus, there is an urgent need for more leaders to step up and assume this new, worthy, and radically different role for "Better Normal" leaders. Leaders have a higher calling. We see examples of bold new leadership emerging related to the Covid-Delta surges in 2021. Religious leaders, many political leaders, and business leaders are showing their moral courage and their empathy for the most vulnerable and are being more assertive. As we have noted, there are already many leaders leading for a better normal. It's the right thing to do, and leaders, this is your new role.

You are the voice for the most vulnerable with whom you live and work. You must be an advocate for your people.

BE HOPE-GIVERS ANYWHERE ANY PLACE

So, fellow humans, those of you who seek to lead and those already leading for a Better Normal, you have a new inspiring practice to add to your leadership role in this new world. This is a big challenge to navigate. It will require the best of the new "hard skills" that inspire and bring hope. The rock you stand on is the people you lead. As you know, they are your number one asset. Honoring and taking care of them is good for all your stakeholders and good for business.

You can change lives, make lives better, and be a hope-giver wherever you are. This new role of leaders calls to leaders in any organization, business, or religious setting to make life better for those you lead and serve.

We wouldn't be talking about this new role if it weren't for the magnitude of people directly affected to some degree by structural inequities. I am fully aware how often I have used the term "millions." It is staggering to realize the number of people who fit into the groups of people who have historically been slightly to grossly diminished by systems and structures. There are also millions of people who have fought extra hard all their lives to overcome some lack of opportunity. They are resilient and persistent. Their stories are at the heart of the American dream. And again, we inherited this, and it isn't going to change unless new leaders change it. You didn't build the inequities into the system, but you now must acknowledge those inequities and work to remove them where you are, however you can. Otherwise, you will unintentionally come across as insensitive or uncaring. You care immensely. None of us saw 2020 coming. But you can rise to the opportunity. The American dream should never be as hard as we have made it for many. Think about any time you have been treated unfairly. You don't like it. It hurts, angers, disappoints, and discourages.

And, if the system treats you unfairly over and over, you don't want incremental change. You want big change now.

> "Making progress" is not good enough. Equity is equity.
> Fair is fair. "Shades of gray" may be good reading but is
> lousy policy when it comes to making things right.

I want to call out again the names of the groups of people who have been historically marginalized by man-made systems and structures since the scope and magnitude of those directly affected is so large. They make up a large percentage of the workers, employees, and associates in most companies and organizations. If we needed any more evidence of the inequalities and their painful impact, 2020 was the year that brought them to our living rooms and into the reality of homes and workplaces. In no specific order:

- Women. Traditionally have been and currently are paid less than men and often for similar jobs. Black and Brown women make even less than White women. Women make up only a small portion of senior leadership positions and seats on corporate Boards. The "MeToo" movement exposed the broad scope of sexual harassment in the workplace. Jodi Kantor and Megan Twohey, investigative reporters for the New York Times, write in their 2019 book, *She Said,* about the difficult job of uncovering the truth when businesses systemically have protected the abuser and colleagues of the abuser remain silent. They also write about the courageous and inspiring stories of the women first willing to come forward. The "She Said" reporting is a model for the type of gritty work and determination that leaders for a "Better Normal" must embrace for changing the policies that sustain the long-standing inequities that exist in most every organization and community.

- People of color have traditionally experienced and currently live with structural or systemic inequities in the workplace, the criminal justice system, educational systems, financial systems, home buying, with pollution, and in law enforcement. The "Black Lives Matter" movement joins the long struggle for "civil rights" and has become a major force in the moral and ethical call for significant reform in the various systems noted above. White supremacy is real. Racism is real. Hate crimes are dramatically increasing.

> The "She Said" reporting is a model for the type of gritty work and determination that leaders for a "Better Normal" must embrace for changing the policies that sustain the long-standing inequities that exist in most every organization and community.

- LBGTQ people have consistently been discriminated against and dehumanized by unfair policies and practices that make their lives more difficult in almost any arena, even in many places of worship that should be sanctuaries or havens for all.
- Indigenous people are the first people to live in a region. In America, of course, this means Native Americans. Our history with Native Americans is indeed a "Trail of Tears" filled with broken treaties, promises, and inequities, as well as years of brutal and deadly forced institutional education of indigenous children. The deadly practices of those institutions are just now being exposed. Imagine being punished for speaking your native language. Imagine being murdered for just being who you were created to be. Imagine your child disappearing forever.
- Poor people. The gap between the wealthy and the poor widens each year. In 2019, 35.2 million people lived in food-insecure

households meaning that at times during the year, these households were uncertain of having, or unable to acquire, enough food to meet the needs of their family because of insufficient resources. According to Statista, almost 1 in 4 American households make $25,000 or less per year. Add to this the lack of affordable healthcare and daycare, our response to the poor among us paints a dark picture for the wealthiest country in the world. Livable wages ($15 minimum wage is inadequate), healthcare, and daycare are huge issues for working poor. Being poor is systemic and not a moral weakness.

As many as 70% of working Americans fall into one or more of the above groups. Every leader should feel uncomfortable with the realities of inequities and lost opportunities. Guilty? No. Uncomfortable, bothered, and compassionate enough to act and make things right? Yes.

I am thinking again of Brené Brown's work as I am writing now and know she would be your biggest champion as you "dare to lead" with your new role. She sites vulnerability as the prerequisite for all daring and courageous leadership behaviors. Recall her assertion from her new book, *Atlas of the Heart*. "If we can't handle uncertainty, risk, and emotional exposure in a way that aligns with our values and furthers our organizational goals, we can't lead."

Dennis Waitley said years ago that "the seeds of greatness are within you and those you lead." And Robin Williams would whisper in your ear as he did with the young men in the movie, *Dead Poets Society*.

Envision this scene in the movie where Williams, as teacher John Keating, invites his students to leave their classroom and join him in the hallway where pictures lined the walls of young men, graduates many years earlier. Keating asks them to lean in and look closely at the faces in the pictures. "They're not that different from you, are they? Same haircuts. Full of hormones, just like you. Invincible, just like you feel. The world is their oyster. They believe they are destined for great things, just like many of you, their eyes are full of hope, just like you. Did they wait until it was too late to make from their lives even one iota of what they were capable? Because, you see gentlemen, these boys are fertilizing daffodils. But if you listen really close, you can hear them whisper their legacy to you. Go on, lean in. Listen, you hear it—Carpe—hear it?—Carpe, carpe diem, seize the day boys, make your lives extraordinary."

This is your opportunity to make your leadership extraordinary. This moment in this troubled country, mirrored in your organization and in your community, is the ideal time to make a difference. Your new role and your new "reset mission" as a leader are to know the people you lead, know their history, get up to speed on the structural inequities that you did not create. It's high time to show empathy with all your teammates by acknowledging what you have learned, commit to being there for those you lead and their families in the community, and take the actions you need to take to make things right and make their lives better.

> This is your opportunity to make your leadership extraordinary.

Remember Kyle Kover of the Milwaukee Bucks? I shared his story of discovery related to the reality of 2020, Black Lives Matter, and the growing awareness of police brutality in response to black men and women? Kover's story is so powerful and relevant to your new role, I want to mention it again. It is a story of one man and one team that were intentional with empathy and their actions.

The decision this team made to not play a game minutes before tipoff in late August of 2020 was a defining moment for the character of this Bucks basketball team. Fast forward to July of 2021, this team of character, empathy, and action would use their resolve to surprise most observers of the game and win the National Basketball Association (NBA) Championship title. As you might guess, there are stories within the story. In short, you must know that one of those stories is about the most valuable player (MVP) in the finals, a humble young man who migrated from Nigeria to Greece where a few coaches learned of his amazing athletic skills. (If you have read John Grisham's novel, *Sooley*, this might be the real Sooley, alive and well in Milwaukee.) Now, a young 26, Giannis Antetokounmpo understands what his journey means to people around the world. Here is his reflection just after winning it all. "I represent my country, both countries, Nigeria and Greece. A lot of kids from there. But not just from Nigeria—all Africa and all Europe," he said. "Eight years ago, eight and a half years ago, when I came to the league, I didn't know where my next meal will come from. My mom was selling stuff in the street. Now I'm here sitting at the top of the top. I'm extremely blessed. I'm extremely blessed. If I never have a chance to sit on this table ever again, I'm fine with it. I'm fine with it." And, Giannis continues with this hopeful wish, "I hope this can give everybody around the world hope. I want them to believe in their dreams." Giannis Antetokounmpo's journey includes several people who found the leader within to support and encourage the "one wild and precious life" of this young man. Leaders for a Better Normal will make it their job to discover the amazing gifts of the ones they lead, nurture their potential, and inspire the extraordinary in them.

You will recall Kover's August 2020 moment. Hear Kover again as he shares why he felt his role was necessary and important. "It's always interesting for me as a white man in these spaces. What to do? How do I help as a white man? What do I say as a white man in this space?" Kyle then expressed his poignant "Aha" experience, "You know what you do? You stand with the marginalized. And when you can, you amplify their voice, and you listen to their thoughts, and you listen to their ideas, and then you find your way to help out."

I want to paraphrase Kover for this moment and the new role of leaders for a Better Normal.

"Leaders, you know what you do. You stand against the leaders who helped create and enable a Malignant Normality or leaders who are content to get back to a Bureaucratic Normal. You stand with the marginalized people with whom you work, you stand with their families and lead in the community."

You listen to their history, their thoughts and ideas. With empathy, you engage your associates and inspire them to want to take actions for the common and better good, the shared aspirations." Why is this so darn important? Without empathy and understanding, you simply will never fully engage your associates. Empathy doesn't offer solutions, but it is the first step in conveying you understand and are willing to walk in their shoes.

A recent Korn Ferry article led with the thought, "It's not your imagination. There are way too many people working 24 hours every day to make our world a worse place to live: meaner, dumber, angrier, more selfish, more hurtful, and less understanding." The culture wars, the malignant normal political leaders, and those complicit or silent to the normalizing of destructive and dehumanizing behaviors are dangerous. Leaders who cannot stand up for their marginalized people, speak out against inequities, hate crimes, and gun violence cannot lead. The worst types of betrayal are from powerful leaders and organizations that protect the system over people, stay quiet to protect their power, and become a part of a cover up culture. They use anger and shame to keep people quiet. Power, control, and fear are standard operating tactics, and the practices of the ethical heart are ignored. The threat is real. It's not your imagination.

WAKING UP TO THE NEW WORLD AND BETTER NORMAL LEADERSHIP OPPORTUNITIES

Lessons learned from the pandemic and what the new world will look like are many. It is clear that people now think much differently about work and have discovered what their "want to do" is, and what they deep down value. As part of the listening process and getting to know those you lead better, I suggested earlier that leaders spend time with those they lead clarifying personal values and organizational values. People have reflected on their own during the pandemic what is most important in their lives. They are not as willing to jump through more bureaucratic hoops. The myths of "have to," "must, should and ought" have been exposed as people traps. Just because there are low paying jobs available with few benefits does not mean they will be filled. People are smarter now and value themselves more. The belief that a livable wage with benefits is just not possible has become probable. Profitable companies can invest their profits more in their people and their people will pay them back with greater loyalty and productivity. Most of us are willing to pay more for hamburgers, toilet paper, and basic necessities if it means the people that work at McDonalds, Walmart, or serve others in any capacity make a living wage, have health insurance, and more reasonable childcare options.

I am recalling the humorous story about the experience of one young man who felt led to pursue a monastic-like lifestyle with a premium on silence and reflection. Part of his code of silence was the admonition that he could break his silence by returning to his spiritual mentor every few weeks and would be allowed to speak only two words. The first time back, he said, "bed hard." The second time back with his mentor, he shared the two words, "food cold." And the third time, when asked by his spiritual mentor, "Yes, my son, what two words do you have to share today?" The young man, who had had enough of this experimental lifestyle, blurted out, "I quit." At any rate, the 4 million who said "I quit" in April 2021, according to the Bureau of Labor Statistics, was the highest "quit" rate since the agency began publishing these rates in 2000.

A Washington Post business article of June 17, 2021, did a deep dive into the lives of people who said, "I quit" during the pandemic, asking "why the big change?" Their responses are instructive and helpful in understanding why we are never going back to normal. Let's look at the rationale for quitting from two people representative of those interviewed.

Emily Jump, 25, from Columbus, Ohio was working for a cosmetic dentistry business when facemask wearing became common. Jump said she became fixated on reading people's emotions through their eyes. Then she started researching microblading and permanent makeup and discovered her calling. She had always wanted to start her own business but kept putting that desire into the "pipe dream" and unrealistic category. Here was the "Aha" thought. "But I think the pandemic helped me realize that maybe life is too short to think about something instead of just doing it." Despite the financial risk, she was confident she could do it. And she did. Jump said she's the happiest she's ever been.

Vladi Kuschnerov, 37, from Brooklyn, had wanted his own business for more than 20 years, but it took the pandemic for him to take the plunge. His thoughts were thoughts that many share. "I always wanted to give back to the community with a mission-driven kind of vision, but as corporate life cycles go, you're always pursuing the next thing, the next promotion." He goes on to share his lesson learned. "The pandemic has shown us there is no line between people's lives and their work. They will merge and merge, more and more together, and I think the best way to enjoy and have fulfillment in your life is to find something that fulfills you in your work as well as your personal life."

"Something that fulfills you at work as well as your personal life." The St. Jude challenge is for companies to make their missions and visions about making a difference in the lives of people and/or with the environment, regardless of the product or customer.

From another Washington Post article came an interview with a young couple with whom many can identify. Tim and Sara Wojtala did a total rethink about their careers due to the pandemic. They both changed careers. This was Sara's underlying reason. "The problem is we are not making enough money to make it worth it to go back to these jobs that are difficult and dirty and usually thankless. You're getting yelled at and disrespected all day. It's hell." And finding childcare with two young kids has been a huge issue she added. Tim and Sara are joined by many who had time to reflect on more purposeful work and work environments that value and respect people.

The big moment of reflection gave people time to consider, reconsider, and ponder more important things than long hours, uninspiring jobs. No more "it is what it is" thinking and the hopeless feeling of "what can I do?" The once-in-a-lifetime experience caused people to look at the world differently, ask questions of themselves and others they had never dared ask before. Many, many people did find carpe diem courage. The time was therapeutic. What happened is similar to what I saw when people came to me when I was a practicing psychologist. Most were perfectly normal, imperfect people who needed someone to listen to what they could not share with others. They wanted someone to hear them, understand how they were feeling, help them hear themselves and gain the courage to act on their new understandings. So, the pandemic led to a lot of therapeutic self-discovery and new-found courage to act.

For writers like me who could not get out and conduct personal interviews during the pandemic, investigative reporters and leadership consulting firms did the work for us. Thanks to these colleagues and the "big time-out," much of my research on the workplaces and environments of the future come from capitalizing on the excellent research done by others. The research and early outcomes from the experiences of an estimated 1.1 billion people who worked remotely in

2020 tell us all we need to know. There is nothing normal about the future of work, and insights are pouring in from "future" observers, thinkers, and writers. I want to highlight a few thoughts that are particularly helpful in grasping the opportunities of this pivotal moment for leaders for a Better Normal.

Paul Daugherty, Marc Carrel-Billiard, and Michael Biltz, all technology leaders at Accenture, shared these insights from their research related to the reset leaders need to make based on what we have learned from people like Emily, Valdi, Tim, Sara, and others. "The past year has poked holes in long-standing norms about how companies operate and how people live. Companies looked at their operations and saw fragile supply chains, untrustworthy information and radically new customer needs . . . While it will be tempting for companies to retreat to what they know, 2020 brought the need for a different path to light." They continue with this powerful challenge to leaders. "Companies have also learned that leaders don't wait for the "new normal," they build it themselves," sharing that "91% of executives agree capturing tomorrow's market will require their organization to define it." In short, we must all learn to be pioneers and explore new territory. With words that speak directly to our journey in this book, the writers add, "In this (new) future, companies are poised to have an outsized impact on the world around them---and financial success will only be one measure of leadership. It's a unique moment to rebuild the world better than it was before the pandemic. That means expanding our definition of value to include how well people thrive, the impact left on the environment, growing inclusivity and more." Hear their insight for enterprises that want to succeed in the future. "As the future takes shape, there will be no room for enterprises that cling to the past." Should you want to read more of their thinking, the article is entitled *"Every leader is a technology leader: Embracing a new mindset to shape a better future."*

> It's a unique moment to rebuild the world better than it was before the pandemic.

As mentioned above, "expanding our definition of value" means we have discovered how undervalued, marginalized, and vulnerable most people are. These are the people that have fallen off the radar screen of most leaders, believe it or not. These are the people that need empathy, understanding, and compassion if they are to volunteer their best work and discretionary energy to help the organization be successful. You know who they are by now, but you may need a few more pieces of information to know how critical this information is to your success as a leader.

I confess, for years I did not appreciate or understand fully the significance of our structural and systemic issues. Fortunately, I have learned from my marginalized friends, many researchers that have captured the negative impact of decades of inequality, and the stark images that were captured live for all to see in 2020. In addition, I have learned much from the three most important women in my life. They have helped me understand the multiple ways they are forced to think differently every day as women, just because they are women. The "Me Too" experiences are shared by most women. We men may not have intended to be the problem, but we often are. As a result, women must worry more about their physical and emotional safety at work and home much more than men. The message is simple for us men. Stand with the women you care about and all women. Understand, advocate for them, and be part of the solution.

There are multiple examples of structural inequities. We can no longer claim, as I once did, "I just didn't know it was this bad." Now we know.

My goal is to provide a few stark examples and simply say
all of these are on your plate as a leader for a Better Normal.
We simply must acknowledge them as leaders.

Then we must acknowledge them directly with all the people whose lives has been diminished in some way by the inequities. For example, if leaders want women to give their best at work, leaders must help fix some big problems. "We've now had 50 years of the revolution of women entering the labor force, and most necessities that make it possible for parents to fully participate in the work force are still missing," said Betsey Stevenson, a professor at the University of Michigan and former Presidential Advisor in Economics. She adds, "It's absolutely stunning." According to Stevenson, if we really wanted to be serious about ensuring equal opportunity, parents would have the opportunity to get affordable high-quality early-childhood education, parents would have the opportunity to stay home with children when they are sick, and the opportunity to do more bonding with a child after birth. And here's why "it's absolutely stunning." The United States provides less support for women in the work force compared to almost every industrialized country. In short, inequities in our systems have discriminated against women and people of color for years.

Let's jump to one more systemic issue that many young leaders would never hear about unless they sought it out: "redlining." Over the years, a mountain of evidence has brought to light a stark injustice: Compared with White Americans, people of color in the United States suffer disproportionately from exposure to pollution." According to Justin Onwenu, a Detroit-based organizer for the Sierra Club, "Communities of color, especially Black communities, have been concentrated in areas adjacent to industrial facilities and industrial zones, and that goes back decades and decades, to redlining." Redlining became a systemic issue and was used by the federal government to mark certain neighborhoods as risky for real estate investments because their residents were Black. Then Blacks were denied access to federally backed mortgages and other credit, fueling a cycle of disinvestment and environmental problems in those areas. In addition, years ago decision makers made some horrible decisions related to the interstate system in several cities, including Nashville where I lived. Onwenu points out, "a lot of our current infrastructure, our highway system, were built on—built through—Black communities, so we're breathing in diesel emissions and other pollution just because we're located right next to these highways." As inequalities for women and people of color are "stunning," so are the results of decades of redlining, federal policies that set the stage for segregated pollution. Dr. Robert Bullard, Distinguished Professor of Urban Planning and Environmental Policy at TCU, says the evidence is so obvious and that you can go to any community of color, and they can tell you exactly where the environmental issues are, whether it's the chemical plants, the highway, or the refineries, and the legacy of pollution left over from decades ago, in the air, water, houses and playgrounds. You see, we just don't think about this kind of impact if you haven't lived it, or if your children haven't suffered from the impact. Leaders have to know the history of inequities to appreciate the need for leaders to actually lead change.

There are many sources of great information for leaders who want to be informed and lead for a Better Normal. For example, one institute that helps business leaders make equitable policy decisions is the Economic Policy Institute (EPI). Its mission is to inform and empower individuals to seek solutions that ensure broadly shared prosperity and opportunity. It is a nonpartisan, nonprofit think tank created to include the needs of low- and middle-income workers in economic policy discussions. The Economic Policy Institute is one voice that speaks the truth for working people, believing that every person deserves a good job with fair pay, affordable healthcare, and retirement security. The research they have done debunks as myth the old "trickle down" theory. (Let me quickly insert that economics is not my field of expertise, but in short, trickle-down policy, according to the experts, rests on two basic assumptions. One, it disproportionately benefits wealthy businesses and individuals in the short run. Two, it is supposed to boost standards of living for all individuals in the long run, which is much harder to prove.) Even if we are not economic experts, we can seek the truth from those who study and research economic trends as does EPI. "Rising wage inequality has been a defining feature of the American economy for nearly four decades," reports EPI in May of 2021. Why? "Largely because policy choices made on behalf of those with the most income, wealth, and power have exacerbated inequality."

> For example, from 1978 to 2018, CEO compensation has grown 940% while the typical worker compensation has risen only 12%. During this same time frame, productivity increased 72.2% and hourly pay increased only 17.2%, making productivity growth 4 times more than hourly pay growth.

Even to the casual observer of trends, it would seem that "trickle up" theories would make much more sense. Why not go directly at the staggering wage inequalities, pay living wages, provide health insurance, day care, and increase buying power for those who need it most?

Let's put the above information together with other significant inequity information and we see why millions of people who had time to reflect while working from home during the height of the Covid crisis decided to leave their jobs permanently or demand the opportunity to continue to work from home. We can also see how millions of people struggle from paycheck to paycheck. A few leaders have dug more deeply and listened more closely to the people with whom they worked. They have been so touched by how many people in their enterprise are hurting and struggling that they have already taken significant steps to increase pay and benefits as well as seek to understand better how important the people are who do the work every day.

Korn Ferry CEO Gary Burnison shared this related insight in his regular column in June 2021. "Leadership absolutely does evolve," Stu Crandell, global leader of our firm's CEO and Executive Assessment Practice, told me this week. "The change in leadership that we're seeing now was already underway, but it's been massively accelerated by the pandemic and calls for social change." "Gone are the days of vertical leadership that focuses on driving results up the chain," says Burnison. "Today, we need more horizontal leadership that's all about leading across the enterprise. It takes a strong sense of purpose, awareness of how we impact others, courage to go beyond our comfort zones and challenge old ways of thinking, an inclusive mindset, and the willingness to embrace ambiguity and paradox . . . We are leaving the old world and leading in the new."

The words of Burnison speak directly to all of you who are on board for leading differently and accepting your new role of "empathy and action." Burnison continues, "As we look to the future, companies need to think how to rebuild better on the other side of the crisis to better support its workers and stakeholders. About four in five Americans agree the pandemic has exposed underlying structural problems in our society and opened their eyes to acceptable and unacceptable corporate behavior. Americans overwhelmingly believe that the pandemic has landed our society at a critical crossroads, with nine in ten agreeing that this is an opportunity for large companies to hit "reset" and focus on doing right by their workers, customers, communities, and the environment." Yes, you read correctly. Ninety percent of Americans basically affirm your new role to do what is right for those you lead, those you serve, those you live among, and the environment that impacts us all.

> Ninety percent of Americans basically affirm your new role to do what is right for those you lead, those you serve, those you live among, and the environment that impacts us all.

As I write in early August 2021, the need for intentional and collective action related to the environment hits a new high. A just released United Nations landmark report on climate change evoked a "code red for humanity" response from the U. N. Chief, noting that humans have pushed the climate into "unprecedented" territory. I want to highlight this information because it means leaders have a ground swell of support and permission for doing what is right, internally with your colleagues, externally in the community, and acting both locally and globally with the environment. The leadership practice of Ethical Heart: leading with compassion and your moral compass is lifted up. This is another stamp of approval. Sure, it takes courage to develop these new practices and habits. Sure, you will feel vulnerable and exposed, but you know you have legions of silent deep-down encouragers and supporters who are looking for leaders to model the way and lead with a moral compass and compassion for humanity. And the urgency with every inequity and our response to the environment is indeed a "code red for humanity." And, as you begin to lead differently, you will inspire and encourage those silent supporters to find their voice.

Here is how one well-known company assumed advocacy for the environment years ago, signaling their commitment to lead for a Better Normal. A new survey from Axios and The Harris Poll found Patagonia to be the most respected brand in the country. Founder Yvon Chouinard was passionate about environmentalism and knows that some people are turned off by that passion. But, at Patagonia, they've decided they don't need to appeal to every American as an employer or a retailer---they want the most engaged employees and the most loyal customers. Here's what former CEO, Rose Marcario, had to say about living out their environmental value.

"Whenever we make these decisions (based on our values), there are two outcomes. We do better business---we make more money—and the other part of it is, we attract people to the company who want to work for a company that has a greater purpose than just selling stuff."

Swedish climate activist Greta Thunburg has brought a real sense of urgency to all leaders about climate and, in truth, all human issues that matter most when she spoke at the World Economic Forum in 2019: "I don't want you to be hopeful. I want you to panic. I want you to feel the fear I feel every day, and then I want you to act. I want you to act as you would in a crisis. I want you to act as if the house was on fire. Because it is." There's nothing normal about climate change.

"The impacts of these events are unfolding moment-by-moment— on streets and in living rooms, in board rooms and on the factory floor, in hospitals and in supermarkets—across the country, where Americans contend with illness, with inequity, with loss," concludes Burnison. "What future comes of this time of turmoil remains to be seen, but what's clear is that it has revealed an economic system that propagates inequality and instability—a system that we now have the opportunity to repair and rebuild together." So future leaders need good information about the inequalities in order to be empathic with the magnitude of the problem and the number of people they lead who are negatively impacted by the inequalities.

Patagonia is an excellent example of how leaders in the new world after 2020 must deal with pushback from potential customers. They value and are passionate about environmentalism. The environment, systemic racism, women's rights, protection of voting rights, social justice, affordable healthcare, daycare for working parents, vaccines, masks, and gun violence have all become a part of the polarization of America and the great culture war. Business leaders and leaders for a Better Normal must know the truth and stand for the marginalized people with whom they work. Avoiding these issues will never make the conflict go away and will only embolden Malignant Normal leaders and those complicit with them. So, if equity, diversity, psychological safety, and inclusion are values of the company you lead and values of the people you lead, look to Patagonia and St. Jude and others like them for how to deal with the blow-back from the culture war. New evidence tells us that most people want leaders to do right and will appreciate your courage. Gen Xers or Millenniums and Gen Zers and most talented older people are now seeking cultures of inspiration and places where they can make a difference.

JUST Capital is one group of people that saw the writing on the wall concerning the inequities in our economic system. Like the Economic Policy Institute we discussed earlier, JUST Capital was founded to provide better information for more informed decision making by companies and organizations. We look to groups like this because they are committed to helping companies and leaders find a better way to lead. The founders of JUST Capital were a group of concerned people from the world of finance, business, and civil society who collectively said, "We are capitalists committed to stakeholder capitalism." Their mission is "to build an economy that works for all Americans by helping companies improve how they serve all their stakeholders—workers, customers, communities, the environment, and shareholders. We believe that business and markets can and must be a greater force for good, and that by shifting the resources of the $19 trillion private sector, we can address systemic issues at scale, including income inequality and lack of opportunity. Guided by the priorities of the public, our research, rankings, indexes, and data-driven tools help measure and improve corporate performance in the stakeholder economy."

Look at just one of the shocking research findings that drives the work of JUST Capital. Get this. Fifty percent (50%) of workers at America's 1,000 largest public companies were not making enough to support a family of three, even with a spouse working part time. JUST Capital is the only independent non-profit that tracks, analyzes, and engages with large corporations and their investors on how they perform on the public's priorities of equity and fairness. In other words, Mr. Large Corporation, what are you going to do with the fact that 50% of your colleagues are not making enough to support a family of three, even with a working spouse? What are you going to do about the fact that women traditionally make less money than men doing the same job? What are you going to do about the fact that Black and Brown women traditionally make even less? What do you plan to do with all the people you work with who have been traditionally marginalized? What will you do to create living wages, affordable health insurance, and affordable day care for all your people? So, JUST Capital provides the tools to organizations and leaders to be intentional about their most important assets, set goals, and measure progress toward those goals.

The crisis and opportunities that simultaneously emerged in 2020 have been a wake-up call for companies and organizations. Because of established federal and independent groups like the Economic Policy Institute and JUST Capital who had already compiled rich information and data related to structural inequities prior to 2020, companies and leaders can take quicker actions as they realize they have great power to improve lives in the world around them. Social contracts make sense. Taking actions not only to improve the lives of their employees but the lives of those in the community around them makes sense. Intentionality makes sense. Belief and hope are turning into reality. There are role models and good examples of leaders and companies making a difference. We are changing our behaviors. We are seeing empathy and actions resulting from new understandings.

THE NEW ROLE OF LEADERSHIP FOR THE BETTER NORMAL: TURNING EMPATHY FOR OTHERS INTO STRATEGIC ACTIONS FOR A BETTER COMMUNITY AND BETTER WORLD

Better Normal Leadership is dramatically different from the inadequacy of Bureaucratic Normal Leadership or the dangerous trend of Malignant Normal Leadership. Better Normal Leadership is a bold new approach for a better world.

In the opening pages of this book, I suggested that leaders must see the world from a different perspective, a perspective with a world view where there is significant hurt and pain from man-made violence, systemic inequities, winning at the expense of others, a growing number of powerful people leading for a "malignant normal" as opposed to a "Better Normal," and increasingly destructive outcomes from climate change. In addition to leaders finding their moral compass and leading with the leadership practices that inspire others they lead; I am advocating a new role for leaders. This new role will add value to the lives of colleagues, their families, and the community in which all of you live. The new role means that you serve in new ways, build products in new ways, interact with associates in new ways, and you add value around you in new ways. Michael Lit, CEO and Co-Founder of Vidyard, an on-line video platform for business, wrote a recent Forbes article describing how the pandemic changed everything about normal. As a software business leader, he witnessed and experienced, along with other enterprises around the world, a historic software adoption curve during Covid. Everyone had to adapt to new ways of working that upended normal assumptions about employee productivity and how to get the most out of your associates. Lit and his colleagues see a decade of disruptions to established industry structures. For example, he suggests we are in the midst of a generational shift and that Gen Z folks will dominate the world in a few years. They are, he says, "far more comfortable using video to interact with fellow employees and the outside world . . . they came to maturity in a convenience economy where the expectation was that everything should be available immediately, as conveniently as possible. So, how do you expect the average Gen Zer to commute two hours to a job?" In short, they are not going to and "we're not returning to the old normal. Why should we?"

Although Lit is making the case for technology and video interactions as a new way to interact with associates, at a deeper level he is making a case for empathy with a new generation. He is saying leaders need to be sensitive to building a new kind of relationship with those they lead, one that does not depend on the organization needing large quantities of physical space. We older generations will have to give up

> The new role means that you serve in new ways, build products in new ways, interact with associates in new ways, and you add value around you in new ways.

our preference for more face-to-face interactions, realizing that relationships are not sustained by physical proximity alone. Far from it as a matter of fact. It's word of wisdom to leaders, "Too many business leaders remain stuck in an old mindset, seemingly desperate to justify their existing expenditures in real estate . . . Any company that still thinks it can issue an edict and its people will happily return to the office is living in a bubble."

Relationships with and empathy for those you lead has always been about intentionality, whether you are in person or miles away. Leaders must now be more intentional and focused on what we all have learned during the lingering pandemic and increased awareness of inadequate leadership models. It is no less than a reawakening of the human spirit and new perspective on the value of life itself. The following issues have risen to "strategic planning" level. They directly impact the quality of life for people at work.

- Work-life balance. We have a new understanding that there is more to life than work, and life is short. We want to be inspired and live fully at work and home. And millions of people discovered this on their own.
- Remote work. We have discovered through a Covid-forced "time out" that remote work does create a new work-life balance and adds a new dimension to life. The added surprise for everyone has been the insight that hybrid models work, and productivity holds steady or increases.
- Childcare needs and flex-time opportunities. Most parents have to work. As we gradually shifted from a one-income household to two-income households years ago, there was no shift accommodating the need for convenient, affordable childcare. Nor did we provide enough flexibility for parents with small children to respond quickly to sick kids, doctor visits, and extra time to bond after birth.

- Predictable hours. Hours that change quickly from week-to-week drive people crazy. Hours that regularly hit 50 and 60 a week suck the joy from life. People thrive on predictability.
- Pay equity. The disparity between pay at the top and the bottom of the pay scale has steadily increased over the past 50 years. Pay for women over that same period has been consistently less than men and is even worse for Black women, much worse for Latino women.
- Opportunity to grow in the job. People are much more likely to quit jobs now if there is no opportunity to grow. Also note that "grow" in the job doesn't just mean "climb the ladder" or be promoted. More importantly it means being rewarded for expanding your influence, your learning, your ability to make others around you successful.
- Psychological safety and vulnerability. Physical safety has always been a basic core need, a steppingstone to higher order needs and reaching full potential. Now we have learned the power of a psychologically safe work environment that frees and engages us to be our vulnerable, imperfect, innovative, creative, and collaborative best self.
- Systemic and structural inequities and the environmental crisis have been exposed and laid bare. I have addressed these issues in a variety of ways. Addressing these issues and advocating for immediate change is the new role for leaders of a "Better Normal." It is the most powerful way to turn your new awareness and empathy for those you lead into actions that have a lasting impact.

Mike Haynie is Vice Chancellor for Strategic Initiatives and Innovation at Syracuse University and Barnes Professor of Entrepreneurship at the Whitman School of Management. He has studied leadership for over 20 years and interviewed thousands of business leaders, entrepreneurs, military officers, and coaches. He has especially focused on better understanding the few leaders who are able to lead transformational change. So, I was particularly drawn to an article he wrote with the intriguing title, "What Maya Angelou Can Teach Us About Post-Pandemic Leadership." "This has to good," I thought to myself, already appreciating the implications for leadership having briefly spent time with Angelou and been inspired by her work for years. Haynie says that what he learned from his studies of those who fit the traditional leader stereotype (what I have called the "Bureaucratic Normal" leader) may be a skilled executive but not a transformational leader and that Maya Angelou has an ability and gift that traditional leaders lack. Drum roll, please. "The ability to understand and translate the human condition." Haynie indicates, "I realize I'm not breaking news when I suggest that the 'soft skills' of leadership are, for many, the most elusive" and that most business schools, while claiming ownership of leadership as their academic domain, often find it difficult to introduce topics like "empathy, perspective taking, and emotional intelligence." In my new model, "Better Normal" leadership, I have affirmed that the old "soft skills" are now the "hard skills" for leaders based on the realities of 2020 and the challenge for leaders to be much more engaged with those they lead.

> Maya Angelou has an ability and gift that traditional leaders lack: "The ability to understand and translate the human condition."

Hanie goes on to say that "Angelou's writings, when viewed through the lens of contemporary leadership theory, represent a masterclass in empathic and humane leadership. That is, she offers insights into the nuances of human connectedness and belonging that illustrate and illuminate---in ways that are prescriptive and actionable—the attributes and abilities that have historically distinguished competent managers and executives from once-in-a-generation leaders." How powerful is that? And then he shares an oft quoted Angelou thought that takes on an entirely new meaning in the post-pandemic world, "At the end of the day people won't remember what you said or did, they will remember how you made them feel." And he concludes with this instructive thought for those who chose to lead for a better normal. "The extent to which leaders are prepared and willing to routinely exercise the soft skills of leadership—and commit to a culture where employees are and feel valued and supported—will ultimately define who wins and who loses the war for human capital in the post-COVID workplace."

> **Simply put, the new leadership role for the future requires sensitivity, empathy, compassion, and understanding, skill sets that most traditional leaders don't have or don't practice.**

Now, these required hard skills are a must for all leaders, including traditional supervisors and managers. Personally, I would encourage leaders to invite all the people they lead to join them and engage with Empathy 101 and Emotional Intelligence 101 learning. Talk about Maslow's Hierarchy of Needs and creating a culture of inspiration where people feel connected, loved, and belong. See this as learning the basics of a new leadership language with rich dividends for all relationships at work and home. Leaders are not only the hope-givers but also the ones who lead change to make things better. Leaders are the ones who must bring a new intentionality to their leadership. Leaders for a Better Normal must turn empathy for others into actions for others, "understanding and translating the human condition" with their colleagues.

I want to highlight three models of "empathy into action;" 1) philanthropic and organizational acts of empathy and compassion, 2) individual acts of empathy and kindness, and 3) structural actions with empathy that reduce or remove inequities in the system. All three speak to being intentional and using your platform for a greater good.

PHILANTHROPIC AND ORGANIZATIONAL EMPATHY IN ACTION

Americans are generous givers. In 2019 alone, we gave $449.64 billion, a 5.1% increase from 2018. The largest source of charitable giving came from individuals or 69% of total giving followed by foundations (17%), bequests (10%), and corporations (5%). Most of the charitable dollars went to religion (29%), education (14%), human services (12%), grant making foundations (12%), and health (9%). And this next statistic may be no surprise based on the number of solicitations appearing in our mailboxes and the number of fundraising events we could attend. Based on recent data, there are more than 1.54 million charitable organizations in this country. In addition, over 30% of the U.S. adult population volunteer talent, time, and energy to making a difference in their communities.

There are so many people in need and a multitude of worthy causes. As a leader, one way you can help others is to be a model for leading in efforts to give and serve others in your community. There is great precedent for being sensitive to the needs around us and doing our part to make a difference. The more leaders engage those they lead in making collective shared decisions about how to make a difference is a step forward for leaders for a Better Normal. It is a step in the right direction if you make this a process of discerning with your colleagues the greatest long-standing inequities in the community or communities you serve. Then, you will be opening the door to a discussion of structural inequalities or inequities that many of your colleagues may have grown up with and experienced personally. This can be a double insight for your team. Think of it as learning about inequities and learning about your colleagues. This sets the stage for thinking more deeply about how you will lead in making a difference on a more permanent basis.

INDIVIDUAL ACTS OF EMPATHY AND KINDNESS

We mentioned earlier that your imagination was not failing you, that yes indeed there were people working 24/7 to make the world more mean-spirited, more angry, more divisive, more hateful, and less empathic and compassionate. So, I pay attention to people who act in contrast to the growing malignancy of bad behavior. I was recently inspired by the 2021 version of the 2020 Tokyo Olympics and the numerous celebrations of the human spirit that go beyond borders and boundaries. There were many moments to salute, but one that particularly touched me was an interchange between two superstar women, one in gymnastics and one in music. Unexpected empathy from unexpected sources is powerful, and we saw this rare display of empathy play out in real time between Simone Biles and Taylor Swift. As you know, Biles was heavily favored to win at least 5 medals. You will recall that she had to withdraw from all the competition that required the masterful twisting in the air for which she is known. The cause for withdrawal? The "twisties," a phenomenon that causes gymnasts to feel "lost in the air" and can result in horrific injury. If you have ever had positional vertigo, as I have, you have a small sense of Simone's feeling. It is scary. Her twisties was likely triggered or exacerbated by the enormous stress she faced from high expectations. As it turned out, she did compete in one final event, the balance beam, that did not require twists. She earned a bronze medal for her scaled back performance and showed great courage in the process. Because she shared her vulnerability with mental health and her humanity on a world stage, helping all her teammates win medals she might have won, Simone won much more than gold medals. She won our hearts, the hearts of the world. She also showed us her character, her moral compass, and her win-win collaborative mindset.

Among her many fans, Taylor Swift appeared in a moving video tribute to Simone, just before Simone competed in the balance beam competition, in which Swift asks: "What do we want from our heroes?

What do we expect of them? What do we need from them? What happens when they surprise us? When you have the attention of the world, everything you do takes on a bigger meaning. It can be a heavy burden. It can be a chance to change everything." Taylor talks from experience. She has used her huge stage to speak for equity for women and respect for the LGBTQ+ community. She has also called for political leaders and other leaders to use their moral compass and work for the better good. So, she salutes Simone for using her stage to help change the way we think about mental health and our one humanity. Taylor finishes her video with these sensitive words about Biles. "Throughout the last week, her voice has been as significant as her talents, her honesty as beautiful as the perfection that has long been her signature. But don't you see? It still is. She's perfectly human, and that's what makes it so easy to call her a hero. Simone Biles, back on the beam in Tokyo."

Don't you see, dear leaders for a better world, being perfectly human is our calling. We are all vulnerable, we all feel enormous pressure at times, we don't have all the answers, and none of us is perfect. Our willingness to be honest with ourselves and those we lead as we struggle together for shared aspirations reveals something even bigger: our shared humanness. Biles, who many have called the greatest athlete of all time, touched our hearts because she hit our empathy button with her vulnerability. And Taylor's creation of an empathic and understanding response evoked this from Simone. "I'm crying. How special. I love you, Taylor Swift." This is what empathy does, over and over, time and time again. Empathic responses capture the essence of how others feel. Empathic responses demonstrate an understanding of the other person. Therefore, empathy is your way to get through to family members and teammates. You can say "I understand" a million times, but showing you understand so the other person affirms they have been heard is the only way to get through. Empathy always gets through and the person who is heard always wants to share more after being heard. The "listened to" person always feels closer to the one who listens and understands. Finally, here's Taylor's response to

Simone. "I cried watching YOU. I feel so lucky to have gotten to watch you all these years, but this week was a lesson in emotional intelligence and resilience. We all learned from you. Thank you." Rarely do we get to witness this kind of interchange, especially between two powerful women with big influence on big stages.

I want to call attention to one other factor that is key to empathy. Notice who is the center of attention. Swift keeps the focus on Biles. She responds basically by saying "this is about YOU, not me." When seeking to understand and appreciate someone else, keep the focus on the other, as is done here. Google this video. You will see Biles performing and hear Swift's words. It's all about Simone. As I am writing today, just after this video came out and just after this exchange between Simone and Taylor, I just feel grateful for what we all had a chance to see and hear. What a model for leaders. Think about it. Taylor Swift's distinctiveness is her amazing ability to "connect" and be empathic with others. She hits a cord of shared vulnerability with her music. "It all begins with a song" is the tag line for songwriters, and Taylor writes most of her songs with that special gift of empathy and understanding. Millions of people believe in her because "She knows how I feel, she understands me, she gets me." As a result, people feel a little closer to her. They trust her. That's what empathy and understanding do. Leaders for a Better Normal, take note. Taylor Swift is a role model for the "hard skills" of sensitivity, empathy, understanding, acting from an ethical heart of compassion, and leading with a moral compass.

Unexpected acts of kindness and empathy are available every day to leaders. They demonstrate that the leader "sees" the other person. We all want to be seen and heard. We all are vulnerable. We all are imperfect. When the leader lives these truths, acts on empathy, the leader helps create the psychological safety necessary for high performing teams and extraordinary individual performance.

EMPATHY FOR PEOPLE MARGINALIZED BY STRUCTURAL INEQUITIES AND ACTIONS THAT REDUCE OR ELIMINATE THOSE INEQUITIES

Leaders have an opportunity to be real heroes in the new world. Leaders for the Better Normal who focus on making others successful by trusting them and inspiring them will separate themselves from other leaders. Leaders who actively work to remove structural/systemic inequities will bring an even more uncommon distinctiveness to their leadership. This is the empathy arena where leaders can have the most impact. This is the arena where you show you genuinely care about all the people you lead. Being transparent about commitment to removing structural inequities is essential to the leader's new role of making others successful and inspiring the best in others.

There are two basic opportunities for leaders to make a difference with long-standing structural inequities:

1. Internal, within the organization. Leaders can make a significant impact in their organizations within their scope of influence. Be brutally honest about existing inequities related to women, Black and Brown colleagues, diversity, inclusion, and the impact your organization has on the environment. Little will change unless policies changes or strategic initiatives with accountability are implemented to create greater equity. These are internal changes over which you have more influence and control.

2. External, in the community and world. Leaders can make an impact in the community when they personally help with community projects, invest philanthropically in the community, and more importantly, when they are willing to take a stand with their voice or company brand. Willingness to take a stand with the company or organizational brand is the most difficult, but it has become more important because of the magnitude of social justice and environmental concerns. Because of Malignant

Normal political leaders and complicit Bureaucratic Normal leaders, leaders for the Better Normal must see this as "lobbying" with a moral compass and standing up for the right thing.

OPPORTUNITIES WITHIN THE ORGANIZATION TO ADDRESS INEQUITIES

In terms of responding with empathy to an inequity that had festered for years internally, no one has answered the call for a Better Normal world more than St. Jude Research Hospital. I have referenced St. Jude in two previous chapters, the Ethical Heart and Creating Shared Vision. We left their story prior to the release pf their new five-year strategic plan (2022-2027) which outlines the strategic goals associated with their Global Initiative to significantly reduce the inequities between childhood cancer cure rates in America and the world. No child in the world! The impossible dream? Not anymore. St. Jude has taken the ultimate "leap of faith" from its successful model for America to a model for the world, ensuring that every child with cancer and other catastrophic disease will have access to quality care and treatment no matter where in the world they live. The implications of the St Jude Global initiative for the impossible dreams of a Better Normal future are enormous. It is an empathy-to-action model for any organization. Any organization can model St. Jude and inspire their people to reduce or eliminate a structural inequity in the organization. The mission doesn't have to be "finding cures and saving lives." It can be any mission that is life-changing for those with whom you work.

As a leader anywhere or any place, know that people will be inspired to be a part of eliminating any long-standing inequity as part of the larger strategic plan to make a difference. At Belmont University, we strategically addressed an inequity in opportunity by increasing our cultural and ethnic diversity through a full scholarship program designed to provide opportunity for high-need, high-achieving students in Nashville public schools. By 2021, over 280 students, mostly first-generation college students, had enriched the Belmont experience for everyone. Initiated in 2013, "Bridges to Belmont" came alive with a substantial gift in 2015 from a Belmont alumnus who graduated from one of the underserved Nashville public high schools. He would have never attended Belmont without a scholarship. This "pay it forward" gift was an inspired higher-calling response from a Better Normal leader, then Hospital Corporation of America (HCA) CEO Milton Johnson and his wife, Denice.

As a leader, you can identify the inequities in your organization that have been around for years. Listen to your colleagues and discover the stories that make the inequity real. Help people see and experience the inequity and its negative impact. Many CEOs have listened closely to their marginalized people who struggle every day to make ends meet. They have heard "I can't provide for my family." "We live day to day unsure how to pay our bills." "I am never comfortable at work because I can't do daycare." Some leaders who have realized for the first time the hardships of their people are raising salaries and benefits significantly.

"Our people are our most important asset" can no longer be an empty PR phrase used by bureaucratic normal or status quo leaders to describe their enterprise. We know better. There is so much new information. Like the song, "we can see clearly now" that people are our most important asset, and we see the companies that act on that belief and those that do not. Companies that treat people as "wild and precious" increase value for all their stakeholders and are simply more successful by all measures that count most. Now we know that long-standing inequities in our organizational structures demand immediate action, as does the environment.

EXTERNAL OPPORTUNITIES TO ADDRESS STRUCTURAL INEQUITIES IN THE COMMUNITY

Leaders, we must also be clear about the structural inequities in our larger community related to systemic racism and the impact on Black and Brown people. An unlevel playing field was built into the systems years ago. Some inequities are a continuation of discriminatory policies, (as in housing, bank loans, policing) that never were "named" as unfair or bias but have had lasting negative impact on millions of people. The inequities negatively impact every leader and every workplace. They directly impact the people you work with and thus they directly affect everyone. The marginalized people are our people, our friends, our associates, and our fellow human beings. This is the "lobbying role" for senior leaders particularly. You can make it easier for the significant number of your marginalized colleagues in a multitude of new ways:

- Listen to your people. Many may need help with housing, banking, home loans, or discriminatory practices within the community. Get engaged with your Chamber of Commerce and letting community leaders know how their behavior impacts the people with whom you work.
- Learn from athletes like Simone Biles, Naomi Osaka, and Michael Phelps who used their platform to courageously influence how people think about mental health issues like depression and anxiety that impact all people and all families. As a result of gaining new empathy for what had been the silent suffering of those depressed, anxious, and even suicidal, many organizations are taking bold new actions. The United States Tennis Association, for the first time this year at the US Open, provided quiet spaces for tennis pros to unwind, make mental health professionals available on site to determine if players were

too stressed out to conduct an after-match interview. Mental health issues gained par with physical health.

- The CEO at St. Jude used his influence internally to keep the vulnerable St. Jude Children's Research Hospital children, doctors, staff, and families safe during the pandemic by requiring vaccinations, masks, testing, and tracking. They isolated the clinical facilities where the children were, far in advance of the worst part of the pandemic, always being proactive and staying ahead of what seemed "normal" in the community. Then, Downing spoke openly to the Memphis community and asked they do the same to reduce the surge of the Delta variant as over 98% of hospitalizations from Covid were coming from unvaccinated adults and children. He spoke to the moral obligation to put the lives of vulnerable children and older adults over personal agendas.

- Patagonia, the outdoor clothing and gear company, was founded on a commitment to the environment. They proudly affirm that they "are in business to save our home planet. We aim to use the resources we have---our voice, our business and our community—to do something about our climate crisis." They put their associates in touch with a host of environmental volunteer opportunities and make it easy for associates to personally make a difference. Patagonia has found that doing what is morally right increases the loyalty of their people, their customers, and is good business.

- Can leaders make a difference with the deeply ingrained social justice issues and the structural inequities of systemic racism and sexism that create an unequal playing field for the women, black, brown, LGBTQ, and indigenous people with whom you work? Absolutely. It has been my experience that most of us want to do the right thing. Now that we know more, we can search for ways to use our influence, our brand, to make a difference as Patagonia did, aligning business strategies with their core environmental value.

LEARNING TO BE BETTER HUMANS

Rotary International is a humanitarian service organization which brings together business and professional leaders in order to provide community service, promote integrity, and advance goodwill, peace, and understanding in the world. Rotary is perhaps best known for leading in the eradication of polio, saving an estimated 20 million lives. With over 46,000 member clubs world-wide and a membership of over 1.4 million, Rotary has an unusual opportunity to make a difference in this world. Rotary is perfectly positioned: Global clubs, 1.4 million community leaders around the world, commitment to a higher calling of the common good, and service above self. In 2022, Rotary International made a further commitment to a global leadership role for a Better Normal with the selection of its first woman President in its 117 years of existence. Jennifer Jones, a member of the Windsor-Roseland, Ontario, Canada, Rotary club, made Rotary's commitment to diversity, equity, and inclusion a key part of her presidential platform. "Diversity has long been one of our core values and continues to serve as a foundation for how we interact with each other and our communities," said Jones. "I know that my experiences and perspective as a woman mean that I bring a different lens to how I see and approach opportunities and challenges for our organization. I hope to be a catalyst for similar opportunities for leaders from all backgrounds that comprise the global mosaic of our organization. We are stronger, more creative, and more effective when we ask for and leverage those diverse perspectives to tackle the world's most pressing challenges." Jones theme for the year? "Imagine Rotary." Her message resonates with me as a fellow Rotarian and author who is writing about the need to reinvent leadership and enlist an army of new and existing leaders to lead change for a better normal. My take on her challenge. "With

46,000 clubs around the world and 1.4 million diverse and influential members, imagine your power to make a bigger difference in your local community, in your region, in the world. Why not Rotary lead the way with new commitments to equity, diversity, and inclusion?" Rotary International is already an army of leaders for a Better Normal. They are creating and sustaining positive impact in communities around the world. Keep Imagining.

Rotary members in this country are already becoming even more proactive in leveraging their influence for good by living into their values since the events of 2020. Tom Gump, a Rotarian in Minneapolis, for example, shared the story of his personal "change of perspective" experience and that of his fellow Rotarians after the death of George Floyd. "Real leaders are made when you have tough times," says Gump, a former prosecutor turned real estate lawyer and Rotary leader. "When George was murdered, that changed everything." Gump and others were going to work hard to raise money for the Rotary Foundation to fight polio and increase club membership, but they changed directions after Floyd. "We figured that if Rotary is going to be a leader, we need to be a leader in the equity portion of our existence. Because if we don't, nothing else is going to work," Gump said. Over 150 Rotarians, many Presidents and President-elects, partnered with the YMCA of the North's Equity Innovation Center of Excellence, asking the YMCA executive, James White, a Black man, to lead learning sessions for the Rotarians. He called the sessions "creating a better story," an honest story about the history of Black people in America. "In reality, all we are trying to do is learn how we can become better humans," says White. "And as better humans, we're going to be more inclusive, and Rotary will be a place where everyone comes in and feels like they belong." Rotary is a "learning organization," committed to making local communities and the world a better place. Leaders for a Better Normal listen, learn, and then act differently based on what they learned.

Most CEOs know policy makers in local, state, and federal government and can advocate in some form for policies that address structural inequities. Advocate for voting opportunities. Create time during working hours for those who make you successful to get out and vote. Make transportation available. Work to reduce gun violence and create common sense gun policies. Every Fortune 100 company has a team of lobbyists. Since people are your most important asset, you can no longer just lobby for your best financial interests or your stockholders. You must lobby for fairness and equity for your people and doing what is morally right for your people.

A closing thought. What if the Business Roundtable, an association of the CEOs of America's leading companies, expanded their influence to make a difference, a tangible policy difference in police reform? What if they led the way to diversify their Boards to include many more women and Black and Brown people?

What if some led the way in reducing the huge disparities in salaries within their leading company and what if they made living wages, affordable healthcare, and daycare for all their people a real part of their strategic plan. What if top CEOs learned more about the lives of the marginalized people they lead, the people who make up a large portion of their leading company, turned up their empathy level long enough to understand, became more compassionate, and then committed to doing more to reduce the structural inequities? Recall the research that revealed that fifty percent (50%) of workers at America's 1,000 largest public companies were not making enough to support a family of three, even with a spouse working part time.

And what if politicians at every level thought more about good solutions and less about winning. Highly partisan politics as seen daily through the culture wars simply means we rarely use our collective best thinking. That's how people get marginalized. Win-lose and lose-lose thinking and acting are the prices we pay because of poor solutions or no solutions. The human costs are great, as we noted in chapter one. Organizations with compelling, complex, and worthy missions challenge all their people to be creative, listen to each other, be collaborative, and reach the best solution possible. Fortunately, there are emerging examples of politicians who have accomplished much through collaboration in business and politics and are willing to lead the way in seeking solutions to complex problems. One healthy example is a podcast coming from the Howard H. Baker Jr. Center for Public Policy at the University of Tennessee featuring former Tennessee governors Phil Bredesen and Bill Haslam, a Democrat and Republican, respectively.

"It really does matter how we approach governing," Haslam said. "I think our fear is, in today's world, it really has become a game where we're just trying to win the argument, we're not trying to get to the best solution. That's sad to me, that the method of moving people is to stir outrage and not to provide solutions. I think that bothers both of us." Marianne Wanamaker, executive director of the Baker Center, said the podcast format is in part aimed at college students, who often "don't have a thoughtful model for a functional political debate." She goes on to say that the toxic nature of the culture wars environment discourages young people from fully participating in civic life and politics. "They've been raised in a generation and taught to believe that people who disagree with you are evil, that you're in a battle, you're on the good side and they're on the evil side. It's your job to stand your ground. We want to turn down the heat on that and remind people that's actually not public debate, that's not constructive, that's not the way you solve problems." Both former Governors said they came away from their conversations with new insights into complex issues like gun violence, affordable housing, and climate change.

It's amazing what happens when people actually talk to each other, listen to each other, and learn from each other.

It is hard to believe that it was 20 years ago when U2's lead singer, Bono, paid a visit to George W. Bush in the White House with the goal of getting the new President to join the worldwide fight against HIV AIDS. Bono's visit and passion for his fellow human beings worked, and Bush created the President's Emergency Plan for AIDS Relief the following year, bringing life-saving drugs to millions of people. Even people with radically different political views can find common ground.

A NEW HEDGEHOG FOCUS FOR TURNING EMPATHY INTO ACTION

You recall the *Good to Great* hedgehog, laser-focus concept. Any organization with any product or service can energize their culture, brand, and attract passionate people by committing to eliminating existing inequities and/or enhancing the environment in their organization and community. This is intentional and worthy work and would become a part of your vision and strategic initiatives.

1. Pick your "passion:" equity in pay, livable wages with healthcare benefits, pay increases, daycare for working parents with small children, anti-racist policies and actions across the organization, leadership education for all and creation of a common leadership language, more people of color and women in leadership positions within and on the Board, a culture of inspiration, a hybrid work-home arrangement, environmental enhancement, or any significant improvement in quality of life for the talented humans with whom you work.
2. Choose what "you can be best at" in your world of business.
3. Decide on the "economic engine" that will sustain your chosen strategic vision-initiative over time.

Remember, you are competing for talent, you are competing for people who want to make a difference and give their discretionary energy to meaningful work, and you are competing for the future.

> So, the opportunity to make a difference is deep and
> wide. There is hope when we seek to understand,
> learn from each other, and struggle together to reach
> solutions that create a better human condition.

This chapter has been fueled by the passion of both our daughters who have always imagined a better world. This chapter, calling for a new role for future leaders, is the chapter they have most strongly encouraged. Ironically, the very first day of drafting this chapter, award-winning artist, Common, released a new song called "Imagine." The song captures the themes of healing, inspiring, uplifting, as we deal with all the injustices that have been revealed in 2020. "The truth is," Commons shared, "there is still so much work to do . . . we need to make sure things do not return to the status quo." John Lennon wrote another song called *Imagine* in 1971 in which he encourages listeners to imagine a world of peace, without materialism, borders, and religion to divide humanity. We desperately need to imagine a new leadership narrative where thousands of new leaders lead to make things better, turning their imagination for what is possible into reality. I also hope existing leaders, and those who imagine themselves for the first time becoming a leader, can sense the urgency of the moment. By accepting this new role, this new voice, this new visibility well beyond the status quo, leaders for a Better Normal can inspire a better future and a better world. The practice of turning "empathy into action" can be life-changing and hope giving for millions of people.

"The only thing necessary for the triumph of evil is for 'good people' to do nothing."

THE ST. JUDE MODEL FOR TURNING EMPATHY INTO ACTION

"St. Jude is where those with a passion for making a difference come to break new ground." – CEO James Downing

I offer a summary review of St. Jude's journey of reimaging their vision as a template for you to reimagine or imagine the new vision opportunity you have to operationalize your empathy into making a greater difference with your colleagues, customers, community, and the world. St. Jude chose to expand their vision for pediatric cancer and catastrophic disease cures to underdeveloped countries around the globe, reducing the inequities in cures between America and the rest of the world. You might choose greater economic security for your colleagues, a more compelling vision, or expanding the ranks of leadership to include many more women and people of color. Imagine being known for making a difference with the environment in your community. I encourage you to lean into the miraculous St. Jude story that I have featured throughout the book. You will see, hear, and feel the power of an organization being intentional about using the brains and talents of all its people and all its resources to focus on an even more compelling vision. The vision is a bold "great to greater" leap. The long-standing "no-child-should-die-in-the-dawn-of-life" empathy for children with cancer has expanded exponentially from America to the world. The inequity of cures for pediatric cancer in America and pediatric cancer cures in less developed countries will be greatly reduced by 2030 as a result of this giant step that turns compassion and empathy into life-changing actions. Any organization anywhere can make a similar leap with greater organizational empathy, a culture of inspiration, and an even more compelling vision for making a difference.

"IF NOT ST. JUDE, THEN WHO? WHY NOT US?"

According to James Downing, MD, President and CEO, the decision to expand their empathy for children to a global stage came from numerous strategic discussions that centered around the question, "If not St. Jude, then who?" Why not us? Who is going to do this is we don't do it? They were encouraged by their ability to get a lot of smart people to collaborate, and they saw a potential pathway to success. They were attracting the best and brightest stars to be a part of the St. Jude vision and, as Dr. Downing said, "St. Jude is where those with a passion for making a difference come to break new ground."

As you continue to imagine your "mission impossible" to make a difference with structural inequities, think about making your workplace a place where those you lead can bring their passion for making a difference to work every day and be a part of breaking new ground.

The spark from the small dying child who said, "Tell someone I am here" years earlier became a flame, and, in March 2018, the World Health Organization (WHO) saw all the potential St. Jude saw, designating St. Jude as the first WHO Collaborating Centre for Childhood Cancer. Shortly afterwards, in May 2018, St. Jude Global was officially launched with the commitment to ensure that every child with cancer and other catastrophic diseases will have access to quality care and treatment anywhere in the world they live. By 2021, there were already partnering centers of excellence in Mexico, Central and South America, Sub-Saharan Africa, Asia Pacific, China, Eurasia, and Eastern Mediterranean, creating a network and opportunity to build more partnerships. Every new protocol, every new breakthrough that saves a child's life in Memphis can be shared across the St. Jude Global Alliance, saving thousands more children around the world. The 2030 vision and strategic goal for St. Jude Global Initiative and WHO is ambitious. "To cure at least 60% of the children in the world with six of the most common cancers." The survival rate now is 20%, the same survival rate in this country when St. Jude was founded in 1962.

"It's a daring dream, but one that's within our reach. In science and medicine, collaboration is the engine that drives progress. Imagine what great feats we can achieve together, working across disciplines, across borders and around the world. Together, we will give children the best hope for their futures—no matter where they live," says Downing.

> *Here's the thing about huge, audacious, near impossible dreams. The person or organization who dreams and accomplishes the impossible dream knows how daring it is but believes its within reach.*

St. Jude has listened. They have heard the voices of children with cancer and catastrophic diseases in Nicaragua, Memphis, Beirut, Amman, Ukraine, and in the poorest, most hurting regions of the world. They have seen a fragile and vulnerable humanity in the voices and faces of children everywhere. The magnitude of need was almost overwhelming. Their cup of empathy for what they saw and heard was running over. They understood the human condition of children with cancer. They had the numbers. They knew how many children would die if they did not act. They never gave up. "If not St. Jude, then who?" St. Jude chose to make a lasting difference in this world by doing what no one had imagined before.

Their cup of empathy for what they saw and heard was running over.

The leap to St. Jude Global is another "giant step for mankind." It is only appropriate that as I write this reference to outer space, a Physician's Assistant at St. Jude's and former patient, Hayley Acre, blasted into space as part of a first-ever four-person civilian crew to make such a venture. The spaceship is named Inspiration 4 and part of the mission, in addition to research, is to inspire people around the world to learn more about St. Jude and its expanded global vision. Now, even the sky is not the limit!

The question now for leaders everywhere is this: What's your giant step for making a difference by reducing structural inequities and improving the lives of others where you are? What strategic commitment could your organization or team make to improving the environment? How will you stand up for your people with political leaders who seek to diminish the opportunities for some of your people and the opportunities for the children of the people you lead? Leaders for a Better Normal do have a new role and it comes from answering these questions. For most leaders it will mean thinking more deeply than ever about creating a better world and adding value in new ways to the lives of those you lead.

I trust you can begin your journey to answering the above questions from what you have been reading as well as from the models emerging from the growing number of open organizations, some of which have been cited in this work. However, the lessons you need for Better Normal leadership are all in the featured St. Jude model. I chose their model because it represented an already great organization becoming even greater, expanding its difference-making capacity to the world. St. Jude leaders have been most gracious in sharing with me during this difficult time. Sharing and kindness are a part of the St. Jude DNA. I must add, in my career-long search for leadership excellence, what has fascinated me most about the St. Jude phenomena is HOW St. Jude went from great to greater. It is the St. Jude "process" for doing things that creates the headlines and takeaways for the Better Normal organizations of the future. They are medical researchers and medical doctors, somewhat "nerdy" people by trade. They had to learn to collaborate, think and act collectively, and get out of their comfort zones. They did it because they shared a compassion and vision for finding cures and saving lives.

Let's face it. Think of all those beautiful minds, big brains, and international mix at St. Jude. Had they not gotten in the same boat, agreed to row in the same direction, and give their absolute best to the moonshot of St. June Global, none of this would have happened. As we capture the lessons learned from St. Jude, we see a diverse, international group of extraordinarily talented individuals who realized they had to become an extraordinary team to accomplish the new global vision. Then, they worked back from the new vision. An overarching lesson right here. Always go to the dream, the vision, and work your way back to now. What must happen to get us to our vision?

After Danny Thomas was inducted into the inaugural class of the Tennessee Healthcare Hall of Fame in 2015, I wrote Marlo Thomas. Marlo had received the award with a moving video tribute to her father at the close of the Hall of Fame event at Belmont University. Part of my message to her was, "St. Jude is such a rich blessing to Memphis and the world. Your telling of the St. Jude story served as a perfect close to the induction event and I can tell you that there were no dry eyes among the 640 people present. Thank you for continuing to be the face of the St. Jude miracle."

Leaders must keep the dream alive and lead the way in implementing the dream. Dr. James Downing became CEO of St. Jude in 2014. St. Jude was already wildly successful with new cures for pediatric cancer in this country. So, as he tells the story, his first directive from the Board was "don't screw up." Downing had been at St. Jude for 30 years at this point in his career. He immediately asked himself what challenges he thought he would face as the new leader. His response to his own question was a response that any leader should consider. "And the first challenge was me." "As a scientific director, I was the bad cop. I was the analytical, aggressive scientist that took no prisoners. . . . But that's not the job (of a CEO). I needed to get up. I needed to lead this organization and be the face. And I needed to communicate and inspire and motivate."

Leaders often need coaches, which is exactly what Downing did to learn the new rigorous "hard skills" of inspiring others. He continues to seek feedback and learn from his coach, willing to be vulnerable with another person about the doubts, questions, and leadership challenges he faces. This means leaving his own ego at the door and seeking to do what is best for St. Jude. He believes so strongly in coaching that he makes leadership coaches available to all people in leadership positions.

Remember how only 50% of new supervisors and managers are trained to manage, even fewer trained to lead. We know that only a small fraction of people promoted into leadership positions are taught leadership skills. As a result of Downing's own realization that he needed to learn a new skill set in order to lead, St. Jude initiated a Leadership Academy in 2016 that will eventually reach hundreds of people throughout the organization in a variety of roles who influence others. When I interviewed Leadership Academy Director of Learning and Development, Dennis Reber, and his colleague Thonda Barnes, I was pleasantly surprised to walk into the Marlo Thomas Center for Global Education and Collaboration. I had never been to any stand-alone building with the words "global" and "collaboration" as prominently placed at the entrance. Talk about being intentional with the importance of collaboration to their Global Initiative. Wow. There are 116 national flags prominently displayed which represent the diversity of people working at St. Jude, a powerful visual of the difference-making collaborative work required by the compelling global vision.

The Leadership Academy's goal is to provide every leader at every level the development needed to be able to lead "The St. Jude Way:" Be the Model, Unleash Talent, Ignite Innovation, Lead with Compassion, and Dare to Excel.

The Leadership Academy is extremely focused on the distinguishing features of St. Jude. Everyone knows they either serve the children directly or serve someone who does. Teaching and learning are values-driven, and intentionally capture the head and heart of St. Jude, a neat combination of recruiting bright people with emotional intelligence that fit the St. Jude culture. Reflecting on their "hedgehog" concept, they are **passionate about** children with cancer and catastrophic diseases, they believe they can be **best in the world at** finding cures and saving the lives of those children, and their **economic**

engine is ALSAC and the millions of donors who want to be a part of their global vision and core mission. They want all their people to understand what differentiates St. Jude from others and dare everyone to excel at what they do by aligning their daily work with the strategic plan. They teach collaboration and use the fuel of their vision and mission to inspire the discretionary energy in their associates for innovation and new discoveries.

Niraj Trivedi, a lab operations leader in Developmental Neurobiology, hosted me for a brief tour of his St. Jude facility. I got more than a tour. I got some additional insight into how deep the St. Jude Way permeates the organization. As we walked and talked, I asked him about his career at St. Jude. "My colleagues and I came into this field with a new approach to an old problem. Being at St. Jude inspires us to look at things in a new way." He then, without my asking, started enthusiastically sharing a story about microscopes and the revolution that had occurred in the capabilities of both light and electron microscopes. Trivedi went on to tell me how the microscope was so important to St. Jude research and the biggest challenge to microscopic discovery was simply "resolution," how to get a better picture of organs and cells. "The good news," he continued, "is that we have made great progress and are even working and partnering with the best people in this field, like a 2014 Nobel Prize recipient who has been a part of revolutionary discoveries and inventions related to better resolutions and images. Of course, this will allow St. Jude to make new discoveries in pediatric research." At this point, we were ending the brief tour, but I wanted to hear more about how St. Jude was working with a Nobel Prize recipient in Chemistry. This accidental story was beginning to sound like a Leadership Academy and "St. Jude Way" lesson of "unleashing talent," "igniting innovation," and "daring to excel."

EUREKA MOMENTS

Niraj referred me to his colleague, David J. Solecki, PhD, who had blog-posted an article on the St. Jude website in January 2020 directly related to this conversation. Solecki indicated that the impetus to reach out to Eric Betzig, the Nobel Prize recipient, came with one of the inventions Betzig help create, the cryo-SR/EM microscopy. "Just like astronomers needed the Hubble Space Telescope to peer deep into the universe, cryo-SR/EM microscopy is a powerful tool to peer into the depths of cells for biologists to get their 'eureka moments.'" Solecki said, in short, that he and another colleague were the first to utilize another of Eric Betzig's bleeding-edge inventions and the first to "ask a neurobiology question." When they did ask their question, as being curious and "daring to excel" often does, "the unexpected happened: we were soon not only in contact with Eric Betzig but were quickly in the thick of discussions to utilize one of his newly developed microscopes!" I have always been fascinated with the power of teamwork through my own research and excited that Solecki made a point in his blog article to talk about the collaborative process it took to unleash the collective talent of people from St. Jude and the Janelia Research Campus at Howard Hughes Medical Institute, bringing groundbreaking optical microscopy and new nanometer resolution to the research world of St. Jude. "How" they worked together led to a eureka moment that will further the bigger process of finding cures and saving lives.

This is the essence of organizations and leaders who are creating a better normal. They bring a new perspective, a new way of looking at old problems, and finding new ways to make a difference.

St. Jude also provides a good model for being brutally honest about their "current reality" and the threats and opportunities they faced with the global initiative. They chose to turn the threats into opportunities. According to Dr. Asya Agulnik, leader of the Eurasia Regional program, because of their partnership with WHO and other global partners in Ukraine, Poland, Italy, Spain, and Germany, St. Jude was immediately able to facilitate the evacuation of hundreds of families in Ukraine with children who needed medical care including many with cancer. St. Jude became the first hospital in this country to welcome 4 children in cancer treatment and their families from Ukraine. The global network of active compassion is working, even during war-time conditions.

I mentioned earlier how impressed I had been with the process of HOW St. Jude made the leap from great to greater. The Ethical Heart is activated by core values and compassion for others; Urgency about strategic initiatives keeps first things first, and Win-win collaboration assures maximizing the collective talents of all, as with the Solecki story above. If St. Jude's intellectual property is a gold mine for the medical communities around the world, the process (the How) they used to create the St. Jude Global strategic initiative is another gold mine for leaders anywhere.

"DON'T SCREW IT UP" TO REINVENTING

Downing not only changed his leadership style to inspire others, but he also thought St. Jude could be even better than the Board's admonition of "don't screw it up." So, he immediately challenged the organization to rethink everything through a strategic planning process. Everything. The five-year strategic plan of St. Jude provides the strategic direction and "wayfinding process" of getting to the future. The Global Initiative, one part of the strategic plan, has its own "wayfinding process," with specific deliverables by 2030.

Leaders in any organization can make sure their colleagues understand the most important strategic initiatives and how they personally contribute to those initiatives. This means intentional investment in time to do this with your colleagues. Five-year cycles of strategic planning are part of the culture at St. Jude as was true at Belmont.

With measurable and tangible goals, short-term wins are frequently reached and celebrated at St. Jude. There are successful patient cure parties, new cure celebrations, recognition events for those who model contributions to core values, and many other wins to celebrate. Remember the Kotter "Gloves on the Conference Room Table" story becoming an immediate company celebration and a beautiful example of what one person can do to lead change?

We discussed earlier the 10 core values of St. Jude. The annual peer recognition process invites associates to identify their colleagues throughout the organization who are living out one of the core values, supporting the vision and mission. They name the recipients, tell their stories in written form, and share throughout the St. Jude community. People can see what values and guiding principles look like!

St. Jude leaders were eager to share with me what they call "The St. Jude Way." They are proud of what they do, and they should be. Just as they have shared their life-saving medical protocols with medical centers and medical doctors around the world, they were eager to share the underlying non-medical protocols of leadership. I trust you have found them as hope-giving, inspiring, and difference-making as I have.

BEING INTENTIONAL WITH THE LEADERSHIP PRACTICE OF EMPATHY INTO ACTION

The Change Process:

Moving from Malignant Normality to the Inspiring "Better Normal"

Phase 1. Current leadership. Inadequate, uninspiring, and dangerous has become "normal." Unfortunately, current leadership practices are unconscious, automatic, comfortable, and systemically broken.

Phase 2. Changing to Inspiring Leadership Practices. Change will be conscious, intentional, uncomfortable. Trust the process of discomfort.

Phase 3. Leading Change with Inspiring Leadership Practices will again become unconscious, automatic, comfortable. The "Better Normal."

Notice again that being uncomfortable is a part of any change process. Uncomfortable is embedded in the learning and growing arenas. No discomfort, no change. No growth. No learning. This simple model of the change process can be useful to leaders with the people they lead. Being vulnerable and uncomfortable is on the pathway to great work and extraordinary outcomes. Traditional Bureaucratic Normal leadership practices are so unconscious, automatic, and comfortable that they have gone unchallenged for decades. Malignant Normal leadership practices are becoming unconscious, automatic, comfortable, and more dangerous the longer good people and good leaders do nothing to challenge their brutal and hurtful impact on people.

Our goal is to make cultures of inspiration unconscious, automatic, comfortable, and consistent with our shared human values. Doing the right thing, like with WD-40, can become the "knee-jerk" response of any organization.

BEING INTENTIONAL WITH THE SHIFT TO MORE INSPIRING PRACTICES: ACTION STEPS

Keep Asking: "If not us, who?" "Why not us?"

1. Consider starting with your colleagues and those you lead by discovering together the greatest, perhaps long-standing structural inequities in your organization and community. You can facilitate this meeting or ask a trusted facilitator in your organization to facilitate it. Start by focusing on the organization, then the community, remembering that structural inequities in the community have a direct impact on your colleagues. This could basically be a focus group to understand and share empathy

with those affected by the inequity. Begin with a few ground rules. First, people will feel some degree of apprehension and vulnerability about sharing honestly. You and others must agree to confidentiality and honor the thoughts and feelings of all. This may be the beginning of the creation of a more psychologically safe environment where people can share freely, without fear of repercussions. This will also build trust. Second, the goal is to identify and understand the inequities, not seek solutions at this point. Third, it is important that everyone in the group be heard so invite people to prepare in advance and write their thoughts on paper. Fourth, ask people to share their personal experience with the inequities they identify and the negative impact they see on the organization and the community. Anticipate learning a lot about perceived inequities and a lot about your colleagues.

2. From what you learn in step 1, consider what would have to happen to make significant changes and make things more equitable, both in your organization and the community. As a leader for a Better Normal, you are committed to making a difference.

3. Pick one inequity in your organization and develop a plan for making a difference by helping create greater equity. Think Hedgehog.

4. Pick one inequity in the community and develop a plan for making a difference by helping create greater equity. Think Hedgehog.

5. At some point, you may want to consider connecting a day of service in the community for the team you lead, find a way to support a family whose home has been destroyed by fire or natural disaster, or do a habitat build together. The key, connect the service to a structural inequity you have discovered from talking with your people. Remember, you are helping others see through new lens what the people you are serving see every day.

OPPORTUNITIES WITH THE ENVIRONMENT

"B The Change" offers great opportunities for getting started in making a difference with your empathy and compassion for existing inequities and with the environment. One of the strengths of the Certified B Corporation community is its collective power and network of like-minded businesses. Many others have already acted for a Better Normal and have developed programs and products that can help any organization, large or small, get started. Go online to bthechange@bcorporation.net.

Better Normal leaders will want to tap into the resources of the #ListenFirst Coalition, a community of over 400 organizations (the bridging field) that bring Americans together across differences to listen, understand each other, and discover common interests. The goal, in part, is to build a new foundation of trust and grace where shared humanity is recognized and celebrated, violence is avoided, division doesn't sell, common challenges are solved, and democracy and organizations become healthier, more resilient, and more robust.

Be The Light
Inspire Others
Act to Help
Others Rise

CHAPTER ELEVEN

LEADERSHIP CHALLENGE: HUMANIZING ORGANIZATIONS AND COMMUNITIES

"What counts most in life is not the mere fact that we have lived. It is what difference we have made to the lives of others that will determine the significance of the life we lead."

— NELSON MANDELA

As we come to the end of our leadership journey together, I hope you have been inspired to make a difference with your leadership in new ways. My wish has been and is that those who lead at any level in any organization, company, place of worship, educational institution, or home have discovered a few insights that change the way you think and act with your personal leadership. I have deeply wanted to make a difference with this new model of leadership for a Better Normal.

I authored this book with the strong conviction that the four powerful forces that emerged simultaneously in 2020 created the greatest leadership crisis and opportunity in our lifetime. During the writing of this book, that conviction has only deepened, and my sense of urgency intensified. The culture wars are literally killing us, putting even more pressure on leaders to lead change and do right. As we discussed in the last chapter, this historic time calls all leaders to be better leaders who see, empathize, and act to protect and inspire all those they lead and serve.

It is a time for leaders to find their voice. It is a time for advocating for equity, fairness, and justice. Non-political leaders must assume this new role of changing structural inequities since many powerful political leaders won't.

This is why it is an historic time, a once-in-a-lifetime opportunity to speak up and speak out to make a difference.

It is a delight to see young role models using their influence to make a difference. Kim Namjoon, also known as RM, the 24-year-old leader of the K-pop superstars BTS, spoke in 2018 to the 73rd session of the UN General Assembly. The occasion was the launch of new partnerships with UNICEF and other world leaders of Generation Unlimited and "Youth 2030." The goals of the initiatives are to ensure that every young person is in education, training, or employment by 2030. BTS had launched the "Love Myself" campaign the year before as a part of UNICEF's #ENDviolence program, a global initiative "aimed at ensuring children and teens in the world lead safe and healthy lives without the fear of violence." In short, these young men have been committed to making a difference with their lives and influence. They have sought to listen to young people and understand their life experiences, then write and sing songs that empower and encourage them. As I listened to the words from Namjoon's brief address to the General Assembly, I imagined him speaking to all of us who want to make a difference where we are and in how we lead. As you know, we have made the case that leaders for a Better Normal are responsible for finding their voice and turning their empathy for others into actions that make lives better. Take note of the questions BTS is asking. "So, let's all take one more step. We have learned to love ourselves, so now I urge you to 'speak yourself'. I would like to ask all of you. What is your name? What excites you and makes your heartbeat? Tell me your story. I want to hear your voice, and I want to hear your conviction. No matter who you are, where you're from, your skin color, gender identity: speak yourself. Find your name, find your voice by speaking yourself." BTS are hope-givers. They represent light for millions of young men and women. Hopefully, their spirit will touch your leadership.

I sense, in the next few pages, a kinship with my attorney friends as I have a chance to make my closing appeal. I know that over 50% of books that are started are never finished, but if you are seeing this appeal, then, you are still reading! Rather than making a closing argument or appeal, I want to invite you to make a commitment to personalize your insights from this book and the additional insights the book has sparked for you. Hopefully, you have begun to do some of this already from the "Implementing" section at the end of each leadership practice chapter. If you have begun talking more with the people you lead, really listening and making it psychologically safe for your people to be honest with you, you are learning things you never knew before. Being heard is so powerful and inspiring to those you lead. Remember the marble jar and trust building. Listening to others earns marbles of trust. And hearing is so powerful for leaders who listen. Leaders earn the right to lead by listening. I hope this is empowering to you since one of the key insights for Better Normal leaders is the realization that your new job is to make those around you successful in their new way of working.

As you know, the "Better Normal" leadership model was conceived during an extraordinary moment late in my career that compelled me to write exclusively about leadership for the first time. I have written often about teamwork, collaboration, and the practices of great teams but never directly about leadership per se. As I shared earlier, leadership is an old friend. In fact, my entire career has centered around helping others lead change in their personal lives or their journeys with others. What changed for me were the four startling revelations of 2020. Those revelations became the tipping point for me with the sudden realization that current and emerging leadership models were inadequate for the post-2020 world. Yes. There were and are many excellent books on leadership to help individual leaders. However, no one seemed to be addressing the magnitude of the leadership changes needed for leaders to both lead change within the organization and in the broader community related to long-standing structural inequities and organizational impact on the environment.

The context of leadership has changed dramatically. We need a totally new perspective. "In an environment of constant change, rapid technological advances, social and demographic diversity, leaders can no longer rely on the toolbox of the past," said Nanette M. Blandin, a leadership scholar and president of the Nexus Institute, based in Washington, D. C. "The mechanical model of organizations in the past has produced hierarchies, static positions and rigid organizational charts, and has produced leaders who, however charismatic they may be, rule from the top and rule unequivocally. They control and direct and others follow. That model doesn't really work anymore."

In my view, making leadership tweaks and shifts to navigate differently after the virus -related pandemic stopped far short of addressing the new awareness of how many people are marginalized by existing policies and practices within most organizations and by existing laws and practices in the larger society. Our established systems simply don't protect us. For example, we are aware that the three systems designed to protect our star Olympic women gymnasts protected the abuser and the systems rather than the young women, repeatedly. The gravity of the leadership crisis in government and the private sector became a flashing red light for me, telling me that:

1. The traditional bureaucratic management model was broken,
2. The emerging toxic malignant normality leadership model was dangerous,
3. Leadership literally needed reinventing. A new leadership model was needed in addition to the management model most business schools were teaching with much more emphasis on leadership, the new "hard people skills," and greater leadership accountability built into the system,
4. Business ethics, a moral compass, and aligning actions with values were deal breakers for leaders without them: no character, no moral compass, no leadership, and
5. Most organizations needed to equip far more of their associates to be leaders.

Leadership, in brief, needed reinventing. A quantum leap forward. Incremental steps would be too small. We need many more people to lead and all leaders to lead differently.

In this final chapter, I will borrow the term "Eureka moments" from my research friends at St. Jude, the rare moments of discover that we all seek as learners, to summarize why reinventing leadership is so critical for all leaders. 2020 set off the alarm and the flashing lights. Then, a number of "Eureka" moments followed that allowed me to see leadership from a different perspective, one that was not only different but unique. A review of excellent books on leadership from the past, the ones that had influenced me and others immersed in leadership for years, led to a "blinding flash of the obvious." The "Eureka" moments led to the creation of a new leadership narrative and reinvention of an outdated concept.

The first "Eureka" was finding a common thread running through the best of the best leadership books. Connecting the dots, insights, and gifts from all these books led to an obvious conclusion for me: the very best leadership practices could be reduced to a few, seven, and they were all inspiring. Inspiration is the magic of great leadership, the "only" way to tap into and sustain individual and collective discretionary energy and unused human potential for great outcomes. As Gary Ridge, CEO and Chairman of WD-40 says, "Our job is to make sure that we create an environment where our tribe members wake up each day inspired to go to work, feel safe while they are there and return home at the end of the day fulfilled by the work that they do, feeling that they have learned something new and contributed to something bigger than themselves." Any organization, regardless of the product, can create a culture of inspiration: from St. Jude to Patagonia to WD-40 to W. L. Gore and Associates to Belmont University.

> Inspiration is the magic of great leadership, the "**only**" way to tap into and sustain individual and collective discretionary energy and unused human potential for great outcomes.

One of the biggest lessons learned from the pandemic was the striking success of remote work and hybrid work models. According to Paul Hill, a Utah State University professor who specializes in remote work research, remote work is here to stay. He indicates that "Gallup reported that 60% of employees said they would be "extremely likely" to look for other work opportunities if their employer decided not to offer remote work options some or all of the time. In the end, the data we have suggests employees who can work only in the office do not feel supported to do high-quality work or live their best lives." Cultures of inspiration, therefore, will include hybrid work models that inspire people to commit their discretionary energy and do their best work. Hill adds, "In Utah's competitive labor market, leaders must design the experience employees actually want on purpose, with purpose. As employees desire greater flexibility, leaders who ignore the crucial development by putting their heads in the sand will do so at their own peril." Intentionally creating a more humanizing and purposeful work environment adds the value that millions of employees discovered they wanted during the pandemic. This is one more piece of research that underscores our conclusion that talented people want a culture that cares. As Hill suggests, ignore this information "at your own peril."

Based on the flashing red light of the rise of toxic leaders and malignant normality with the inherently missing moral guard rails, it became obvious that the foundation of a new model had to rest on a foundation of ethics, character, courage, and compassion for people. This second, awakening "Eureka" moment seemed to be so fundamental to normal functioning, core religious values, and democratic process that we had placed it in an "assumption" category. We thought, of course, that "leaders don't intentionally lie, lead to create fear, openly ridicule minorities and create conspiracy theories, consistently blame others, or politicize and worsen a pandemic that has exceeded deaths from the monstrous Spanish Flu pandemic of 1918." Thus, the foundation of the new model had to be named and taken out of the assumption "that leaders will lead from a moral compass" category. Business ethics had to rise in importance in Business Schools, as it has at the Fuqua/Coach K Center on Leadership & Ethics at Duke, and become the foundation of leadership.

We can no longer assume that political leaders and business leaders who are compliant with Malignant Normal political leaders have the ability and/or willingness to be guided by ethical and moral rules of engagement and do the right thing.

Another recent discovery in the world of leadership, that only Brené Brown had named clearly, was the relationship of innovation and vulnerability. The road to great leadership and innovation runs through vulnerability. A third "Eureka." Therefore, inspiration, discretionary energy, and vulnerability are inextricably connected. Inspiring leaders give permission for others to be their beautiful imperfect selves. Being perfect, not good enough, not smart enough, and the shame associated with those imperfections are the enemies of creativity and innovation. Great leaders create a culture of inspiration that encourages risk taking and invites people to volunteer their best thinking and acting skills. They simply model vulnerability and the creation of psychological safety. With an environment where it is psychologically safe to risk, explore, question, and challenge, we see innovation flourishing. How many companies do you know that intentionally train their associates to be innovative and entrepreneurial and appropriately vulnerable?

> With an environment where it is psychologically safe to risk, explore, question, and challenge, we see innovation flourishing.

The seven leadership practices which are consistently inspiring to others have all been written about widely and eloquently. That said, to my surprise and the fourth "Eureka," these 7 practices had never been connected under the one umbrella of inspiration.

THE INSPIRATION UMBRELLA

The 7 Inspiring Leadership Practices

1. *The Ethical Heart: Character, Courage, and Compassion*
2. *A Sense of Urgency: Increasing Intentionality and Reducing Complacency*
3. *The Collaborative Mindset: Win-Win Thinking and Acting*
4. *Shared Vision: Create Your Own Future or Someone Else Will*
5. *Wayfinding: Strategic Direction and Short-Term Wins*
6. *Difference-Making: Recognizing and Celebrating of Individual and Collective Contributions*
7. *Empathy into Action: The New Leadership Role to Lead Change for the Common Good*

Each practice has been called inspirational at times, but the magic I mentioned earlier is magical for three reasons: 1) When inspired, the motivation comes from within. Forget incentive and fear motivation, although both external incentives and fear incentives can lead to short-term motivation. Inspiration taps into discretionary energy and the talent that is hidden otherwise. So, the entire new leadership model is built around practices that inspire and motivate others to want to do best work, 2) Because each of the seven leadership practices inspire in a unique and different way, no one practice can be ignored. The seven practices are non-negotiable, meaning that all are critical to being and being perceived as an inspiring leader, and 3) the seven leadership practices hang together and form a synergistic unit, freeing the hidden potential and sustaining individual and collaborative innovation for extraordinary results. Like the Disney experience, the seven practices engage everyone and create the whiffle dust magic of Better Normal leadership.

The fifth "Eureka" moment was the realization of the outsized dominance and longevity of bureaucratic management models and the heavy use of limiting titles like boss, manager, supervisor, director, and coordinator. We seem to have gone out of our way to make sure that only senior leaders would be called leaders. In addition, managing the process from the top down reinforced the even older concept of "command and control" and the assumption that only a few were capable of real leadership. As a result, people and relationship skills were minimized and reduced to "soft skills" status, easily dismissed as "nice to have" and "touchy feely." In the Better Normal leadership model, the soft skills of listening, assertiveness, conflict resolution, emotional intelligence, and compassion become the "hard skills" rarely taught in business schools and rarely permeate leadership training in most organizations.

In addition, when we look closely at the systemic gender trend toward men leaders and systemic bureaucratic command and control management practices, these trends run counter to what we know about the bottom-line value of the new "hard relationship skills" and the high positive impact of women leaders. The harsh truth is this: Most toxic leaders are men. I know that some of my male friends will give me grief about calling out men, but the evidence is overwhelming. Just don't call it Critical Gender Theory! This is no theory. Most violence in relationships comes from men. Most abuse in homes comes from men. Men are the ones most likely to support open-carry laws, easy access to guns, and assault weapons. Sex trafficking depends on a market of willing men. Most people in supervisory, management, and leadership positions in the public and private sectors are men. Most corporate Boards are men dominated. Men politicians are at the heart of multiple flawed federal and state policies/laws that continue to marginalize people and create systemic inequities. We certainly have made the case for more women in leadership positions everywhere. It's not that men haven't accomplished amazing and great things. We have so much to celebrate about the good in our America and the good work of men. The issue is the continuing systemic inequities that women face and the masculine tendencies to choose aggressive behaviors, use anger and power to control, all harmful. We can celebrate the good and still learn from the systemic inequities at the same time. It's not an either-or proposition.

Several of my wife's good friends recently shared with me the video and lyrics to Keb Mo's hit song "Put a Woman in Charge." This song was dedicated to his mother after her death, describing her as a woman of strength, courage, and "a leader." Men, google the song, listen to the lyrics and learn. The themes throughout this song underscore some of the themes of this book: Men have built the walls and started the wars. People in charge need more sensitivity, kindness, and understanding. All are a part of reinventing leadership. It's time for change.

Leaders for a Better Normal will be a healthy mix of men and women who are kind and understanding and know how to make those around them successful. Real men eat quiche, are vulnerable, compassionate, strong, assertive, and stand up for gender equity. Traditional management models of leadership will yield to Human Growth Models of Leadership as we move toward a Better Normal future.

A sixth "Eureka" moment in my personal road to the creation of the Better Normal model was examining the critical relationship between supervisors and managers and those who report to them. In traditional management models, those who lead have "direct reports." It is the most critical relationship in the normal work environment and has been largely neglected despite years of research that shows how poorly most people rate their "boss." Bosses are uninspiring at best. The relationship between leader and "people led" requires use of all the leader's new "hard skills" and the creation of a level of psychological safety that permits associates to risk being vulnerable, creative, and innovative. After 2020, future leaders who earn the respect of those they lead must reset based on what we learned from hybrid work arrangements, the big timeout, and the new value people place on work-life balance and personal values. Millions of people quit work, sought new careers, and underscored the fact that they were never going back to normal. People want to be led by people who care. Combine the learnings from the pandemic itself, the wide-spread exposure of long-standing structural inequities and those marginalized by those inequalities, leaders for a Better Normal are morally obligated to humanize their relationships, help reduce the inequities in the organization, use their influence for greater equity in the community, and lead in protecting the environment. This leadership model is the first that invites leaders to enter the culture wars and use their voice for those marginalized and vulnerable, many of whom are colleagues and associates.

In short, for those many of you believing for the first time that you can lead and want to lead, you will quickly separate yourself from most who currently supervise, manage, or who are considered "bosses." You can quickly change the culture that you influence by living out the 7 practices of leaders that inspire.

People will want to work with you because you care and inspire. Organizations could change their culture if senior leaders chose to do so by committing to new leadership practices that unleash the potential in people to do great work. People are seeking a culture where leaders inspire rather than boss.

My songwriter friend, Wayland Holyfield, wrote a song entitled *"My Grass is Green Enough."* I have always loved this song. I know I have been blessed with a lot of green grass. I shared in the last chapter my loss, my personal grieving and attempt to honor my daughter through my writing. I have a new sense of connection to the human family through this loss. We all have or will have painful losses. My dream is that we can create cultures of equity, hope, support, and inspiration where we can share and embrace together our personal joys and hurts, our one humanity, and through it all have a common sense that together our grass is still green enough.

Kerry Hannon wrote about *Visionaries with the Courage to Change the World* in a New York Times Leadership publication adapted from an article which first appeared on May 24, 2018. Hannon's writing is instructive for the new role of all leaders to be visionary and courageous.

"Acting as a guardian for not only people but also the planet is a concern that's inextricably woven into the fabric of this new generation of leaders. It's nonnegotiable."

Then Hannon quotes Sanyin Siang, executive director of the Fuqua/ Coach K. Center on Leadership & Ethics at Duke University. She says, "Things aren't linear anymore. We are living in an ecosystem world. It is more complex." Speaking about the new world and the leadership required for next generation-leaders, Siang adds, "They are deeply aware of the context in which their organization is operating, and it is beyond the marketplace—politics, globally, society. It's a long game and one where doing good is good business."

The final "Eureka moment." Most organizations simply need many more people to lead. W. L. Gore & Associates was created back in 1958 by Bill and Vieve Gore with the belief that all people were capable of leading and that managers and bosses and bureaucratic structures inhibited innovation and creativity. In 2021, Gore was certified as a Great Place to Work in the U.S., France, Germany, and U.K. They were selected as #2 on Fast Company's Best Workplaces for Innovators 2021 list. Gore was recognized as a Best Workplaces for Millennials by Fortune in 2021.

With multiple awards for innovation and being a great place to work, major business articles about Gore from Gary Hamel and others touting the work environment that I call a "culture of inspiration," isn't it shocking that only a very few companies and organizations have tried to replicate the Gore model??? You see, the "how" Gore treats people centers on Maslow's hierarchy of needs, a personal growth model applied to the workplace, and the fact that the Gores knew people worked much better if they worked in small collaborative teams! The Gores discovered the secret to "how" people innovate and work best. Yet, for over 60 years after their discovery, bureaucratic models and practices continue to rule the day. In fact, most writers continue to call the Gore model a management model. Let's call it by its true name: a human growth model for building a culture of inspiration. And it is a leadership model, not a management model. Most people who work at Gore say their culture is the competitive advantage. Companies and organizations have loved the Gore outcomes, products, and the results they accomplished, but haven't had the courage or the wisdom to try to replicate the growth model and the team model, the underlying processes that made their extraordinary results possible. Gore is a "Better Normal" model for the organizations of the future. They have lived the connection between vulnerability, psychological safety, and innovation. They have humanized the system. As a result, people and teams are inspired. They consistently exceed expectations.

Leadership for a Better Normal capitalizes on these "Eureka" moments, the discoveries and insights that have been waiting for the year 2020 when we witnessed the worst of leadership. The magnitude of the inequities uncovered in 2020 call for non-political leaders to do what political leaders may not be capable of doing in the highly polarized environment in which we live. Our human vulnerability as well as the value of life itself has been exposed. Now we know that "Normal" has become a strategic threat to organizational and community life.

Jon Meacham, in his recent book, *And There Was Light: Abraham Lincoln and the American Struggle*, reminds us through Abraham Lincoln that with every threat to our one humanity there is opportunity for new possibilities and our best selves. Lincoln is one of us, a beautifully imperfect human being who wrestled with such a big decision. We all know what Lincoln did, but Meacham wanted to write more about "why" Lincoln did what he did. Lincoln had the choice of normalizing slavery as a way-of-life or prioritizing emancipation above his own political future. His moral decision to do what was right makes him a role model leader for this moment in history. Each of us can decide in our own way every day, even in small ways, how we can create light and influence others for good. Think of these moments as "Lincoln moments", another moment to shine from your platform, big or small.

Going forward, leaders must embrace the words of Siang and become "a guardian of people and the planet." The beauty of the opportunity for a new leadership model is one to embrace. We know the leadership gifts, the 7 leader practices that inspire the very best in others. The gifts are waiting for leaders to accept, open, embrace, and personalize. This moment is the greatest leadership opportunity of our time.

I wrote earlier in this book that I was on a mission to recruit thousands of new leaders and invite current leaders to rethink how they lead. I shared with you the burning question that my daughter frequently asked, "What is the end game for people who have the power and resources to make a difference in the lives of hurting people and don't? What do they want?" My appeal to you is that you step up and use your power and resources to lead for an "end game" that makes a difference in the lives of hurting people with whom you work and live.

> Going forward, leaders must embrace the words of Siang and become "a guardian of people and the planet."

The hope of leadership and this young democracy, in this historic test of both, lies in the numerous profiles of courageous leaders that have emerged in the past and are emerging now. We have always risen to the challenge.

The challenge now is for a multitude of new leaders to dare to dream big, dare to lead, dare to advocate for all people, and dare to create healthier organizations, healthier communities, and a healthier democracy.

I invite you to find your "Lincoln voice," join the new younger voices of those who have appealed to "our better angels." We are "we the people." We still have a critical mass of people who believe in doing what is right for the common good. Billions of people around the world place their hope in this beacon of light to lead the way in modeling leadership that inspires the best in others. At this unprecedented moment, we need this "critical mass of people" to raise their voices to be the light that reinvents leadership for a better world.

We have seen the fragile and vulnerable world that astronauts have seen, and we have a new perspective. We have the opportunity as leaders to answer Mary Oliver's question from our new perspective. So, tell me leaders, "What is it you plan to do with your one wild and precious life?" How will you lead?

BIBLIOGRAPHY

Notes

INTRODUCTION

17 *The phrase, "one wild and precious life:"* Mary Oliver, *House of Light* (Beacon Press, 1990).

17 *In the book, The Mission of a Lifetime: Lessons from the Men Who Went to the Moon:* Basil Hero, (Grand Central Publishing, 2019).

19 "In the end, perhaps the greatest blessing:" Krista Tippett, *Becoming Wise: An Inquiry into the Mystery and Art of Living, (Penguin Press, 2016).*

PART I THE NEW LEADERSHIP PERSPECTIVE

Chapter 1: Normal is the Enemy of a Better Normal

37 *According to estimates from the Center:* (Centers for Disease Control and Prevention, 2022).

38 *According to the U. S. Bureau of Labor Statistics:* (U. S. Bureau of Labor Statistics, 2022).

38 "You know the table has been set:" Lisa Quigley, (Nashville, TN, 2020).

39 "This isn't a snow day where you're waiting for the sun to shine…" Jamie Metzl, *The stakes have never been higher as America reopens.* (USA TODAY, May 28, 2020.)

41 Ninety-one percent of 1,000 employees surveyed: Lou Solomon, Survey: *91 Percent of 1,000 Employees Say Their Bosses Lack This 1 Critical Skill.* (Inc.ThisMorning, August 10, 2017.)

41 The trailblazing Gallup Research: Marcus Buckingham and Curt Coffman, *First Break All the Rules: What the World's Greatest Managers Do Differently,* (Simon & Schuster, 1999).

42 "We need to avoid uncritical acceptance of this new version…:" Robert Jay Lifton, M.D. *The Dangerous Case of Donald Trump: 27 Psychiatrists and Mental Health Experts Assess a President*: Bandy Lee, M.D., M.Div. (Thomas Dunne Books, 2019).

44 "What we've learned is that organizations that can…:" John Kotter, Vanessa Akhtar, and Gaurav Gupta, (*The Kotter Chronicle,* January 2022).

44 *"Dark times lie ahead of us and there will be a time…:"* J. K. Rowling (Harry Potter and the Goblet of Fire, Scholastic, 2000.)

47 *One of the movies we have watched many times by popular demand is*: Ferdinand, Blue Sky Studios, (20th Century Fox, 2017).

Chapter Two: The Leadership Opportunity of a Lifetime

56 This is new territory…willingness to interact in: Brené Brown, PhD, *Daring Greatly* (Gotham Books, 2012).

56 "Talking about social justice issues and past inequities…:" Elizabeth Thomas, PhD, *Community Psychology: Linking Individuals and Communities,* (American Psychological Association, 2021)

57 We know from the Gallup research alone that: Marcus Buckingham & Curt Coffman, *First Break All the Rules,* (Simon and Schuster, 1999).

58 Be proactive, begin with the end in mind: *The Leader in Me*, Stephen R. Covey, Sean Covey, Muriel Summers, David K. Hatch, PhD (Simon & Schuster, 2008).

58 Well, if you're familiar with: Stephen Covey, *The Seven Habits of Highly Effective People*, (Simon & Schuster, 1989).

62 New territory just means new learning opportunities: Jodi Picoult, *Wish You Were Here*, (Ballantine Books, 2021).

Chapter Three: Creating a Culture of Inspiration

65 Your work is going to fill a large part of your life: Steve Jobs, *Stanford University Commencement Address*, (June 12, 2005.)

70 Only recently has inspiration been researched and translated into meaningful and explosive: Todd M. Trash, PhD, and Andre J. Elliot, PhD, *Inspiration as a Psychological Construct*, (Journal of Personal and Social Psychology, 2003).

72 "In a culture obsessed with measuring talent, ability, and potential, we often overlook…:" Scott Barry Kaufman, *Why Inspiration Matters* (Harvard Business Review, November 2011).

73 Even fewer felt that their leaders fostered engagement or commitment: Eric Garon, *How to Be an Inspiring Leader*, (Harvard Business Review, April 2017).

74 "Our competitive global economy requires leaders to shift their focus…:" Gregory G Dess and Joseph C Picken, *Changing Roles: Leadership in the 21st Century*, (Organizational Dynamics, Winter, 2000).

75 "I like you just the way you are.:" Fred Rodgers, *Mister Rogers Neighborhood*, (Debut on February 19, 1968.)

76 "Rebbe, why are you so sad?" Reb Zusha, *The Torah of Reb Zusya*, (Moshe Givental, November 2017).

79 *The seven non-negotiable leadership practices are intentionally designed to:* Abraham Maslow, Maslow's Hierarchy of Needs, Motivation and Personality, (Harper & Brothers, 1954).

81 "CEP is a common-sense way to get food straight into the mouths…:" Bradley Tusk, *New Jersey made sure no kid went unfed.* The same should be true for all kids. (Opinion article NJ.com, December 16, 2021.)

83 "I think one of the most important to me, and it was to Bill…:" Vieve Gore. Gary Hamel, *The Future of Management*, (Harvard Business Review Press, 2007)

84 Our enterprise is strongest when we tap into diverse talents and perspectives: Jason Field, W. L. Gore and Associates, (W. L. Gore website, 2022).

84 We have long had a love affair with excellence, greatness, and peak: Thomas J. Peters and Robert H. Waterman, Jr. , In *Search of Excellence*, (HarperCollins, 1982).

86 "It's not about me." Sam Walton, (personal conversation, 1994.)

87 Loehr's book was the first to document: James Loehr, *Mental Toughness Training for Sports*, (Forum, 1982).

89 "Leadership is the art of mobilizing others to want to…:" Jim Kouzes and Barry Posner, *The Leadership Challenge*, (Jossey-Bass, 1995).

90 I focused my research and writing on peak team experiences: Bob Fisher and Bo Thomas, *Real Dream Teams*, (CRC Press, 1996).

91 High levels of emotional intelligence permeate the most productive: Daniel Goldman, *Emotional Intelligence*, (Bantam Books, 1995).

93 "The most general lesson to be learned from the more…:" John Kotter, PhD, *Leading Change*, (Harvard Business School Press, 1996).

95 "The Level 5 Executive builds enduring greatness through…:" Jim Collins, *Good to Great,* (Harper-Collins, 2001).

105 "Some see things as they are and ask why. I dream things that never were and…:" Senator Robert Kennedy, (Theme quote as Presidential candidate, 1968).

107 "Courage, compassion, connection seem like big…:" Brené Brown. *The Gifts of Imperfection*, (Hazelden, 2010).

107 Brown's work was seen first by most readers…: Brené Brown, *Dare to Lead*, (Random House, 2018).

110 "The leader of our amazing tribe of dedicated and…:" Gary Ridge, (Retirement announcement, March 16, 2022).

PART II THE SEVEN NON-NEGOTIABLE LEADERSHIP PRACTICES THAT INSPIRE OUR BEST

Chapter 4: The Ethical Heart: Character and Compassion

123 "The health of both the leader's and the organizations' soul depends on:" Margaret Benefiel, *The Soul of a Leader*, (Crossroad Publishing Company, 2008).

126 The movie is about the Battle of the Bakaara in: Peggy Noonan, *'Everybody's Been Shot'*, (Wall Street Journal, January 11, 2002).

128. "We realize the importance of our voice… Malala Yousafzai. *I am Malala,* (Little, Brown, and Company, 2013).

129 All major religious faiths are shaped by prophetic mandates: Jimmy Carter, *Our Endangered Values: America's Moral Crisis*, (Simon & Shuster, 2005).

129 Familiar guiding values come from the Golden Rule: Duane Short, *The Native American 10 Commandments*, (Catholic Rural Life, April 17, 2018).

129 Gandi summed up his guiding value principles as social sins: *Mahatma Gandhi, Seven Social Sins,* (Young India, October 22, 1925).

130 *"Christ gave us the goals and Mahatma:"* Clayborne Carson and Martin Luther King, Jr., *The Autobiography of Martin Luther King, Jr.* (Warner Books, 2001)

130 "As our distrust of 'the other' beyond our borders hardened and:" Parker Palmer, *Healing the Heart of Democracy*, (Jossey-Bass, 2014).

131 *"There are too many times in our world today when:"* Steve Simon, CNN Interview, (CNN, December 2, 2021).

132 "We had actually sold people a lie:" Mark MacGann; Paul Lewis, Harry Davies, Lisa O'Carroll, Simon Goodley and Felicity Lawrence, *The Uber Files*, (The Guardian, 2022).

134 "Well, it's really important that you lead based on:" Theodore Hesburgh, Bob Fisher and Bo Thomas, *Real Dream Teams*, (CRC Press, 1996).

134 *"Conscience is when God sends a text to your head."* Jeff Keane, (*Family Circus*, January 7, 2021).

135 "I just sat there with tears running down my face, and I was looking at my:" Scott Gleeson, Kyle Korver details emotional backstory of Bucks' boycott during NBA playoffs, (USA TODAY, October 28, 2020).

137 "It's that I exist, you exist…but we don't exist autonomously." Arthur Brooks podcast episode with Tavia Gilbert, *A Case for Spiritually Informed Democratic Capitalism,* (Templeton World, 2021).

138 "Leadership without ethics has no heart and ethics without leadership has:" Coach K Center on Leadership, (Fuqua Business School, Duke University, 2022).

140 "All I saw were talented women players that just wanted an opportunity Betty Wiseman (Personal correspondence with Bo Thomas, 2023).

141 I am not sure where the "marble jar" concept of building trust: Brené Brown, Dare to Lead, (Random House, 2018).

143 *Harvard MBA graduates have been asked the Mary Oliver question just prior:* Tony Deifell, HBS Portrait Project, (Harvard Business School, 2002).

143 Deifell's "inquiry produced surprisingly deep insights into the hopes… Katie Koch, Harvard staff writer, (Harvard Business School, 2002).

145 *"In my most recent research on courage and leadership…:"* Brené Brown, Atlas of the Heart, (Random House, 2021).

145 "We live, breathe and play by our values. Every day." Garry Ridge, WD-40 website and articles by Garry Ridge, (2022).

146 "I pick the first team member. The two of us pick....:" Lou Whittaker, Bob Fisher and Bo Thomas, *Real Dream Teams*, (CRC Press, 1996).

149 "Show me my way in life and I will build You a shrine:" Danny Thomas, (Dedication ceremony of St. Jude, February 4, 1962).

150 CEO Downing and other senior leaders wrestled with their core values: James Downing, (Personal interview, September 27, 2021).

151 "We set up an intranet site and ask employees to nominate co-workers.:" Summer Freeman, (Personal interview, September 27, 2021).

151 "AT ST. JUDE, WE ARE DRIVEN BY A SET OF CORE VALUES.": *St. Jude Living Our Values*, (2021).

154 Working on the premise that values are the internal control system: Paul Ingram, PhD, (Columbia Business School, 2022).

155 "With these principles as our foundation, we unleash the innate.:" W. L. Gore & Associates, (2022).

156 Since so many people relate to spiritual development or a faith community: West End United Methodist Church, (Nashville, 2021).

161 Belmont sought to identify churches that were working to be relevant, creative: Curb Center for Faith Leadership, (Center for Healthy Churches, 2022).

161 There are now 18 churches engaged in a collaborative partnership: Thriving Congregations Initiative, (Lilly Foundation, 2019).

164 "If any of the team gets to the top, we all get to the top.:" Lou Whittaker, Bob Fisher and Bo Thomas, *Real Dream Teams*, (CRC Press, 1996).

167 "What I really aspire to do in the poem is to be able to.:" Amanda Gorman, Presidential Inauguration, (January 20, 2021).

Chapter 5: Sense of Urgency: Increasing Intentionality and Reducing Complacency

173 "Say old man, we are stuck here, surrounded by ice." Tim Maltin, *Crucial ice warnings never made it to Titanic's bridge because the wireless operator was too busy and tired."* (timmaltin.com, March 3, 2019).

174 The human capabilities that are most critical to success: Gary Hamel, foreword to Jim Whitehurst's *Open Organizations: Igniting Passion and Performance*, (Harvard Business Review Press, Boston, 2015).

179 "Major change efforts have helped some organizations adapt.:" John Kotter, *Leading Change*, (Harvard Business School Press, 1996).

183 Six years later, I was asked to review, critique, and write a recommendation…: John Kotter and Dan Cohen, *The Heart of Change*, (Harvard Business School Press, 2002).

188 A company or organization's Hedgehog concept comes from "a deep understanding…:" Jim Collins, *Good to Great*, (HarperCollins Publishing, Inc. 2001).

190 Management systems that treat people as factors of production: Tom Peters and Bob Waterman, *In Search of Excellence*, (HarperCollins Publishers, 2004).

195 We learned in the fall of 2021 about a young Kentucky University football player: *ESPN Special*, (October 16, 2021).

196 More good news, we don't have to reinvent the wheel on vulnerability education: Brené Brown, *The Power of Vulnerability*, (Ted Talk, January 3, 2011).

197 "Brené visited Pixar to talk with our filmmakers.:" Ed Catmull, Brené Brown, Dare to Lead, (Random House, 2018).

206 Another learning companion who has helped thousands of people with their process of becoming: Tara Brach, *Radical Compassion*, (Penguin Books, 2019).

206 Tippett resonates with me as she has spent her life committed to listening: Krista Tippett, *Becoming Wise*, (Penguin Press, 2016).

Chapter six: The Collaborative Mindset: Win-Win

209 My model for business is the Beatles. Steve Jobs, "60 Minutes" Interview (CBS, 2003).

210 Sister Sledge's song *"We are Family"* is dancing in my head: Nile Rodgers and Bernard Edwards, *We are Family*, (January 22, 1979).

210 I'm also hearing Michael Jackson's: Michael Jackson and Lionel Richie, *"We are the World,"* (July 8, 2009).

211 "Are you proud of what you've designed?" Donald Petersen. Bob Fisher and Bo Thomas, *Real Dream Teams*, (CRC Press, 1996).

212 "I told him that we had two choices for the years.:" John Wooden. Bob Fisher and Bo Thomas, *Real Dream Teams*, (CRS Press, 1996).

217 "This is beyond sport. This is the message we deliver to…:" Mutaz Barshim, *World Athletics*, Bob Ramsak, (August 1, 2021).

218 "I know first-hand the sexism and racism institutions and.:" Serena Williams. Rachel Brodsky, *INDEPENDENT*, (March 8, 2021).

218 "Once we call it by name, we can start having a real conversation:" Rebecca Solnit, *Call Them by Their True Names*, (Haymarket Books, 2018).

221 In this song, he describes the secret dream we all have of not having to: Steve Azar, *I Don't Have to be Me (Til' Monday)*, (Mercury, October 1, 2002).

223 "To be nobody but yourself in a world which is doing its best…:" E. E. Cummings, *A Poet's Advice To Students*, (Ottawa Hills School Spectator, October 26, 1955).

229 Leaders inspire others when they are open and honest about their expectations: Joseph Luft and Harry Ingham, The Johari Window, (1955).

233 I suggested that Nashville became a magic place to live, work, and play primarily…: Bethel (Bo) Thomas, *Big Dreams, Bold Leadership, and Collaboration*, Nashville Tennessean, (September 29, 2016).

234 Helen Riess, M.D., writes about the power of empathy in: Helen Riess, *The Empathy Effect* (Sounds True, Inc. 2018)

236 We need to "be felt.:" Mark Goulston, *Just Listen*, (AMACOM, 2010).

245 "The motto for our change initiative was 'Working Better Together.':" Admiral James Loy, *Working Better Together*, (July 2000).

251 It is a beautiful account of one woman's journey to be: Michelle Obama, *Becoming*, (Crown, 2018).

Chapter 7: Shared Vision: Create Your Shared Future or Someone Else Will

254 Envision Charlie Brown and Lucy together: Charles Schulz, *Peanuts*, (1950-2000).

259 Bookends personally mean a lot to me as a former college professor in the: Peter Senge, *The Fifth Discipline*, (Currency Doubleday, 1990).

260 "The more clearly we see the reality of the world, the better equipped:" Scott Peck, *The Road Less Traveled*, (Simon & Schuster, 1978).

262 "You ain't seen nothing yet!" Robert Fisher, Inaugural Address, (Belmont University, 2000).

262 Seeds of Greatness: Dennis Waitley, *Seeds of Greatness*, (Fleming H. Revell Company, 1988).

264 "Never budge, that's my rule." Dr. Seuss, *The Sneetches and Other Stories*, (Random House, 1953).

265 "Come on Tom. We're no worse than anybody else.:" Tom Peters, Stanford University, (Lecture, Summer, 1981).

267 Every night, Dr. Fernando Silva, director of the children's..": Carlos Rodriguez-Galindo, M.D., *Tell Someone That I Am Here*, (Inspire Magazine, St. Jude, Fall, 2019).

270 "I decided that nobody should suffer that much." Gertrude Elion. Bob Fisher and Bo Thomas, *Real Dream Teams*, (CRC Press, 1996).

272 "From all this, we had a choice." Shanelle and Chris Montana, Du Nord Craft Spirits, (New York Times, July 7, 2020).

273 Patagonia is a manufacturer of upscale outdoor clothing: Patagonia.com., (Vision Statement, 2022).

274 "Leadership is the art of mobilizing others to want…:" James M. Kouzes and Barry Z. Posner, *The Leadership Challenge*, (Jossey-Bass Publishers, 1997).

275 If you want to dig deeper into the power of vision, read: Simon Sinek, *Start with Why,* (Portfolio, Penguin Books 2009).

Chapter 8: Wayfinding: Strategic Direction and Short-term Wins

286 "Women who have spoken out for what's right.:" Chelsea Clinton, *She Persisted: 13 American Women Who Changed the World,* (Philomel Books, 2017).

286 I think we're going to look back on this moment and: Megan Rapinoe, *'It's a great day*:" US women's team nets $33m payout in landmark equal-pay settlement, (Fox Sports News, February 23, 2022).

289 "Level 5 leaders are fanatically driven, infected with…:" Jim Collins, *Good to Great*, (Harper Collins, 2001).

294 This new vision for what can be in the world "will provide the tools.:" Dr. James Downing, Personal Interview, (October 8, 2021).

Chapter 9: Difference-Making: Empowering Individual and Collective Contributions

302 79% of employees who quit their jobs cite a lack of: O. C. Tanner Learning Group , Performance Accelerated and Adrian Gostick and Chester Elton, *The Carrot Principle* (Simon and Schuster, 2007).

306 "Our beliefs and principles are not just about creating.:" Terri Kelly, *4 Guiding Principles* at Gore, (mlabvideo, September 2010).

308 The Gores left a huge legacy that few leaders have: Gary Hamel, W. L. Gore: *An Innovation Democracy, from the Future of Management*, (Harvard Business Press, 2007)

314 "I like you just the way you are.:" Fred Rogers, Mister Rogers Neighborhood, (PBS, February 19, 1968-August 31, 2001).

318 "We have strong organizational momentum.:" Jason Field, Statement in assuming new CEO position, (April 1, 2018).

320 I have mentioned before about Friday night and movie night: Don Hall, Carlos Lopez Estrada, Paul Briggs, and John Ripa, *Raya and the Last Dragon*, (Walt Disney Animation Studios, 2021).

322 "Always recognize that ADVANCING treatment for children with.:" Summer Freeman, *Living Our Values*, (St. Jude Communications, 2020).

326 "An organization that engages participative communities.:" Jim Whitehurst, *Open Organization*, (Harvard Business Review Press, 2015).

Chapter 10: Empathy into Action: Leading Change for the Common Good

336 "Apart from the practical advice, the most invaluable part.:" Ian Morgan Cron and Suzanne Stabile, *The Road Back to You,* (InterVarsity Press, 2016).

337 "Over and over, participants talked about their concern that.:" Brené Brown, *Braving the Wilderness*, (Random House, 2017).

340 The "Me Too" movement exposed the broad scope of sexual harassment: Jodi Kantor and Megan Twohey, *She Said,* (Penguin Press, 2019).

342 According to Statista, almost 1 in 4 American households earn less than…:" *Planet Money*, (July 16, 2012.)

342 "If we can't handle uncertainty, risk, and emotional exposure..: Brené Brown, *Atlas of the Heart,* (Random House, 2021).

342 "They're not different from you, are they:" Robin Williams as John Keating. Tom Schulman, *Dead Poets Society,* (Touchstone Pictures, June 9, 1989).

344 "I represent my country, both countries, Nigeria and Greece…:" Giannis Antetokounmpo interview after winning the MVP of 2021 NBA Championship.

344 Sooley: John Grisham, Sooley, (Knopf Doubleday Publishing Company, February 2022).

345 "It's not your imagination. There are way too many people working 24 hours.." Korn Ferry article.

347 Why the big change?: Marisa lati, Lindsey Bever, and Paulina Firozi, *Millions of workers are quitting their jobs during the pandemic. Meet six who made a big change.*(Washington Post, June 17, 2021).

349 "The past year has poked holes in long-standing norms about.:" Paul Daugherty, Marc Carrel-Billiard, and Michael Biltz, *Every leader is a technology leader: Embracing a new mindset to shape a better future,* Technology Vision, (Accenture, 2021).

351 "We've now had 50 years of the revolutions of women in the.:" Betsey Stevenson, University of Michigan professor, (2021).

351 Over the years, a mountain of evidence has brought to light: Justin Onwenu and Nicholas Leonard, *It's time to change the way we measure pollution*, (The Hill, 12.10,2020).

352 As inequalities for women and people of color are "stunning," so are: Dr. Robert Bullard, Environmental Racism Lecture-Race, Place, and the Politics of Pollution, (University of Utah, College of Law, January 31, 2019).

352 "Rising wage inequality has been a defining feature of.:" Economic Policy Institute, (May 2021).

353 "Leadership absolutely does evolve." Gary Burnison, Korn Ferry column, (June 2021).

355 Here is how one well-known company assumed advocacy: Patagonia Has Top Corporate Reputation In Axios Harris Poll, (SGB-media, May 18, 2021).

355 "Whenever we make these decisions there are two outcomes.:" Rose Marcario, *Patagonia's Former CEO Retreats to the Rainforest*, (The New York Times, February 18, 2021.)

356 "I don't want you to be hopeful. I want you to panic.:" Greta Thunburg, (World Economic Forum, 2019).

357 "We are capitalists committed to stakeholder capitalism." (Just Capital mission statement, 2022).

360 "Too many business leaders remain stuck in an old mind-set.:" Michael Lit, *Work Isn't Changing Back to 'Normal'—Get Ready for What's Next*, (Forbes, 2022).

362 "I realize I'm not breaking news when I suggest that.:" Mike Haynie, *How Maya Angelou can prepare leaders for the post-Covid workplace,* (USA Today, July 13, 2021).

366 "What do we want from our heroes? What do we expect of them?": Holly Ford, *Watch Taylor Swift's Olympics Promos for the Tokyo Games,* (NBC, August 4, 2021).

373 "Diversity has long been one of our core values.:" Jennifer Jones, Presidential Platform, (2022).

374 "Real leaders are made when you have rough times.:" Tom Gump. Frank Bures, *The Business of Healing,* (Rotary Magazine, May 2022).

376 "I think our fear is, in today's world, it really has become.:" Marianne Wanamaker. Melissa Brown, *Bredesen and Haslam launch podcast diving into complex topics,* (Nashville Tennessean, September 14, 2022.)

378 "The truth is there is still so much work to do:" Common. *Imagine*: (Concord Music Group, July 2021.)

379 St. Jude is where those with a passion for making a difference: James Downing, Personal Interview, (September 27, 2021.)

380 "To cure at least 60% of the children in the world with.:" St. Jude Strategic Plan, (2022-2027.)

383 "And my first challenge was me.:" James Downing, Personal interview, (September 27, 2021.)

385 "My colleagues and I came into this field with a new approach to…:" Niraj Trivedi, personal interview with Bo Thomas (August 29,2022).

Chapter 11: Summary and Leadership Challenge

395 "So, let's all take one more step.:" Kim Namjoon, UN General Assembly, (73rd session, 2018).

396 "In an environment of constant change, rapid technological.:" Nanette M. Blandin, *Visionaries With the Courage to Change the World,* (The New York Times, May 24, 2018).

398 "Our job is to make sure that we create an environment.:" Garry Ridge, Glint, Inc. (W-D 40, 2022).

398 "In the end, the data we have suggests employees who can work.:" Paul Hill, Opinion: *Remote work isn't a pandemic phenomenon----it's here to stay,* (Opinion Utah Business, September 14, 2022.)

402 "This song was dedicated to his mother…describing her as a woman of strength.:" Keb Mo, Composers Beth Nielsen Chapman, Kevin Moore, John Lewis Parker, *Put A Woman in Charge feat* with Rosanne Cash*,* (Rosanne Cash Music Label. (September 2018).

404 My songwriting friend: Wayland Holyfield, *My Grass is Green Enough,* (Unpublished. Nashville, 2022).

405 "Things aren't linear anymore. We are living in an ecosystem.:" Sanyin Siang. Kerry Hannon, *Visionaries With the Courage to Change the World*, (The New Your Times, May 24, 2018).

405 With multiple awards for innovation and being: Gary Hamel, *W. L. Gore: Lessons from a Management Revolution,* (Wall Street Journal, 3.18.2010).

406 This is why it is an historic time, a once-in-a-lifetime opportunity: Jon Meacham, *And There Was Light: Abraham Lincoln and the American Struggle,* (Random House Publishing Group, 2022)

ABOUT THE AUTHOR

Bethel E. Thomas, Jr., PhD, widely known as "Bo," has spent four decades as a student and teacher of peak individual and team performance. Bo now writes after a career of leadership and the implementation of his discoveries as a transformational leader, university professor, psychologist, coach, and organizational consultant. His capstone leadership experience is his 12-year inspiring journey as Vice President for Advancement at Belmont University in Nashville where he helped lead the transformation of a good regional university to a great national university brand. During the same time frame, Belmont collaborated with the Nashville community on multiple public-private-university partnerships, helping Music City become a true destination city. He is the co-author of *Real Dream Teams*, an engaging focus on the characteristics of peak performing teams and team leaders in a variety of settings from business to mountain climbing, to religion, to top gun flying teams, to national champions, to music, to a school of business.

Personal Note from Bo: My Passion for this Book and Why We Must Reimagine Leadership

Reinventing Leadership: Leading to Inspire a "Better Normal" is my piercing new examination of leadership after 2020 when four unprecedented forces converged to forever change how we think of leadership and what leaders do. I was compelled to write this book after what we learned. Traditional management models are simply inadequate and uninspiring for the challenges of the new world, and toxic leaders are dangerous. The best of individual and team performance can only be inspired when people tap into their unused human potential. A majority of people across the country say we can "do better." I concluded that we "must do better" and we know how. We now know that everyone is capable of leading and we know the 7 practices of inspiring leaders.

Since there are many powerful toxic leaders and millions of good people complicit or silent in response, I am the first writer to openly challenge the leadership crisis and threat created by the disturbing rise of toxicity and "malignant normality." All people are called to embrace the opportunity of a lifetime to reinvent leadership and lead with character, courage, and compassion. If "how" we lead is not right, nothing is right. It is up to all of us to humanize leadership. I invite everyone, wherever they live or work, to learn to lead, inspire, and become hope-givers for a "Better Normal."

Bo Thomas

EXHIBIT A: INSTRUCTIONS FOR USE OF THE WORKSHEET (EXHIBIT B BELOW)

THE INSTRUCTIONS FOR ROLE CLARIFICATION WORKSHEET

Every relationship can be improved with more information. Therefore, be honest, there are no right or wrong feelings or requests, seek first to listen and understand, you both want to live or work together differently, and the discussion will be beneficial to both.

This discussion is designed for two people. Each person uses the worksheet to first write the three things the partner can do that would help make working or living together easier or more productive. For example, I might give my partner information such as, "I would like more information from you about key assignments and how the assignment fits with our mission and vision," "I hate surprises. Giving me as much lead time as possible when you need something from me would really help." "If there is something you are concerned about related to my performance, I want to hear it from you directly, not someone else." "I would like for both of us to clarify what we expect from our vacation, what each of us perceive as fun or relaxing."

"I would appreciate any good feedback or even a thank you. I never seem to please you."

The first half of the worksheet is for the requests each person is making to the other. This is the responsible assertiveness piece. After both have completed their requests, they take 15-20 minutes to share the requests with each other. As the two listen to each other, each wants to be sure to listen and understand what the partner wants and writing what is heard in the lower half of the sheet. The only way you really know you understand fully what your partner wants is to repeat back what you heard to confirm it. This is the active listening piece of the discussion. Your partner may want to clarify more if your reflection of what they want is not quite accurate. Stay with it till your partner is fully satisfied that you heard correctly.

At the end of the listening and understanding what each of you would like from the other, both of you will have new information about how to enhance your communication and work with each other. Any actions or behaviors that are causing friction or conflict can be identified and known, open to be resolved. In short, there is opportunity with new information to actively move to conflict resolution and a healthier relationship. Now, you want to commit to behaving and acting differently with each other going forward.

EXHIBIT B: THE COLLABORATIVE MINDSET/ ROLE CLARIFICATION WORKSHEET

Just below is a model for *Worksheet* designed to clarify and specify what two people would like from each other to live or work together more effectively. The instructions for the worksheet are in Exhibit A.

COLLABORATIVE MINDSET WORKSHEET FOR COUPLES OR ROLE CLARIFICATION WORKSHEET FOR TEAMMATES

"We are in this together, wanting to communicate better about misunderstandings, how to work together better, or more specifically (name a project, work assignment, upcoming vacation, etc.) _____.

We are on the same team, in the same family, and have a common mission. Understanding what we need from each other to best communicate, and work together, will be very helpful.

Three things that I would like from you or like for you to know about me that can make it easier for me to work better with you (things you are asserting about yourself to your partner):

1.

2.

3.

Three things you would like from me or would like for me to know about you that can make it easier for you to work better with me (three things that you listened to and understand about your partner).

1.

2.

3.

What we commit to do differently going forward that will help our communication and working/living together.

1.

2.

3.

EXHIBIT C: ANTI-RACISM COVENANT

West End United Methodist
Church, Nashville, Tennessee

In the first chapter of Genesis, God creates all of humankind in God's image. At West End United Methodist Church, one of our foundational Bedrock Beliefs is, God loves everyone unconditionally. We believe that all people are children of God, equally loved, gifted, and inspired by the Holy Spirit.

Jesus told a parable about a shepherd who left ninety-nine sheep in the field in order to find one sheep who was lost. (Matthew 18:12-14) As followers of Jesus we are called to seek out and stand with those in our communities who are hurting, oppressed, and crying out. We are grieved by the horror of the deaths of George Floyd, Breonna Taylor, Tony McDade, and many other People of Color killed at the hands of unjust people and policies. Our Bedrock Belief calls us in this moment to stand against racism and white supremacy, and to proclaim that the lives of our Black siblings, neighbors, friends, colleagues, family and church members not only matter but are worthy, beautiful, valued, and beloved by God.

Racism is a sin against God and neighbor. As we seek to uproot racism, we must first name it, repent of our past, lament the injustices of today, and work together in hope for the beautiful kingdom of God to be realized among us.

PAST

As we at West End move into God's future, it is important for us to name the sins in our history. Naming the sin of racism in our past is a vital step in healing and moving forward.

The sin of racism has been at the very root of our cultural institutions--even the church--for over 400 years. The White American Church has a history of complicity in the sin of racism, both through its most recent silence as well as its history of violence against Black and Indigenous People of Color.

Our congregation was established by the Methodist Episcopal Church South. The divide in the Northern and Southern branches of The Methodist Church stemmed from a decision to allow bishops and pastors to own enslaved persons. And in 1940 when the sanctuary of West End was opened and dedicated for the first time, servants and People of Color were only allowed in the balcony.

PRESENT

We recognize that the past has shaped our present. We are a predominantly White congregation in a denomination with few mechanisms in place to address the inherent imbalances in resources and opportunities in our system. We confess this injustice and commit to actions that lead to a more just future for all.

God's love calls us to individual and systemic change. It is not enough to point out the racism of our neighbor; we must see the log in our own eye (Matthew 7:3). We must commit each day, not just to being racist, but instead to the active pursuit of anti-racism in thought, word, and deed.

FUTURE

To that end, we covenant together with one another as a church to:

1. To examine actively and humbly our own hearts, attitudes, and assumptions. Knowing that only God can change a human heart through the power of the Holy Spirit, we will lead the church in prayer and in practicing the spiritual disciplines that cultivate time and space for the Spirit's work. We will encourage one another to grow in humility and love, trusting that the Holy Spirit will work within us to banish racist attitudes and make us more like Christ. The Spirit will also spur us to action, compelling us to work together to abolish institutional and systemic racism.

2. To listen deeply. We must seek out the narratives, truths, and counsel of People of Color, including those within our congregation.

3. To engage resources that help us explore the history of racial oppression in White culture and in our own attitudes. We take responsibility for our own education. Those of us who are White must realize that we participate in a racist system and have received benefits from this system even if unintentionally.

4. To make anti-racism a commitment of the whole church at every age and stage of life.

5. To require all church staff to complete anti-racism training and to offer similar training to laity.

6. To make clear to the Bishop and Cabinet that we invite a cross-cultural appointment of clergy at West End UMC.

7. To recognize the intersectionality of injustice (e.g. discrimination based on things beyond race such as economic status, sexual orientation, gender identity, physical ability) and to root out these injustices in all of our institutions from education, criminal

justice, housing, and food to the one we have most investment in: the church.

8. To partner with local leadership already doing this work.
9. To continue the formation of relationships with historically Black congregations and congregations of color, such as Gordon Memorial UMC, Clark Memorial UMC, and others.
   a. Continue our Racial Justice Journey series when possible.
   b. Engage in dialogue through book studies, pulpit swaps, and relationship-building.
3. To support more businesses owned by People of Color.
4. To work with leaders and organizations that seek to eliminate racial bias in our justice system.
5. To work within our own Tennessee-Western Kentucky Annual Conference with ministries such as Black Methodists for Church Renewal, the General Council on Religion and Race, MARCHA and others to de-center Whiteness and dismantle white supremacy.
6. To work with local, state, and national advocacy efforts to support policies and practices in the public sphere which dismantle institutional racism in every aspect of our society.

We will not be perfect in this work, but we commit to taking the next right step and to being held accountable.

EXHIBIT D

List of Values

What do you value most? Most of us have never taken the opportunity to clarify the very things we value most. Leadership is about being intentional with our personal values and organizational values. We often call them "guiding principles" or ethical guardrails that help us align our actions and behaviors with what we say we believe. Core values and guiding principles can be operationalized to make it easier for you or your company to do the right thing. You may want to start by circling your top ten, but we have found it very helpful to then narrow your choices to your top three. This will be tough, but very helpful.

Accountability	Belonging	Courage
Acceptance	Caring	Creativity
Adaptability	Collaboration	Curiosity
Adventure	Commitment	Dignity
Appreciation	Community	Diversity
Assertive	Compassion	Entrepreneurship
Authenticity	Competence	Efficiency
Balance	Confidence	Emotional Intelligence
Beauty	Connection	Equity
Becoming the Best	Contentment	Ethics

Excellence

Fairness

Faity

Family

Freedom

Forgiveness

Fulfillment

Fun

Generosity

Growth

Happiness

Harmony

Health

Home

Honesty

Hope

Humility

Humor

Inclusion

Independence

Initiative

Innovation

Inspiring

Integrity

Intentional

Intuition

Joy

Justice

Kindness

Knowledge

Leadership

Learning

Legacy

Leisure

Love

Loyalty

Making-A-Difference

Morality

Openness

Optimism

Order

Passion

Patience

Power

Recognition

Reliability

Resourceful

Respect

Responsibility

Risk

Safety

Security

Self-discipline

Self-respect

Serenity

Service

Simplicity

Solitude

Spirituality

Stewardship

Strength

Success

Teamwork

Thrive

Time

Tradition

Transparency

Trust

Trustworthy

Truth

Understanding

Unity

Unique

Useful

Uplifting

Vision

Vulnerability

Wealth

Welcoming

Well-being

Winning

Wisdom

www.ingramcontent.com/pod-product-compliance
Lightning Source LLC
Chambersburg PA
CBHW071537210326
41597CB00019B/3028